Anglo-Saxon Cemeteries

A Reappraisal

PROCEEDINGS OF A CONFERENCE HELD AT LIVERPOOL MUSEUM 1986

Edited by Edmund Southworth

on behalf of the
BOARD OF TRUSTEES OF THE NATIONAL MUSEUMS
AND GALLERIES ON MERSEYSIDE

First published in the United Kingdom in 1990 by
Alan Sutton Publishing · Phoenix Mill · Far Thrupp · Stroud · Gloucestershire

First published in the United States of America in 1991 by
Alan Sutton Publishing Inc · Wolfeboro Falls · NH 03896-0848

British Library Cataloguing in Publication Data

Anglo-Saxon Cemeteries : A Reappraisal.

    1. England. Anglo-Saxon Cemeteries
    I. Southworth, Edmund
    942

ISBN 0–86299–818–2

Library of Congress Cataloging in Publication Data applied for

Typeset in 11/12pt Garamond
Typesetting and origination by
Alan Sutton Publishing Limited
Printed in Great Britain by
Dotesios Printers Limited

CONTENTS

FOREWORD

The Board of Trustees of the National Museums and Galleries was established in 1986 to administer the collections of the Walker, Sudley and Lady Lever Art Galleries, Merseyside Maritime Museum and the Liverpool Museum. The collections in the Liverpool Museum had been previously looked after by the City of Liverpool until Local Government reorganization in 1974 when responsibility passed to the Merseyside Council which was itself dissolved in 1986. 1986 also marked the centenary of the death of Joseph Mayer, a Liverpool goldsmith and antiquarian, who gave his personal collection to the city in 1867. The conference which stimulated the papers in this volume was organized by Liverpool Museum as part of an attempt to draw attention to the diversity and importance of the Mayer Collection. It was organized jointly with the University of Liverpool's Department of Continuing Education with the active support of the British Museum.

My thanks go to all the contributors to the conference for whom this volume is a record of their deliberations, and especially to Leslie Webster of the Department of Medieval and Later Antiquities at the British Museum who did much to ensure the success of the conference and more recently in helping to prepare these proceedings for publication.

Richard Foster
Director, National Museums and Galleries on Merseyside

INTRODUCTION

The curator of a large and varied collection such as that at Liverpool Museum has a constant awareness that he could do more to improve access to the collections under his care. Whilst there may be a familiarity with sections of the whole among a small number of scholars, very few collections are ever displayed or published in their entirety. Liverpool Museum has had more difficulties than most in this direction. From its foundation in 1852 the influx of important collections from the scholars, merchants and philanthropists of the city has outpaced the resources of the museum. A period of stabilization in the 1930s was thwarted with the destruction of the main museum building in the Liverpool Blitz of 1941.

During the 1950s the main building lay mostly in ruins, and the collections that survived remained packed in store with minimal access even for staff. The collections were rebuilt to some extent as many museums divested themselves of material from further afield in favour of local archaeology. The 1960s saw the physical reconstruction of the museum and the transfer of the collections into improved, though barely adequate, storage. Not until 1976 was it possible to open a gallery devoted to the Antiquities of the Ancient World and British Archaeology. Only now was it possible to look at the collections themselves in more detail with a view to cataloguing and publication. A number of catalogues and handlists have been published since then, and computerized documentation has enabled the collections to be organized in a way which encourages study.

From whatever angle the collection was approached, however, it soon became clear that work was needed on the central theme of Joseph Mayer. His donation to the museum in 1867 of nearly 15,000 items had formed the core of our collections and each scholar working on catalogues needed to examine the contribution Joseph Mayer had made in acquiring the foundation deposit. As a successful jeweller and goldsmith in the prosperous city of Liverpool he had the wealth to acquire entire collections and the skills to appreciate what he was buying. A summary of his better known purchases would list Egyptian antiquities from the Sams Collection, medieval ivories and European prehistoric metalwork from the Fejervary Collection, Greek and Roman gems from the Hertz Collection among the strengths. In addition to this he made systematic and inspired assemblages of medieval manuscripts, Etruscan and classical jewellery, Liverpool porcelain and Wedgwood pottery, Chinese ceramics and European arms and armour.

Yet Mayer was more than an inspired collector working in the British and Continental art and antiquities markets. He was an ardent supporter of the new discipline of archaeology, and in particular British Archaeology. Locally, he was a founder member of the Historic Society of Lancashire and Cheshire, and he acquired material from the local archaeological sites being discovered in developments associated with the growth of the railways. Nationally, Mayer played a notable part in establishing British Archaeology as a significant subject by purchasing the Faussett Collection of Anglo-Saxon antiquities for the nation and then publishing the excavator's account for posterity.

The Faussett Collection is described in detail in this volume which represents the proceedings of a conference held in Liverpool in 1986. In planning the conference I was anxious to place the Faussett Collection and Mayer's role into context. The collection itself is one of the finest groups of Kentish cemetery material ever excavated, yet it has never been catalogued and published in its entirety. Every scholar who has used parts of the collection has blessed the standard of Faussett's recording and the foresight of Mayer in publishing the *Inventorium Sepulchrale*. Leslie Webster from the British Museum was particularly supportive and helped to create a programme of speakers who would examine three main themes: first, the circumstances surrounding the excavation of the Kentish cemeteries by the Revd Brian Faussett and the subsequent acquisition of the material by Mayer in 1856; secondly, the validity of the examination of old assemblages of material; thirdly the current philosophies and techniques used to examine Anglo-Saxon cemeteries similar to those excavated by Faussett.

During 1986, the centenary of Joseph Mayer's death, a number of other events which looked at various aspects of his life and collections were organized by Liverpool Museum. As a result, this work is paralleled by a volume of essays on Joseph Mayer and his collecting activities which was edited by Dr Margaret Gibson and published by the Society of Antiquaries in 1989. My thanks go to Dr Gibson for her encouragement and persistence. I am also especially grateful also to Leslie Webster for her most generous support, not only in setting up the conference, but also in assisting with the academic editing of these papers. The contributors to the conference and this volume have shown considerable patience and understanding, for which I am eternally grateful. My own staff at Liverpool Museum and our colleagues at Liverpool University deserve special mention for their contribution towards this work.

Edmund Southworth
Curator of Archaeology and Ethnology
Liverpool 1990

CHAPTER ONE

BRYAN FAUSSETT AND THE FAUSSETT COLLECTION: AN ASSESSMENT

Sonia Chadwick Hawkes

T he Faussett Collection, now part of the Mayer Collection in Liverpool Museum, is the legacy of one remarkable early pioneering excavator in East Kent, the Revd Bryan Faussett, who between 1760 and 1773 excavated no less than 750 Anglo-Saxon burials at sites within carriage drive of his family home at Heppington near Canterbury. Most of these sites, on the now famous Kingston, Sibertswold, Barfriston, Chartham, Beakesbourne and Bishopsbourne Downs, were drawn to his attention because they were then still marked by groups of small barrows (Plate 1.1). The other

PLATE 1.1   THE BARROWS ON KINGSTON DOWN, from *Inventorium Sepulchrale*

PLATE 1.2   THE SAND-PIT AT GILTON, Ash, after Douglas

site, at Gilton near Ash, had been discovered by chance in the digging of a sandpit (Plate 1.2).

Bryan Faussett was born in 1720 at Heppington. He graduated from Oxford, as a commoner at University College, obtaining his B.A. in 1742 and his M.A. in 1745, and was almost immediately elected a Fellow of All Souls College, 'as of kin to the founder, Archbishop Chichele'. His studies at Oxford, according to the syllabus of the time, would have included divinity but would have been chiefly in classical subjects and philosophy, the standard B.A. degree course then being the precursor of the present degree of Literae Humaniores.[1] The form of the examination in the eighteenth century was quite different, however, being wholly oral and generally very lax and corrupt in its conduct and administration, so that a man then could do as little or as much for his Oxford degree as he chose. Bryan Faussett, though playing a full part in the Jacobite enthusiasms and intrigues indulged in by both his family and university in such politically exciting times, seems nonetheless to have become 'a scholar of no inconsiderable taste and acquirements' as 'his works, the library he collected, and the whole tenor of his life, sufficiently show.'[2] He was certainly well versed in Latin, ancient history and antiquities and he may also have made some study of anatomy. Anatomy in the eighteenth century did not form part of the official course of study for the degrees of B.A. and M.A. at Oxford, unless one were intending to become a medic, and such specialists were rare except, interestingly, among the Fellows at All Souls College. However, anatomy was an excitingly novel subject at that time, at Oxford as elsewhere, especially when there were bodies available to be dissected. We do not know whether anatomical dissections took place at Oxford in Faussett's time, but certainly there were rival lectures on anatomy which he could have attended, by Nathan Alcock at Jesus College and Thomas Lawrence in the basement of the old Ashmolean Museum, just around the corner from the Bodleian

Library. And in the early seventeenth-century Old Schools Quad, adjacent to the Bodleian, the Anatomy School apparently contained a whole museum of exhibits, doubtless including skeletons. A man of great intellectual curiosity such as Faussett, living in an age of growing scientific enquiry, is likely to have been attracted to such a subject, in order to study the physical condition of man alongside his mental and spiritual.

Certainly, when he came to do his cemetery excavations in Kent, he showed a remarkable knowledge of human skeletons. His ability to age and sex them, his awareness of the significance of such things as tooth wear and tooth loss, with reabsorption of sockets, as a factor in the ageing process, together with his knowledge of abnormalities such as metopism (the frontal suture remaining open into adulthood) can scarcely have been acquired except by study of anatomy at Oxford. Though the last thirty years of work on Anglo-Saxon cemeteries have brought about an increasing awareness of the importance of human skeletons and the data to be derived from their study, Faussett was unique in his day, and for long afterwards, in the quantity and quality of his observations, as something natural and familiar to him. Within limits, those observations are usable today in comparison with modern studies, and for a man of the eighteenth century that is truly a remarkable achievement.

However, Faussett did not begin his excavations immediately on leaving Oxford. He was ordained in 1746 and, being presented in 1748 by All Souls College to the living of Abberbury in Shropshire, was enabled to leave Oxford and marry Elizabeth Curtois, a lady from a Lincolnshire family, shortly after. Such a rapid transition from the status of bachelor don to preferment and the married state was considered ideal by most young Fellows of Oxford colleges at that time, and Fauseett was luckier still in that his father died as early as 1750, leaving him free to return to Kent, to live near his widowed mother, until her death in 1761 left him in undisputed control of the family estates. According to his great-grandson he was without preferment, unemployed, for many years until almost the end of his life in 1776, but by his own account he was curate at Kingston (*Inventorium Sepulchrale* 1856, 36) from 1750 until 1756 and later an absentee vicar of another or perhaps the same uncongenial living, which brought him in not more than £20 a year and in which he kept a curate in his turn.[3] He was clearly not much enamoured of life as a country vicar, unless he could be close to his home at Heppington. On one occasion he was moved to write:

> I am sincerely sorry that I ever took orders:– nay, could I decently leave them, I declare to you that I certainly would do it; for, thank God, I can live without them – else God help me! I had, indeed, resigned it (his living) long ago but for . . . that, after so much money laid out on my education, I might have it to say that I was not quite without preferment (*Inventorium Sepulchrale* 1856,209).

He was thus a man without clerical duties for much of his middle life, enjoying independent means and ample leisure. He was able to follow his favourite antiquarian pursuits without serious hindrance, except for the periodic attacks of gout which afflicted him during the last twenty years of his life. To quote Thomas Godfrey-Faussett yet again:

> I think few persons of taste and education can pass any length of time in Kent without becoming antiquaries, at heart if not in pursuit; and I have no doubt that the influence of the neighbourhood was strong upon my great-grandfather from an early age. Perhaps no portion of England is more

suggestive of the past, or offers to the antiquary a richer field for his observation and research . . . its downs studded with barrows, or crowned with encampments . . . He could not walk a hundred yards in any direction from his father's house without crossing the ancient camp entrenchments with which it is surrounded; a Roman road, the well-known "Stone Street Causeway" ran through his property within half a mile of the house.

In his preoccupation with such things he found few like-minded neighbours, as we read in another of his letters:

I am just going to eat venison with some of my friends (such as they are) here. The best sauce to it that I can possibly expect will be some hodge-podge disquisition on horses, dogs, hunting, shooting, etc.; but as it is my misfortune not to be a sportsman, it is odds that it will not be cooked to my palate. But I must bear with it, or live alone (*Inventorium Sepulchrale* 1856, 211).

Faussett consoled himself in this cultural wilderness by correspondence with and visits to and from like-minded friends in London and elsewhere; by avidly collecting coins and antiquities; by driving or riding around the countryside visiting churches and, increasingly as time went on, by his excavations of ancient burial grounds. These he thought to be of 'Romans Britonized' and 'Britons Romanized', because of the Roman coins found with some of the dead, but all but one of the cemeteries he excavated, on Crundale Down, subsequently proved to be Anglo-Saxon. He had a vague idea that this might be the case but no real means of proving it (*Inventorium Sepulchrale* 1856, 38–9) since he could not identify the few post-Roman coins from his graves. It was to be left to James Douglas, a like-minded man indeed but of a generation later, to make the breakthrough in deducing that the cemeteries of small barrows excavated by Faussett and by himself on the downland of Kent were, in fact, of Anglo-Saxon date. Further, the coins and Christian artifacts from some of Faussett's graves led Douglas to conclude that they were the burial places of the first Christian converts, between the conversion of Kent by the Roman mission of St Augustine at the end of the sixth century and the transfer of burial to intramural and churchyard sites in the eighth century (Douglas 1793, 122–31), a conclusion accepted today. Of the two, therefore, Douglas was the better scholar.

But the fact that Bryan Faussett was to remain in ignorance of the true identity, novelty and real importance of his discoveries was no bar to his enthusiasm for barrow digging. He described it as 'my hobby-horse' (*Inventorium Sepulchrale* 1856, 214). However, the first Anglo-Saxon site he excavated was not a barrow cemetery but a flat cemetery which was being destroyed by sand extraction. Faussett's account of his first visit to the site, written up meticulously in his excavation diary, conveys most vividly the conditions of the times, the difficulties of the site and, above all, the flavour and quality of the man himself, his powers of observation and narrative, and the excellent practical sense he showed as a novice excavator. Since even the published *Inventorium Sepulchrale* is now a rare book, I make no excuse for quoting him here at length.

At a place commonly called Gilton Town in the parish of Ash, next Sandwich, in the county of Kent, on the right hand of the high road leading from Canterbury to Sandwich, and about a quarter of a mile from Ash-Street, is a large and deep sandpit, in which from time to time for a great many years past, whenever sand has been dug within three or four feet of the surface, or whenever the surface has rushed down after frost or rain, as it usually does, many antiquities of different sorts have been discovered and picked up, either by the servants of the farmer who used the land . . . or perhaps, more particularly, by the servants of a miller, who has two large windmills on the west side of and close to this sandpit.

Happening to be at Ash in the end of the year 1759, on the purpose of copying the monumental inscriptions in that church among others, and enquiring, as I always do on such occasions, whether there were any antiquities or other remarkables in the neighbourhood, I was informed of this famous sandpit, and of the particulars above mentioned.

I immediately visited the place; and having looked about it and examined it for some little time, one of the miller's servants came into the pit to me and shewed me something sticking out, about three or four inches out of the sand, and at about three feet from the surface of the eastern and deepest part of the pit. It appeared to me to be nothing more than some piece of stick or root; but he assured me it was the head of a spear; and he said he was certain there was a grave there from the colour of the sand, which, in a small line of about eighteen inches in length parallel to the surface, and about two inches in thickness, appeared in that place of a much darker tinge than the rest of the sand. He told me also, that, if I pleased, he would get a ladder and a spade and see what was in it.

It was now pretty late in the day, which made me object to his proposal, imagining he would not have time to go through with the work. However, on his assuring me that he had been used to the work, and that by help of another miller, his fellow-servant, he should soon rifle it (for that was his expression), my curiousity prompted me, though at a considerable distance from home, to set them about the business and to wait the event.

The miller and his companion immediately produced two ladders and as many spades; and with these began to delve in a very rough manner into the sand rock in an horizontal manner, as if they had designed to have made an oven. The head of the spear (for such indeed it proved) they, at the first or second stroke of their spades, contrived to break all to pieces. Indeed it was very brittle. At the next stroke or two, part of a skull and a few vertebrae of the neck (all much decayed) were indiscriminately cast down into the pit, without the least care or search after anything. That concern, they said, they left to me and my servant at the bottom, who were very nearly blinded with the sand falling on us, and in no small danger of being knocked on the head, if not absolutely buried, by the too zealous impetuousity of my honest labourers.

I found, in short, that this manner of proceeding would not do; but that if the grave did chance to contain anything curious, it must, most likely, be lost and overlooked. I therefore desired them to desist, and advised them rather to open the ground above, till they should get down to the skeleton, and then carefully to examine the bottom of the grave. This advice, having been used to proceed oven fashion, if I may so call it, they did not at first at all relish; but after a little persuasion and a little brandy (without which nothing, in such cases as the present, can be done effectually), they very cheerfully approved and very contentedly followed, so that in a very short time they got to the skeleton, I mean what remained of it. And though I then went into the grave myself, and very carefully examined every handful of the above-mentioned discoloured sand (namely where the body had lain and rotted), I found nothing but some soft spongy remains of decayed bones. It was now too near night to think of doing anything more at that time, and too late in the season, considering my distance from home, to attempt anything further that year. But I promised myself the pleasure of returning to the work, and making a further and more diligent search, as early as the weather and length of days of the ensuing spring would give me leave.[4]

Faussett returned on 10 April the following year, hired labourers and began his own excavations, digging forty-nine graves in just two days, and, continuing in the next few years, a total for this site of one hundred and six graves in eleven days. His appetite whetted, he went on to dig hundreds more graves in the barrow cemeteries nearer Heppington. He continued this work until 1773, just three years before his death.

Now though this last passage is always good for a laugh from a lecture audience, it has much serious content and gives a very fair idea of how Faussett proceeded. He and his large band of hired workmen laboured long hours and at great speed in uncovering the graves and getting down to the burials (most days opening what today would seem a

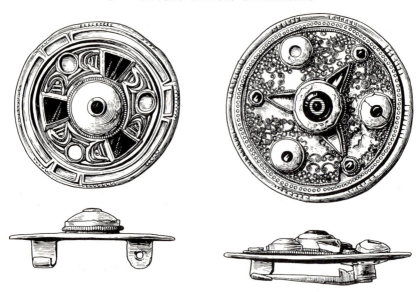

PLATE 2   BROOCHES FROM KINGSTON DOWN grave 299, Marion Cox

48 at Barfriston (Plate 3), and the pendants from grave 172 at Sibertswold (Plate 4).[8] With its Frankish coins of Marsal and Verdun, datable around AD 650, this is one of the key dated grave-groups from seventh-century Kent.

For Bryan Faussett himself, however, the real crown of his achievements must have come with the opening of grave 205 on Kingston Down in August 1771 (Plate 5). A barrow larger than usual was found to cover a huge burial chamber, ten feet long by eight broad and six deep, composed of thick wooden boards reinforced at the corners by iron clamps. Inside was an insignificant-looking female skeleton, but evidently once a lady of the highest rank, because she had at her feet a pottery vessel and two bronze bowls (Plate 7), one Frankish and one Celtic as we now know, together with a wooden casket. At her left thigh was a chatelaine of fine iron links and twin silver safety-pin brooches, perhaps for fastening the side of her shift or even her overdress. At her throat was a single gold pendant and at her right shoulder the largest and most exquisite Kentish jewelled gold composite disc-brooch yet to be found (Plates 5 and 6). This dates the grave to the early seventh century. What makes this grave the more poignant is Bryan Faussett's discovery of the reburied and very well-preserved bones of a child outside the coffin, perhaps with the small glass palm-cup recovered from this grave (Plate 6). Unparalleled wealth and all the signs of a sad human tragedy here must have fixed this grave especially in his affections. In fact its discovery made him wild with excitement. Thomas Godfrey-Faussett makes it clear that his great-grandfather had always been a tremendous enthusiast for his archaeological enterprises:

Of his first success, and thence gradually increasing ardour and diligence in the discovery of tumular relics, his work is, in fact, a journal; but the cool, clear-headed narrative gives the reader no idea of the intense enthusiasm of the author. Tradition tells us of the state of almost boyish excitement in which he superintended the opening of his barrows; of the eagerness with which he sifted every crumb of earth taken from them; of his not unsuccessful endeavours to instil some of his own ardour

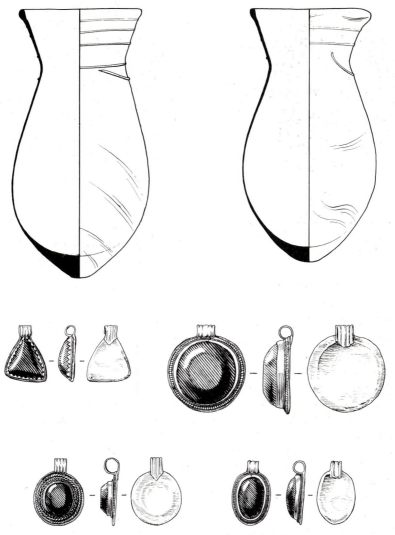

PLATE 3 BARFRISTON grave 48, Marion Cox

into his labourers; of his good humour when they worked well; his anger when they flagged; and his rage and vexation when an unlucky pickaxe shattered a vase or patera; of his even animating his men by seizing spade and pickaxe himself; and, in spite of gout and infirmity, setting no mean example of activity. His good humour and good pay appear to have been more remembered than his occasional outbreaks of wrath; and his cottagers always rejoiced when an interval freer than usual from gout gave the signal for another digging for "the Squire" (*Inventorium Sepulchrale* 1856, 204).

Finding Kingston Down grave 205 must have been an altogether superlative experience. Bryan Faussett, by now suffering severely from recurrent, protracted and extremely painful visitations of the gout, had delegated the active supervision of his excavations to

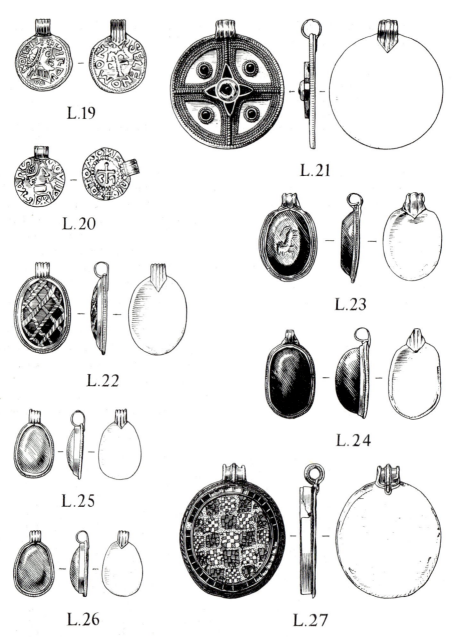

L.19

L.20

L.21

L.22

L.23

L.24

L.25

L.26

L.27

PLATE 4   SIBERTSWOLD grave 172, Marion Cox

his son Henry, but despite his infirmities was nonetheless waiting close by in his coach to hear the latest news from the site. It was in fact Henry who boasted

> through life that he had himself discovered, as he superintended the opening of one of his father's barrows on Kingston Down, that famous fibula, which was the gem of his collection, as it still is, I believe, of all Anglo-Saxon tumular antiquities. . . ..On finding it, he carried it with great glee to his father, who was in his carriage hard by, suffering under an attack of his old enemy: his father drove off with it; and next day a report was spread around that the carriage had been so full of gold that the wheels would hardly turn . . . (*Inventorium Sepulchrale* 1856, 206).

Anyone who has ever dug on a site in a really rural community, even in recent times, can imagine the village alehouse buzzing with gossip and ill-informed speculation about the nature and size of the golden treasure rumoured to have been found. Anyone who has ever found a real treasure such as Faussett's can imagine his euphoria, and the relief with which he carried it safely back to his library, where he could savour it quietly and study its finer details. After resting his pain-racked limbs, he made the finest drawing of his life in committing the Kingston Brooch to the page of his diary reproduced in Plate 5. His account of the grave itself gives a fair sample of his steady hand and elegant style. Bryan Faussett emerges from this brief study as a man with a passion to excavate as much as possible of the hitherto unknown people whose burials and artifacts became such an absorbing interest to him. He was not an innovative thinker like Douglas, but as well as his enthusiasm he had great gifts of dedication, patience, intelligent observation and painstaking recording of everything he saw and handled. His diaries are an eloquent testimony to his literary and scientific skills. 'His plain, clear narrative of facts, daily recorded with cautious attention to the most minute circumstance', praised by Charles Roach Smith in his preface to the 1856 publication, ensures that his excavation diaries,

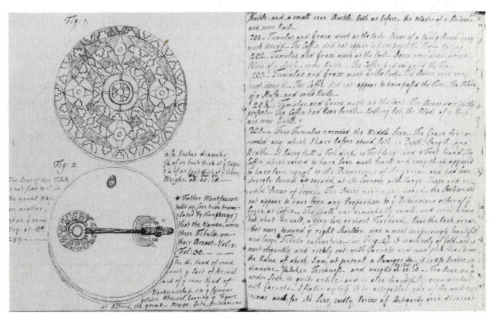

PLATE 5   KINGSTON DOWN grave 205, as recorded in Bryan Faussett's manuscript *Inventorium Sepulchrale*

preserved along with most of his excavated finds in Liverpool Museum, remain an archive of the first importance today.

However, the fact that Bryan Faussett's diaries have survived to this day, and that the finds from his excavation are also extant in large part, is due to a series of very lucky chances indeed. By the end of his digging career Bryan Faussett was still in his early fifties but was dying by slow degrees in great pain. No doubt his cabinet of antiquities was in as good order as his diaries but he can have been in no state to organize a publication. Moreover, there seems to be very little doubt that Bryan Faussett had spent a great deal of money on his collections and excavations, at the expense of the prosperity of the family estate. At the end of his life he might have been quite hard up, for he was grateful to obtain, through the intermediacy of the Archbishop of Canterbury, the rectory of Monk's Horton and the perpetual curacy of his own parish of Nackington (*Inventorium Sepulchrale* 1856, 203). Surely he must have sought these for the income they would have brought him as absentee incumbent rather than as an active occupation for himself when excruciatingly crippled by gout.

The Faussett family kept some of the account books, including the excavation field notebook for 1772, now in Liverpool Museum, which has details on its back page of the numbers and names of workmen employed that year and the wages paid to them, so we do have an idea of what Faussett's excavations are likely to have cost. Some details have been published, namely that his usual daily rate of pay for labourers was 1 s. 6 d. but that exceptionally, perhaps for a surveyor, he paid 15 s. 9 d. On 24 July, when he opened forty-one graves at Sibertswold, Bryan Faussett had hired fourteen men at a cost in wages of £1 15 s. 3 d.[9] The precise modern equivalent of this sum must be in excess of £500. Between 13 July and 2 October of 1772 Bryan Faussett mounted ten such day-long blitzes on the barrows on Sibertswold, Barfriston and Kingston Downs, and though not all were perhaps on the same large scale, the expenditure in modern terms must have run into several thousands of pounds during that one summer alone. The economics of the Faussett excavations could profitably be researched further. There were also the other collections he had amassed, not just the vast numbers of Roman coins, which he rationalized in 1766 by the casting of a bell, but grander follies such as the Faussett Pavilion, built during his last years, where the interior had been decorated by monumental antiquities of all periods brought from all over the county and beyond, each with its descriptive plaque in marble (Jessup 1975, 51–2, Plate 16). One comes reluctantly to the conclusion that Bryan Faussett was no longer entirely sane or at least recklessly prodigal in the spending of money by the end of his life.

To quote Thomas Godfrey-Faussett yet again:

> Every one of experience in archaeology knows how expensive an amusement it is, especially when carried to the length of engaging single-handed in excavations and collections as extensive as his were; and though we, his descendants, are justly proud of his labours and fame, we may perhaps be forgiven for feeling that there is very little to show for the number of acres spent upon it; and for wishing that he had spared more of that energy and practical wisdom which we trace in his works, to the management and preservation of his hereditary property.

Modern posterity would not wholly agree. Faussett's excavations remain immensely important in giving us so much information about these mainly seventh-century cemeteries of his, which otherwise would have been destroyed without any comparable record. Gilton would have been quarried out with just occasional attention from collectors such as William Boys (1792); the Kingston barrows would have gone on being eroded until nearly invisible, as they were when I first visited the site in 1956, and being unrecorded the site would in all likelihood have been destroyed by the progressive widening of the A2 road to Dover, at a time when there was little effective rescue archaeology in this part of Kent. Even with Faussett to testify to the site's importance, modern rescue excavation on Kingston Down has been woefully inadequate. His other sites would probably have been ploughed down and thus have vanished from sight without record. So one can claim that Faussett was an important rescue archaeologist. As to the quality of what he found, one can say with confidence that he has afforded us with an important control sample, and a very big sample at that, of what Kentish Anglo-Saxon barrow burials of their period were really like. There have been no comparable excavations of such sites on such a scale since, nor could there be once the barrows were ploughed away and the circumstances irrevocably changed. So Faussett's contribution to Anglo-Saxon cemetery research is precious and unique; he spent freely of his own patrimony to lay in stores of archaeological wealth for the benefit of posterity.

However, Bryan Faussett's family could not know the long-term value of his archaeological work. Looking at the diaries and the few really valuable things in his museum at Heppington, most of them must have felt even more critical than Thomas Godfrey-Faussett, especially if, as he implies, Bryan Fausett actually sold land to pay for his archaeological work. It is perhaps significant that his son Henry, who had been his companion from childhood in the archaeological ventures, did not go expensively to Oxford. Instead he trained as a lawyer and man of business in London and became best known for carrying out in exemplary fashion 'the duties of a country gentleman', which his father had so despised, and for the good management of his inherited estate, which his father had so neglected. James Douglas certainly, in his extensive correspondence with Henry Faussett, refers several times to his 'good husbandry' and 'plans of agriculture' (Jessup 1975). Apart from farming, Henry's chief enthusiasm was for collecting pictures although he retained a keen interest in the archaeological collections in the museum at Heppington and may well have intended to make a publication himself. He left many draft layouts of illustrations for a folio publication, comparable to Douglas's *Nenia Britannica*, which are now in the safe-keeping of the Society of Antiquaries of London,[10] as well as finished watercolours of exquisite quality of some of the objects excavated by his father and also finds from the 1730 excavations on Chartham Down (*Inventorium Sepulchrale* 1856, 160–176; Douglas 1793, 99–110). These he was able to paint at Mystole House, before the collections of the Fagg family there were sold or otherwise dispersed, and by appending them to his father's manuscript diary devoted to this site, has preserved their likenesses for posterity.[11] The finds themselves are now apparently lost to us.

A like fate could so easily have befallen the Faussett Collection had not Bryan Faussett apparently had the foresight to ensure that his family should not dispose of it, so that 'it remained for three generations in the Faussett home at Heppington, strictly tied by the terms of Bryan's will so as to be of no use to anyone, and almost forgotten' (Jessup 1975, 50). But with James Douglas at large in East Kent from about 1779, for a short while the collection became the subject of intense interest yet again.

Captain Douglas, as he then was, supervised the excavation of Anglo-Saxon barrows

and flat graves found during the construction of the fortifications known as Chatham
Lines and by 1782 had opened something like eighty-six of them. Their contents, which
formed the basis for his own cabinet of antiquities, became a subject of serious study and
reflection and, as we have seen already, Douglas became convinced that he was dealing
not with Romans but with Saxons. Obviously these were exciting times for him, he
became rather full of himself, and, as younger scholars are prone to do, talked publicly
of discrediting the views of his predecessors, in this case notably Bryan Faussett. That he
grated on at least some of his elders seems quite clear from remarks in a letter written
from the historian Edward Hasted to Dr Ducarel on 2 August 1780.

> There have been many more Roman remains lately dug up at the Lines at Brompton, near Chatham,
> which I have had a relation of from the engineer, Captain Douglas, who is just entered on the study
> of antiquity, and is as complete an enthusiast as I ever met with in my life: he seems beginning where
> he should leave off, and talks much of criticising on the conjectures of our late friend Bryan Faussett,
> who was, I do think, as capable and learned a man in that way as this country ever had. (*Inventorium
> Sepulchrale* 1856, 215; Jessup 1975, 26.)

This overestimates Bryan Faussett, of course, and, as we know, Douglas was to be
proven right, but obviously his manner could give offence.

At some point during these years Douglas met Henry Godfrey-Faussett and laid siege
to him to gain access to the Faussett Collection with a view to its publication. The
surviving correspondence[12] is one-sided, the letters being all from the effusive Douglas,
so one cannot follow the finer points of the progress of their relationship, from formality
through friendship to such a final snubbing coolness on the part of Henry that it
defeated even James Douglas's fulsome determination to maintain it. In the beginning
Douglas, presuming on an existing acquaintance, cast himself in the role of interme-
diary in the potential sale of the Faussett Collection.

> 2nd Apl. 1781:– 'Dear Sir,
>   . . . A gentleman high up in the estimation of the antiquarian world and who has himself a great
> and valuable collection of antiquities, has delegated me to treat for your cabinet should you have any
> desire to part with it? I am therefore to request of you the sum, which you would set upon it,
> provided you would listen to a negotiation from me – you will acquiesce with me in supposing that
> antiquarians do not scruple in making bargains for antique rust, therefore any delicacy on this subject
> would be ridiculous – however if you have any inclination to listen to proposals, I make no doubt but
> what I shall be able to introduce your cabinet of *hastie*, umbonae, fibulae etc to a good antiquarian
> market.'

The hopeful purchaser, Sir Ashton Lever as it transpires in the next few letters, never in
fact visited Heppington and never made an offer, but in the letter quoted below Douglas
seems to have had another purchaser in mind. Might it conceivably have been himself?
No one as far as I know has suggested this before, but from the special interests shown,
it seems all too likely.

> 4th May 1782:– 'Dear Sir,
>   . . . I should have no manner of objection in treating with you concerning your collection of
> things found in barrows etc. If the value set upon them is compatible with reason and the scarcity of
> money in general, indeed I should say the poverty of the time. Permit me now to tell you that I am
> empowered to negotiate with you for the purchase but also not to exceed a certain price; the person is

not a very moneyed man, yet if you conclude the disposing of them he will remit you their value on the immediate conclusion of the bargain. Whatever transpires with me, I give you my honour shall remain a secret, but indeed I see no reason why you should have the least reluctance to make your intention public of disposing of them, since it happens every day that the first families in the kingdom are selling their collections . . . I find Dr. Jacobs has sold his collection of medals etc which he has been much disappointed in; they fetched a mere trifle indeed.

I apprehend you have no objection to permit your manuscripts that is your father's to go with the things – you know it would be extremely awkward to have the collection without them.'

Henry Faussett obviously responded by seeking Douglas's opinion about the value of the collections, with which he must by now have become familiar from visiting Heppington, but Douglas demurs about putting a price on them himself.

30th May 1782:– 'Dr Sir,
. . . If you have any *serious* intention of disposing of your cabinet mention your sum and an opportunity will present itself to you which you perhaps will not so soon meet with again to sell it into private hands . . . If your terms will meet with approbation I will have the pleasure to wait upon you and conclude everything to your perfect satisfaction.'

If my reading is right (and the whole scheme on Douglas's side seems so utterly transparent – to acquire the Faussett Collection and the manuscripts of the *Inventorium Sepulchrale* for a bargain price) one feels sure that the lawyer and man of business, Henry Faussett, cannot have been unaware of the subterfuge and may have been teasing the enthusiastic Captain Douglas to get a valuation. From what Jessup tells us of the terms of Bryan Faussett's will, any sale at that time would have been out of the question. The great mystery is how Douglas imagined he could have afforded even the 'fair sum' which Faussett was to have set upon the collections. He was, however, always an optimist and full of enterprise, as Jessup comments about him in a different context, 'All his life he found it hard to forgo what he judged to be a bargain and he was never to be prevented in attempts at dealing' (Jessup 1975, 61). In the event Henry effectively scotched any notion of his disposing of the Faussett Collection, by insisting that his father's enormous collection of Roman coins and medals be included in the sale. This was too much even for James Douglas.

18th June 1782:– 'Dear Sir
I had the pleasure of your favour setting forth your intentions not to part with your collection, unless the medals were to accompany it. As the person who is willing to purchase the cabinet (and who by the way is well acquainted with the particulars) only collects barrow curiousities he will therefore not accept of coins etc . . . so much of this – now to my own proposal – I have very nearly completed a general history of the funeral customs of the antients . . . I have made drawings of the most material part of my small researches . . . my proposal is to request the assistance of your collection – which as it will ornament my work to a great degree . . . so I think you will have an easy opportunity of communicating the discoveries to the world.'

Having abandoned the project of buying the Faussett Collection outright, Douglas turned at once to soliciting Henry Faussett's help in making it available to provide materials for his own embryonic *Nenia Britannica*. This abrupt turnabout, the unsophisticated introduction of the new scheme, cannot but have provoked some reaction from Henry, whether a sigh or a laugh. Unfortunately we know so little of his character and whether or not he had a good sense of humour, although there is a hint in a much later letter, of 16 May 1786, when Douglas was curate at Chiddingfold on £40 a year, that Henry did indeed tease him. 'You said I should be genteel' Douglas writes 'if I kept a cow and two pigs: wishing therefore to appear with gentility in the eye of my friends, I bought my stock of necessary credentials for gentility at a fair a few days back.' I think we can therefore be certain that Faussett was not without humour in his dealings with Douglas; otherwise one feels that Douglas's effusiveness would have become intolerable.

Initially Henry Faussett kept Douglas at a distance and his hands off the diaries and collections until he was much surer of his honesty. From the letters and the rather perfunctory acknowledgements in the *Nenia Britannica* it seems that it was Henry's policy to draw all the objects from the collection that he permitted Douglas to illustrate, thus preventing Douglas from taking them away to work on or even handling them at all. This will have been to reconcile Douglas's ambitions with the terms of Bryan Faussett's will and was certainly prudent, in view, for example, of Douglas's tardiness in copying and returning Sir William Fagg's plan of the barrows on Chartham Down (Jessup 1975, 192) and as subsequent disputes about the unpermitted publication of items from the Faussett Collection were all too sadly to show.

With regard to the Faussett Collection, the 'hands off' measures began quickly upon Henry's hearing of the *Nenia Britannica* project from Douglas and, as usual, we can only surmise Faussett's reply from Douglas's reactions.

> 19th July, 1782:– 'Dr Sir,
> . . . Far be it from my thoughts to entertain any idea of making extracts from your manuscripts . . . I am perfectly contented with yr. permission to make drawings of those things which I may find serviceable to my plan . . . – but I do not wish by any means to give you trouble to draw them yourself.'

But at first that was the procedure and Douglas merely did the *aqua tinta*, the coloured engravings, from Faussett's original drawings for publication, so it is conceivable that Douglas was never officially given free access to the Collection at all. We are indebted to them both for some very fine, accurate illustrations, notably of the finds from Kingston Down grave 205 (Plate 6 and 7). These were finally made available to Douglas only in 1785 and eventually appeared in the *Nenia Britannica* as plates 10 and 11.

> 4th February 1785:– 'Dear Sir,
> . . . I shall readily accept your offer of the drawings of the *rich* barrow with the description of the relics as they were found – and from which I shall make an engraving which I mean to inscribe to the owner.'

> 25th April 1785:– 'Dear Sir,
> . . . I thank you much for your drawings – I have prepared all things for engraving and if I could only commune with you – you little know, the good you would infuse into me for my studies – pray come – pray do – no one will be more rejoiced to see you and yours . . .'

The *Nenia Britannica*, first funded by Douglas himself and later put out to public subscription, began to appear in separate parts in 1786, and included important selections from the Faussett Collection, Kingston Down grave 205 appearing in number 4 in 1787.

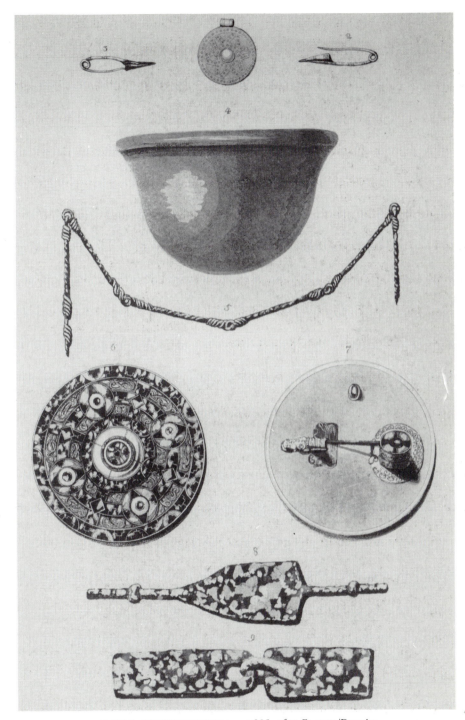

PLATE 6   KINGSTON DOWN grave 205, after Faussett/Douglas

PLATE 7 KINGSTON DOWN grave 205, after Faussett/Douglas

But Douglas was always greedy to illustrate more from the cabinet at Heppington and began to include sketches of his own to supplement Henry Faussett's fine drawings. In Douglas's letters during the years 1786 to 1789 there is plenty of evidence to show that he had considerably offended Faussett. Typically his self-justifications, apologies and explanations are rapidly followed up by further demands for information and drawings. In a letter of 2 October 1786 we find him attempting to rebut an accusation of having read and quoted from Bryan Faussett's excavation diaries, access to which had apparently been expressly denied him by the son. In his next letter of 11 October 1787, he complains of 'epistolary neglect' and simultaneously moves into a more intimate mode of address, perhaps in an attempt to ingratiate himself:

'Dear Faussett
    . . . I here have impressed for your notice an impression of a plate for my next No. which contains miscellaneous relics. Your *cross* and vessels are introduced to ascertain their analogy with similar specimens . . . You will oblige me by marking the other relics found with your *cross* which I fear to have given in too large a scale of drawing; also the other relics found with the *cross* from the barrows at Chartham . . .'

From the final publication it does not appear that Faussett responded. Disenchantment with Douglas notwithstanding, the whole proceeding was going far beyond the terms of his father's will and he could not associate himself with it. On 7 March 1788 there was a further demand:

'Dear Faussett
    . . . I have sent you a slight proof of a plate for my succeeding No. – I could not venture to publish it before you cast an eye over it and returned me a few notes on the relics which you recognise in it. They are taken from my sketch book; the rapid production of a few minutes on a cursory survey of your cabinet; and I am reluctant to make out the description from my own notes which I can not well trust to. You will please to believe that the world will always consider your favours in their just estimation and that you have already made use of my book as the vehicle to make them known.'

This must have been too great an impertinence to be borne. Again there was no reply from Henry and the illustrations in the relevant plate xviii of the *Nenia* are clearly based on Douglas's sketches and have not the accuracy we have learned to expect from Henry Faussett. It is sad to have to conclude that James Douglas behaved very badly towards Henry in the matter of Bryan Faussett's Collection, and that the relationship between the two men was not as mutually cordial as Jessup has led us to believe. The facts extractable from the letters sketch in for us an altogether unflattering picture of James Douglas.

   The practical outcome of all this for modern students of the Faussett Collection and its portrayal in the *Nenia Britannica* is that only those drawings drafted by Henry Faussett can be regarded as wholly accurate.

   The dust of forty years now descends upon the Faussett Collection at Heppington. Henry has died and his eldest son Dr Godfrey-Faussett has inherited the estate but, as Doctor of Divinity and Professor at the University of Oxford, he is not at home for more than half the year. The dust is about to be disturbed and totally dissipated by the advent of Charles Roach Smith, walking the Stone Street from Canterbury to Lympne, and after passing the entrance, turning back to make an unpremeditated call at Heppington.

From this chance event great things were to ensue. The British Archaeological Association, on its first public meeting at Canterbury in 1844, viewed the Faussett Collection at a time when the study of Anglo-Saxon antiquities had become all the rage in influential quarters. From that time Charles Roach Smith was to become the Faussett family's adviser about the fate of the Collection. After the death of Dr Faussett the family was forced to sell but the problem was how to effect this without splitting it up at public auction. The extraordinary story which followed is best heard from Charles Roach Smith himself.

> Consulted on the subject by the Executors, I immediately advised that the antiquities and manuscripts should be valued and offered first of all to the Trustees of the British Museum. In consequence the Executors, very considerately and commendably, gave the Trustees the power of acquiring this extraordinary collection of Anglo-Saxon Antiquities, at a very moderate sum. That the Trustees might have a full chance of understanding the value of the treasures placed within their reach, the officers at the head of the department of Antiquities made a personal examination of them; and the six volumes of manuscripts were forwarded for their examination, and study, if necessary. This was in August 1853. The Trustees declined the offer. The officers, backed by the antiquarian societies, continued to importune them to purchase; but still they refused. In this fruitless negociation, six or seven months were consumed . . . At length, however, the Executors received a final refusal, and Mr. Mayer immediately became the purchaser. (Roach Smith 1853, 182).

There is more, very much more, in this article, which robustly denounced the constitution of the British Museum and the lack of a department of National Antiquities, which makes fascinating reading, but which is not strictly germane to this paper. But I cannot forebear quoting a further passage, which is very relevant.

> Fortunately the Faussett Collection is not lost to the country. In the hands of Mr. Joseph Mayer its integrity will be preserved, and under his liberal and enlightened care it will be made accessible to the public; but Liverpool instead of London will have the honour of possessing the first collection of Saxon antiquities in the kingdom. Moreover it is Mr. Mayer's intention to print the entire manuscripts and illustrate them fully from the original objects. Had the Trustees purchased the collection it is not likely this important step would have been taken; and the manuscripts would only have been accessible to a few under disadvantageous circumstances; now, their contents will soon be at the firesides of antiquaries in every part of the globe.

With hindsight he was absolutely right. When the British Museum did come to acquire major Anglo-Saxon finds, such as the Gibbs Collection from Faversham or the finds from the Taplow Barrow, there was no immediate full publication. Once purchased by Mayer the Faussett Collection fared very well indeed. Thanks to his liberal funding and Roach Smith's tireless energy and enthusiasm, a handsome publication was published with the minimum of delay in 1856 and the numbers of volumes printed, advertised at 300, would have sufficed for the requirements of the day.

Unlike James Douglas, Charles Roach Smith made an honest job of publishing the Faussett Collection and the excavation diaries.

> In preparing the manuscripts for the press, I have judged it best to print them precisely as they stood; preserving the general arrangement and even the orthography as much as possible. As the great value of the *Inventorium Sepulchrale* depends wholly upon the numerous facts which it contains, it is right those facts should be set before the reader just as they have descended to us. (*Inventorium Sepulchrale*, vi–vii.)

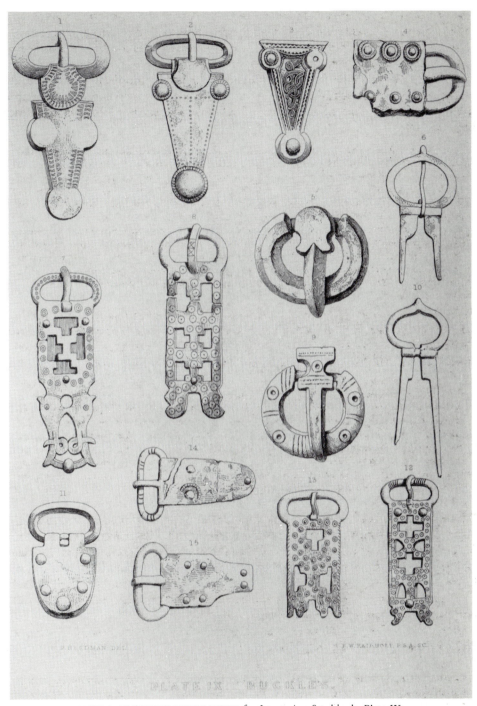

PLATE 8   FAIRHOLT'S ILLUSTRATIONS for *Inventorium Sepulchrale*, Plate IX

PLATE 9 FAIRHOLT'S ILLUSTRATIONS for *Inventorium Sepulchrale*, Plate XX

The only changes were in the footnotes, where he omitted some of Faussett's erroneous observations and added notes of his own where needed. The volume was provided with a lengthy introduction by Roach Smith and an index. The illustrations were entrusted to the best antiquarian illustrator of the day, F.W. Fairholt, who provided both numerous text figures and twenty plates, seven of them in colour. The quality of the illustrations can be appreciated from Plates 8 and 9, which show Fairholt's quality in line and wash. The *Inventorium Sepulchrale* of 1856 is thus both a work of reference and a work of art: besides being a joy to own it remains indispensable to the archaeological bookshelf.

This immaculate publication of the Faussett Collection is doubly valuable today. During the Liverpool Blitz, the museum in William Brown Street took a direct hit and some categories of objects were destroyed. Chiefly these were the metal vessels and the pots, so Fairholt's accurate drawings of them (Plate 9), supplementing the earlier work of Henry Godfrey Faussett (Plate 7), and a few later photographs, are all we have by way of a record of these lost objects.

But the *Inventorium Sepulchrale* of Bryan Faussett, edited by Charles Roach Smith, is now a rare book. Few copies come into the antiquarian bookshops and such as do now cost £150 or more. It is no longer true to say that the volume can be at the 'fireside' of all interested scholars. The need for a new edition was realized many years ago, and between 1963 and 1971, when the material was not on display at Liverpool, thanks to the enlightened courtesy of the museum authorities, batches of it were sent to Oxford. There, thanks to a grant from the British Academy, it was catalogued afresh and redrawn by Mrs Marion Cox, samples of whose work are shown in Plates 2–4. Those drawings, as well as photographs of the jewellery and other susceptible finds by Robert L. Wilkins FSA, await the time and opportunity to prepare a new edition of *Inventorium Sepulchrale*. It will be a challenging task to incorporate all the new information from modern excavation and research while retaining, as Charles Roach Smith did, the integrity of the original diaries. But it should be possible to make an even better job of it, through facsimile of some of the text and all the available illustrative material, from Bryan and the incomparable Henry Faussett, through Fairholt and on to Marion Cox, in a rich mix of old and new together.

Notes

1. Information about the Curriculum and optional subjects at Oxford in the eighteenth century has been taken from Aston (gen. ed.) 1986, Volume 5.
2. The biographical detail is taken from a letter from Thomas Godfrey Faussett to Joseph Mayer, dated 5 August 1854, which is published at the back of the printed *Inventorium Sepulchrale* (1856), 201–7. Thomas Godfrey Faussett inherited the archaeological interest and himself dug the Anglo-Saxon cemetery known as Bifrons at Patrixbourne, Kent, see *Archaeologia Cantiana* X (1876), 298–316 and XIII (1880), 522–56, using the same probe that his great-grandfather had invented to help locate graves. His great-grandson describes him as something of a polymath. 'He was a minute and painstaking herald and genealogist; and actually visited every church, and copied with his own hand every monument and armorial window in Kent; his collections of which, as well as his transcripts of county visitations . . . were, after his death, of much service to Mr. Hasted in compiling his celebrated *History of Kent*. He amassed, too, a cabinet of more than five thousand Roman and British coins' . . . 'but the select of his cabinet; the remainder, chiefly being duplicates, to the weight of one hundred and fifty pounds, he melted down into a

bell, which still swings on the roof of Heppington, and bears the following inscription:
AVDI . QVID . TECUM . LOQVITVR . ROMANA . VETVSTAS .
EX . AERE . ROMANO . ME . CONFLARI . FECIT . B . F . A . s . s .
1766.'

3. Letters from the Revd Bryan Faussett to Dr Ducarel, who was clearly an intimate friend, dated 16 July 1764 and 18 January 1765, *Inventorium Sepulchrale* (1856), 208 ff, 213.

4. *Inventorium Sepulchrale* (1856), 1–3. There is a nearly contemporary illustration of the sandpit at Gilton (Plate 1.2), which was made by James Douglas in 1783; Douglas 1793, at the top of p. 25; Ronald Jessup 1975, plate 4, 283–4. It shows the archaeological stratigraphy of the site and the two windmills precariously close to the edge of the pit, just as Faussett described them. The little engraving on page 1 of *Inventorium Sepulchrale* 1856, shows a later situation with three windmills in a more 'romantic' composition.

5. Jessup 1975, plate 23 (upper), 288. This is a photograph of a watercolour, an extra illustration facing folio 89 in Douglas's own copy of the *Nenia Britannica*, now in the British Museum, MS. G. 6863.

6. This evidence from Kingston Down remains as yet unpublished.

7. For a full study of Anglo-Saxon barrow burials, see Guy Grainger in the forthcoming report on the Finglesham cemetery.

8. Figure originally published in Sonia Chadwick Hawkes *et al*, 'X-Ray fluorescent analysis of some Dark-Age coins and jewellery', *Archaeometry* 9 (1966), pp. 98–138. The majority of the gold analysed came by courtesy of the then authorities of Liverpool City Museums, from the Mayer Collection, and thus included everything from the Faussett Collection except the Kingston Brooch, which was judged too precious to travel to Oxford for the purpose.

9. 'The cost of living, eighteenth century style', Museum Piece, Liverpool Museums, November 1971.

10. In Library of the Society of Antiquaries of London, MS 723, along with the letters from Douglas. Jessup 1975, 286, thinks these drawings were by Douglas, but on the whole it seems unlikely.

11. I am indebted to Dr Stephen Briggs for the information that the original survey plan of the barrows on Chartham Down, made for Dr Cromwell Mortimer, and his illustrations of the finds from them, now resides in the British Library.

12. Library of the Society of Antiquaries, MS. 723. A selection was published in *Inventorium Sepulchrale* 1856, 215–221. The majority appear in Jessup 1975, 182–229.

Bibliography

Aston, T.H. (gen. ed.) 1986: *The History of the University of Oxford: V, The Eighteenth Century* (ed. L.S. Sutherland and L.G. Mitchell).

Boys 1792: *Collections for a History of Sandwich*.

Douglas 1793: *Nenia Britannica: or a Sepulchral History of Great Britain*.

Hawkes 1982: "Finglesham. A cemetery in East Kent", *The Anglo-Saxons*, Campbell, J. (Ed.) Oxford, 24–5, figure 1.

Inventorium Sepulchrale 1856: *Inventorium Sepulchrale*, Smith, C.R. (Ed.) London.

Jessup 1975: *Man of Many Talents: an informal biography of James Douglas 1753–1819*.

Smith, C.R. 1853: "The Faussett Collection of Anglo-Saxon Antiquities", *Collectanea Antiqua* III, 179–92.

Shephard 1979: "The social identity of the individual in isolated barrows and barrow cemeteries in Anglo-Saxon England", *Space, Hierarchy and Society*, Burnham, B.C. and Kingsbury, J. (Eds.) B. A. R. International Series 59, 47–79.

CHAPTER TWO

FAUSSETT REDISCOVERED: CHARLES ROACH SMITH, JOSEPH MAYER, AND THE PUBLICATION OF *INVENTORIUM SEPULCHRALE*

Michael Rhodes

The papers which comprise this volume are the proceedings of a conference to mark the centenary of the death of the Liverpool goldsmith, collector and philanthropist Joseph Mayer (1803–86). That his centenary has been celebrated by a conference on Anglo-Saxon cemeteries is due to his acquisition of the Faussett Collection of Kentish antiquities and the subsequent publication of Faussett's *Inventorium Sepulchrale* (1856), which remains a corner-stone of Anglo-Saxon cemetery studies. The events which led Mayer to purchase the Faussett Collection mark and illuminate a series of important turning-points in British archaeology in which his friend Charles Roach Smith played a central role. This paper will firstly assess these events against their social and intellectual background, and secondly highlight the achievements of Smith and his contemporaries in the then newly internationalized field of Dark-Age studies.

THE FAUSSETTS AND DOUGLAS

The Revd Bryan Faussett of Heppington (1720–76), Kent's premier barrow digger, wrote his will in July 1769, some six years before his death.[1] If he was already crippled with gout, this had not diminished his cultivated eccentricity

PLATE 1   REVD BRYAN FAUSSETT'S TOMBSTONE, Nackington Church (M. Rhodes)

and dry wit, for among various conventional provisions for his wife and family, and the disposal of his corpse in Nackington Church (Plate 1), of which he was Perpetual Curate, he made two less than usual requests. The first was that his sermons should be burnt, every one. The second related to his antiquities:

> . . . as I have been at great pains and expense in collecting them, that they may never be disposed of by sale or otherwise but upon the greatest necessity, but that they may still continue in my family and at Heppington, humbly trusting in God that my posterity will some of them at least wisely prefer polite literature and refinement to ignorance and dissipation, and books and medals to hounds, horses and gaming men.

Thus it was that the collection remained in the family for two more generations.[2]

If few outsiders managed to gain access to the antiquities, Faussett's 'posterity' nonetheless appreciated the importance of their inheritance. His son, Henry Godfrey Faussett (b. 1749) had himself exhumed the famous Kingston fibula, and had drawn many of the skilful illustrations in his father's notebooks, the *Inventorium Sepulchrale*, which provide a grave by grave description of the discoveries.[3] Although Henry's professional duties as a lawyer prevented him from devoting much time to antiquities, he continued to take an interest in archaeology, and became friendly with Captain James Douglas (1753–1819) following a visit to the Chatham Lines in 1779 or 1780 (Jessup 1975, 52).

The significance of Douglas's excavations in Kent is well known (op. cit.). By 1782 his investigations here and elsewhere had almost provided him with sufficient material for 'a general history of the funeral customs of the ancients' (Smith 1856, 217), and he became increasingly anxious to examine the Faussett cabinet. For the past year he had been trying to persuade its owner to sell the treasures to an anonymous collector 'high up in the estimation of the antiquarian world' (op. cit., 215). Henry Faussett not only refused to sell, but was reluctant to allow Douglas even to see the collection, hoping perhaps to publish it himself. Eventually, Douglas was granted access to make notes and drawings, although Faussett apparently did not permit sight of his father's notebooks.[4]

Douglas's *Nenia Britannica* was published in parts between 1786 and 1793 (Douglas 1793). Each part was illustrated, the text being dependent upon the plates. For the first time, a British antiquary had recognized the importance of topographical plans, elevations and sections of tumuli, and the need for a classified description of relics to facilitate comparisons. The work also incorporated the clearest statement so far of the principle of applying relative dating from a known to an unknown source. Whilst only the discovery in a grave of a coin or inscription could obviate dating errors, the historian was able to use such relics to date others found in less favourable circumstances by means of comparison. A grave at Gilton, Ash, in Kent, could be no earlier than the coin of Justinian (527–65) which it contained, and no later than 742 when extra-mural burials were prohibited outside churchyards. A Roman brooch and a circular stone from Gilton could not be used for dating, neither could an associated polished flint, which was best regarded as an amulet preserved from an earlier epoch (op. cit., 92). For the first time, the remains of the Anglo-Saxons had been identified and characterized, and the true date of Faussett's antiquities had been recognized. The Kentish burials belonged to local communities, and not – a popular error even today – to warriors.[5] He was uncertain as to whether they were of pagans or Christians, but favoured the second option.

Unfortunately for Douglas, antiquarian opinion was not ready for a work which replaced dependence upon early literature in favour of the scientific consideration of observations. Even Colt Hoare who adopted his idea of classifying barrows, rejected Douglas's Anglo-Saxon dating for barrows of the 'small conic' variety (Hoare 1812, 46–7, and Tumuli plate IV). A full generation passed before his achievements were truly appreciated.

CHARLES ROACH SMITH

T he major force amongst the next generation of archaeologists, who were active from the mid-1830s, came in the unlikely form of a minor retail chemist (Rhodes forthcoming). Charles Roach Smith (1806–90) was born into an Isle of Wight farming family. After a second-rate schooling, he was apprenticed most unwillingly to a chemist and druggist in Chichester. Here, he developed an interest in coins and antiquities, and studied Cicero, adopting his Stoic philosophy. He also read Camden, noting his choice to remain single 'apprehending that the incumbrances of a married life might prove a prejudice to his studies'.[6] Smith too remained a life-long bachelor.

In 1832 he decided to start his own business, and rented a small shop behind the Bank of England, later moving to Liverpool Street. His arrival in the city coincided with the greatest period of redevelopment since the great fire of London, and Smith was intrigued by the Roman remains which were being exposed. Initially, at least, he made healthy profits, and was able to employ assistants. Thus he had both time and money to pursue his interests, which turned increasingly to purchasing coins, figured and stamped samian, and other minor antiquities. Within a few years he had compiled a large private museum (Kidd 1977). Smith was by no means the only collector; what was unusual was the diligence and clarity of thought with which he studied his acquisitions. A keen Latin scholar, Smith searched the classics for any mention of antiquities. His notebooks record detailed records of finds and find-spots supported by accurate sketches.[7] They evince a clear insight into scientific methods, perhaps shaped by his study of chemistry. From the very beginning Smith avoided unwarranted interpretation, but rather weighed the evidence for and against various possibilities.

By the spring of 1836, Smith had become known to a number of antiquarians and was invited to submit a paper to the Society of Antiquaries (Smith 1837). Towards the end of the year he became a Fellow (Plate 2). Unfortunately, Smith's election was opposed by an anonymous person, supported by Sir Henry Ellis of the British Museum, who maintained that Smith was unsuitable as he was in business. Incidents such as this hardened Smith's views on social prejudice, and he often complained of the respect paid to the ignorant and well connected in contrast to the disregard shown to men of real ability who lacked social standing. His perspective was reinforced by the Corporation's antipathy towards City antiquities. Not only was Smith hindered from recording

PLATE 2 SKETCH OF C.R. SMITH by J. Thurstone, late 1830s(?), Mayer collection, Liverpool Central Library (M. Rhodes)

discoveries, but in 1841 was actually thrown off excavations for the new Royal Exchange on the pretext that he had paid workmen for antiquities destined for the embryonic Guildhall Museum. By contrast, a private developer had allowed Smith to excavate and record two Roman mosaics, opened the site for public viewing, and adopted his suggestion that the pavements should be given to the British Museum (Smith 1859, 56 fn.). Such actions gave rise to a second theme in Smith's writings, namely the phenomenon of private enlightenment and generosity as against corporate meanness and ignorance. Both perceptions were seemingly confirmed by the Faussett affair of 1853–4.

If Smith's heroic struggles on behalf of London archaeology are relatively well known, the same cannot be said for another important aspect of his activities. From the summer of 1836, Smith embarked upon a series of archaeological excursions through the South of England. Whilst he clearly enjoyed an excuse to get out of town, his purpose became increasingly serious. In a country lacking museums and antiquarian publications other than *Archaeologia*, it was the only way to learn about antiquities. By the end of 1839, Smith had visited almost every major archaeological site in the South-East, and made the first of many visits to France. Thus he became the first British archaeologist to travel abroad in search of parallels to indigenous antiquities. Indeed, Smith's hunger for information was insatiable. Snippets of hearsay from fellow antiquaries about finds or collectors were carefully recorded, and newspapers were scoured for reports of discoveries. Every lead was followed up by a visit. Travelling in the late 1830s was by no means easy. Coaches and vans were infrequent, and Smith covered miles on foot, staying at inns by night. Everywhere he went, innkeepers were questioned about local discoveries, jewellers' shops were visited in search of coins, and newly dug earth would be scanned for Roman tiles. Local antiquarians received unannounced visits, and not all were pleased to receive a stranger. Smith's records of these excursions provide a unique insight into the activities of contemporary collectors and the state of antiquarianism in the provinces.

Initially, Smith's interests reflected the strengths of his collection, which comprised coins of all periods, and London antiquities of primarily Roman and medieval date. Early Saxon antiquities were almost never found in central London, but Smith's curiosity was roused in 1841 by seeing some of Douglas's finds in the Ashmolean Museum,[8] and by his first unpremeditated visit to Heppington in August. Having tramped from the Gravesend ferry to Canterbury via Reculver, Smith proceeded to Lymne along the Roman road called Stone Street.[9] Heppington lies to the east of this road, about four miles south of Canterbury (Plate 3). By this date, Faussett's collection had passed to his grandson, Dr Godfrey Faussett, an Oxford professor and Canon of Oxford Cathedral, who was away for much of the time.[10] Smith knew of the collection's existence from Douglas (1793) and Hasted (1790, 185 and 557, etc.), although nothing had been heard of it for years. Smith approached the turning to Heppington – and walked past:

PLATE 3   HEPPINGTON, shortly before its demolition in the early 1950s. Photograph recently acquired by Liverpool Museum

. . . for I had no introduction to Dr. Faussett; and I had heard that he had an objection to shewing the collection. As I walked slowly onwards I reflected; paused; turned back, and went to the house. I was courteously received. Dr. Faussett said that it was partly true what I had heard; and at the moment it would be rather inconvenient for him to shew me the collection; but that there would be no difficulty at some future time . . . (Smith 1883, 67–8).

With this encouraging response, Smith continued his expedition.

If this incident aroused Smith's interest in Saxon antiquities, he was spurred into active research next February, when Lord Albert Conyngham (later Lord Londesborough) and his private secretary, J.Y. Akerman, presented a paper to the Society of Antiquaries on their recent barrow excavations at Breach Downs, near Barham, Kent (Conyngham and Akerman 1844). These were the first Saxon barrow excavations to be reported as such since Douglas, and a rich collection of grave-goods was obtained. Akerman considered that the barrows were probably of the late fifth to early sixth centuries, citing Douglas. Their early Saxon date was soon confirmed by J.P. Bartlett who subsequently opened four more of the tumuli, one of which contained a purse with several sceattas. These were identified by Akerman (1843), and illustrated by Smith (1843a, 7 and plate VI).

It seems likely that Smith recalled having seen objects similar to those from Breach Downs in the collection of the Sandwich antiquary, William Henry Rolfe (1779–1859; see Matson 1961), and that he immediately requested these for exhibition. With his comprehensive knowledge of Roman small finds, the umbos, swords and circular brooches in Rolfe's collection would have stood out in his memory (Smith 1856, 39). A hamper of antiquities from Gilton and other sites near Sandwich was delivered to Smith in March, and displayed to the Society of Antiquaries. According to Smith, these showed close affinity with the Breach Downs finds:

. . . thus the two discoveries will be mutually illustrative, and furnish a store of facts, from the general and distinctive features of which deductions may be drawn with greater certainty towards a classification of the remains ascribed to the northern tribes, who successively over-ran Britain after the withdrawal of the Roman forces. As these nations have a near relation one with the other, with similar habits and customs, the correct appropriation of their works of art . . . can only be expected to be fully accomplished by a patient and systematic arrangement of the materials themselves, and the circumstances under which they are presented to us (Smith 1844a).

In a remarkable intuitive leap of imagination, Smith had described what became the principal aim of European Dark-Age studies for the next twenty years, if not much longer. The problem of establishing the ethnicity of the sepulchral remains of northern tribes had been discussed in the last chapter of the *Nenia*, a work which Smith seems to have read closely whilst preparing his paper. Douglas was unable to suggest a method of approaching the problem, but Smith recognized that the first step was to determine regional differences within burial groups of the same period. For this it was necessary to compile a body of reliable data from which the general characteristics of the various groupings could be derived. Smith began the 'systematic arrangement' of which he had spoken in the same paper, by precisely defining two varieties of Saxon brooch. These were possibly the clearest artifact descriptions since Douglas, whom Smith clearly admired (Smith 1851b, 155–6). During the next year, he met the Danish archaeologist, Thomsen, who would have encouraged this classificatory approach (Smith 1883, 151).

On 17 October, Smith made his long awaited visit to examine the Faussett Collection. This 'far exceeded my expectations, which from the mention made of them by Douglas were rather high'. Dr Faussett confirmed that it had 'been never examined for twenty years, and he said, its being thrown open and rearranged was entirely owning to me . . .'. The collection was not confined to grave-goods, but included 'red Roman pottery from off Margate', and 'tiles from Dover Castle'.[11] So numerous were the coins, that Faussett had melted his duplicates into a bell, which hung in the roof (Smith 1856, 204). The manuscript volumes 'would make two valuable 8vo books of print'.[12] In an excited letter to Rolfe, Smith later remarked that 'nothing less than a regular week's stay would have been sufficient to have properly examined everything'.[13] Even so, he made sure to catalogue those coins which had been found in tumuli.[14] Finally, he went outdoors to examine Faussett's pavilion, which contained fragments of sculpture from Canterbury and London,[15] and having been invited to renew his visit, returned to Canterbury, well pleased.

THE BRITISH ARCHAEOLOGICAL ASSOCIATION

By 1843, Smith had probably examined more small British antiquities than any other, alive or dead, and had gathered a mass of data. His formidable gifts had not gone unrecognized; he had been secretary to the Numismatic Society since 1841, and was on the Council of the Society of Antiquaries. Even so, Smith had failed to breathe life into the Society. He was particularly dissatisfied with *Archaeologia*, which was wordy and scantily illustrated, whereas Smith's research had shown him the need for '*facts*, copiously illustrated but sparingly diluted with theory' (Smith 1848, v). For this reason, he now commenced his *Collectanea Antiqua* – the first journal devoted solely to archaeology. In contrast with *Archaeologia*, Smith's *Collectanea* placed an emphasis on the illustration of minor antiquities – reflecting his interests as a collector and his recent perception that even humble artifacts might be used to characterize ethnic and regional affinities. His enthusiasm for collecting, sketching and publishing minor antiquities later caused Smith to be dubbed 'the British Montfauçon', an honour previously awarded to Faussett.[16]

The Society of Antiquaries' inability to respond to the archaeological destruction wrought by railway excavations and road improvements was also a source of discontent. It had neither encouraged rescue archaeology, nor pressed for government action. By contrast, as long ago as 1818 the French government had formed a *Comité Historique des Arts et Monuments* to publish an antiquarian survey of France, with descriptions and drawings of all its monuments. Its work was assisted by the *Société Française pour la Conservation des Monuments Historiques*, founded by Arcisse de Caumont. It was this society which Roach Smith and Thomas Wright tried to emulate when at the end of 1843 they formed the British Archaeological Association (BAA 1846a).

The first formal meeting of the BAA took place in December, at Wright's house in

Brompton. Wright had settled here shortly after receiving his Cambridge MA in 1836, and was writing brilliantly, if not always accurately, on all manner of historical subjects in order to support himself (Lee 1900). This was unusual – the majority of the Antiquaries enjoyed a private income, and like Smith, Wright may have suffered from social prejudice (Levine 1986, 22). Wright also had academic contacts in France, and in the previous year had been elected a member of the *Institut des Arts et Sciences*. He was a keen Anglo-Saxon scholar.

Within a few weeks the *modus operandi* of the Association had been agreed. A Central Committee would collect from correspondents in all parts of the country information tending to the 'discovery, illustration, and conservation' of national monuments (BAA 1846a). A new inexpensive journal would enable the committee to communicate with the members. Amongst other aims, it would draw attention to foreign finds illustrative of British monuments. The expanding railway system would allow members to attend an annual conference – Canterbury was a possible first venue. Lord Albert Conyngham agreed to become its first president; Wright became its editor; Smith and Albert Way, the Director of the Society of Antiquaries, became its secretaries.

The committee's first opportunity to act in defence of archaeological monuments came in June, when they learnt of plans to erect a reservoir in Greenwich Park. This would involve levelling Saxon barrows mentioned in Douglas's *Nenia* (BAA 1845a, 167). The subsequent controversy reached the correspondence columns of *The Times*, where Smith refuted an argument that Douglas had already destroyed the tumuli (Smith 1844b). The affair blew over only after the House of Commons had been informed that workmen had been ordered to replace on the barrows the earth that had been removed (BAA 1845a, 252). Clearly both Douglas and barrows were gaining in public sympathy. The incident is the more remarkable in that it took place prior to the Canterbury Congress.

Not everyone on the committee was in favour of the congress, and preparations fell largely on Smith. Shortly beforehand, he wrote to Dr Faussett to ask if a visit to Heppington could be included in the programme. Faussett replied that he did not want to cause disappointment, but would like advice on how the more fragile items 'not being under the protection of glass' might be submitted to the 'tender mercies of a numerous party'. Inspection of the coins 'for obvious reasons' would be out of the question.[17] By 9 August, Smith had answered these points and Faussett was prudently included on the congress's General Committee.[18]

Despite prognostications of ridiculous failure by staff of the British Museum and the friends of Albert Way, who were suspicious of its popular appeal, the congress succeeded beyond the wildest hopes of its organizers, with nearly two hundred attending amid full press coverage. Ladies were astonished to find that the philosophers included handsome young men, dressed in the most fashionable attire. After a schedule of lectures which would have exhausted the most ardent enthusiast, the band played and there was dancing until midnight (Taylor 1932). The congress marked a watershed in British archaeology. It confirmed archaeology's growing appeal and was the springboard for many local archaeological societies. Its importance to our present study is that Saxon burials, and the Faussett Collection in particular, became the centre of popular attention. The digging of Saxon graves consequently received a high profile for the next two decades.

PLATE 4   MEMBERS OF THE BAA excavating barrows at Breach Down, Kent, during the Canterbury Congress of 1844. From T. Wright's *An Archaeological Album* (Museum of London)

On the second day of the congress, about fifty carriages transported the entire assembly to Breach Down. Lord Albert had previously arranged for eight barrows to be excavated to within a foot of the interment, so that the company could participate in the process of discovery. A heavy downpour of rain did nothing to dampen their enthusiasm (Plate 4). According to *The Pictorial Times*, even 'the bigwigs stood round with staring eyes and open mouths' as the grave-goods were passed around for inspection (op. cit., 196). After lunch more burials were exhumed in the grounds of Bourne Park, Bishopsbourne, Lord Albert's country seat, and the evening session included a discussion of the discoveries (Dunkin 1845, 97–114).

The visit to Heppington took place at 2 p.m. the following day. Security was tight with policemen standing guard outside. Visitors were admitted in detachments under Smith's personal guidance to the small room which contained the collections. Despite these restrictions, everyone was well pleased with the proceedings, including Dr Faussett (ibid.; Smith 1883, 9–11). Wright later wrote of how the collection had challenged their image of Anglo-Saxons:

> . . . we are accustomed to regard them as half savages, without refinement, rude in their manners, and skilful only in the use of their weapons. But [. . . here] the followers of Hengist and Horsa seem to rise up before us . . . our previous notions vanish . . . we see at once the refinements of Saxon life . . . and the skill and taste of Saxon workmen (Wright 1845, 10).

At the close of the conference, Smith proposed a vote of thanks to Dr Faussett, stating that the Heppington visit had been one of the congress's most important and interesting achievements.

He considered that the collection was 'unrivalled in the value of the objects themselves, as works of ancient art of a particular epoch, and in the admirable manner in which they were arranged, classified and illustrated'. Several speakers had commented on the need to publish the collections along with Faussett's catalogue, and Smith now intimated Dr Faussett's willingness to assist in this respect. Unfortunately the Association had neither the time, money or vision to undertake the work (Smith 1854a, 181).

Smith and his colleagues returned to London elated by their triumphs, but the very fact of success aroused the jealousy of those who had opposed the conference. Again, social distinction probably lay at the root of the troubles. The ensuing events, then described as 'anarchaeology', need not concern us, except to say that by March the next year the Association had split into two mirror images of itself (Taylor 1932). The bitter feuding between the Association and the new Archaeological Institute headed by Albert Way, continued for decades and seriously weakened the chance of obtaining any effective antiquities legislation (Fox 1872, 172). For Smith, who remained secretary of the Association, there was the added problem of the mounting administrative work, which kept him heavily committed for the next five years. The congresses created a particular burden. On the positive side, his position as secretary gave him a rare over-view of contemporary discoveries and research.

TOWARDS A MUSEUM OF NATIONAL ANTIQUITIES

It was at the 1849 congress of the BAA at Chester that Smith and Wright, co-founders of the BAA, became friendly with Joseph Mayer (1803–86), co-founder of the Historic Society of Lancashire and Cheshire.[19] Mayer came from a Newcastle-under-Lyme family, whose prosperity was based on industrial wealth. He had trained in his brother-in-law's Liverpool jewellery shop, but in 1844 established his own business in Lord Street, partly because he wanted to be a manufacturing jeweller, not just a middle man. Like Smith, his business provided the means whereby to purchase his antiquities. Mayer had also remained a bachelor, and the two men found much in common by reason of class and interests. A collector since boyhood, Mayer's first portrait, c. 1840, depicts him as a connoisseur of pottery and classical sculpture. He also had a professional interest in antique jewellery – to sell, for his collection, and as a source of design ideas (Gibson 1988).

Mayer's generosity had been noted by the BAA before the 1849 congress had begun: 'The Liverpool people . . . have already subscribed £300 and will pay the *entire* expenses of our day's visit to that place. We are quite unused to such tokens of generosity'.[20] Mayer later promised to pay off any shortfall, which led Smith to comment that 'such people put one quite in good spirits'.[21] It was a heartening end to an unhappy era for Smith and Wright, both of whom resigned from the BAA shortly afterwards on account of new rivalries. Smith showed his appreciation by sponsoring Mayer's election as an

FSA,[22] and seems to have arranged his entry into other societies.[23] He also made gifts of antiquities and commemorative medals to Mayer's Historic Society, and autograph letters for his personal collection.[24] Mayer reciprocated by contributing to the sponsorship of Smith's excavations at Lymne and Pevensey (Smith 1852b, 46; 1858a, 41).

In May 1852, Mayer opened his Egyptian Museum in Liverpool's Colquitt Street, furnishing it with sale-room purchases. His inspiration was the Egyptian Gallery in the British Museum which had opened in 1846. The museum had two principal galleries: the Mummy Room and the Jewellery Room (Gibson 1988, 8). At about the same time, Mayer wrote to Smith with a request for materials for a study collection of national antiquities, and for some explanatory notes, with which Smith gladly complied.[25]

The need for museums of antiquities had been a campaign theme of Smith's since he had become aware of the scale of destruction in London. The British Museum was generallly unwilling to accept British material, and actively collected only works of artistic merit, with an almost exclusive emphasis on classical and middle-eastern antiquities. The lengthy Parliamentary Select Committee Report on the Museum of 1835–6, included but one passing reference to British antiquities (Parliamentary Committee 1835–6, 417–8). After the Government's refusal to provide the Society of Antiquaries with a room for their projected museum in 1839,[26] Smith donated a number of antiquities to the City Corporation, hoping to encourage their interest.[27] But, following the Royal Exchange débâcle, and other incidents, there were serious doubts about the Corporation's ability to create a museum of suitable quality. A writer to the *Literary Gazette* now called for a new society 'for the *preservation* and *collection* of national antiquities'. Once established, this would attract gifts from the Corporation and local collectors alike ('C.C.' 1843). The current popularity of national antiquities, embodied in the new archaeological societies, increased the impetus for a museum. In April 1845, an article in the *Builder* called for government action, deploring the lack of provision for British antiquities in the British Museum ('E.H.' 1845). Two months later, in Parliament, a private member called for a new museum of national antiquities, but his motion was badly prepared and was quashed (Hansard 1845, 1330–4; Anon. 1845a).

Such calls were based on the need for preservation and education, but a purely scientific reason for a national collection was now introduced. At the BAA's second congress in 1845, T.J. Pettigrew, Smith's co-secretary, spoke of the need 'to form collections from various parts, to study the history of the several localities, and then generalise the observations and draw the historical deductions'. It was for this reason that a museum of national antiquities was desirable (Pettigrew 1846, 3). Pettigrew's knowledge of British antiquities was small, and these words so closely mirror Smith's of 1842 that there is little doubt that these were Smith's views, not his own. Earlier in 1845, Smith had cited the problem of conducting regional comparative studies to establish the ethnic origin of Dark-Age materials, as evidence of a need for local or county museums (Smith 1845, 103). It was this same problem which, in 1852, caused Ludwig Lindenschmit to create the Römische–Germanisch Museum (Böhner 1969, XVII).

The first hint of success came in 1845, when Lord Prudhoe offered to donate his national antiquities to the British Museum, provided that a place was set aside for the reception of British collections (Anon. 1845b); a similar ruse had met with some success in 1837 (Miller 1873, 210). The trustees accepted Lord Prudhoe's terms under pressure from the Archaeological Institute (Anon. 1845c). Nevertheless, it was not until the winter of 1850–51, after a Parliamentary Commission (1850) had presented its report on the function and management of the Museum, that a room was opened for British antiquities. Some months later it was still too inadequately arranged to permit a description of the exhibits, but major advances were at hand with the appointment of a new assistant, A.W. Franks, to look after the British material (Kidd 1977, 126).

Franks (1826–97) had graduated from Cambridge in 1849 and the next year became a life member of the Archaeological Institute. Unlike the Museum's other curatorial staff, who were numismatists or biased towards the Mediterranean and Eastern civilizations, Franks was interested in European medieval art, and therefore in the artifacts of barbarian Europe (Wilson 1985a; D. Kidd, *pers. comm.*). His first task was to improve the British collections, with the aim of creating a national series comparable with that of the Danish National Museum.[28] For three consecutive years after his appointment, Franks published notes on his progress in the Institute's *Archaeological Journal* (Franks 1852; 1853; 1854). In this way he hoped to encourage gifts from private collectors, recognizing that the scientific value of British antiquities depended upon the reliability of associated records, and that antiquities obtained from dealers would always be deficient in this regard. In his article of 1853, despite numerous recent discoveries of Saxon grave-goods, most still in private hands, Franks complained that 'additions to the Saxon antiquities have not been very numerous, and that branch of national archaeology is the most deficient in the whole collection'. Clearly such a man would have done everything in his power to acquire a prize such as the Faussett Collection.

FAUSSETT REFUSED

Although the BAA had shown no interest in the collection since the Canterbury Congress, Smith had never forgotten Dr Faussett's offer to permit its publication. Inspired by the success of his recent research on Saxon and Merovingian finds (see below) Smith now wrote to Dr Faussett, offering to publish the collection at his own expense. This was shortly before the latter's death in 1853. Faussett refused, probably because he was considering the disposal of his collection 'consistent with the preservation of its integrity, and the interests of his family' (Smith 1856, v). He nevertheless asked Smith's advice on this subject, and through him offered the collection to Lord Londesborough for £1,000, who seems to have declined.[29]

Dr Faussett's will was proved early that August. The principal beneficiary was his eldest son, Bryan Faussett, who lived at Oxford 'being in holy orders'. Heppington was placed in trust for his benefit, although much of the rest of his estate, including the Faussett Collection and manuscripts, was left to him directly. The executors were, nevertheless, empowered to sell or dispose of such property as was necessary to settle debts and charges,[30] and it was they who decided the fate of the Collection.

PLATE 5   SKETCH OF EDWARD HAWKINS (British Museum Dept. Prints and Drawings)

There were three executors, namely Dr Faussett's second son, Godfrey, his widow, and his cousin, William Bland of Hartlip. The latter had been friendly with Smith since the mid-1840s, when Smith had helped to excavate and publish a Roman villa found on his estate (Smith 1883, 157–8; 1849). All three executors would, therefore, have been disposed to accept Smith's advice, which now was that the collection should be valued and offered to the British Museum (Smith 1856, v). A few days later, Heppington received a visit from Edward Hawkins, Keeper of the Museum's Antiquities Department (Plate 5), accompanied by Albert Way. Having decided that the collection was 'of the highest importance to the Museum', Hawkins immediately arranged for the manuscript volumes to be forwarded to London, and for a mutually acceptable dealer to visit and to value the collection (BM 1854, 1; Smith 1854a, 182). He was promptly rewarded by a 'brace of birds' sent from Heppington.[31] The approved dealer was the 'numismatist and antiquary' William Chaffers, a friend of Smith's, who was not only a member of the BAA but had an important collection of London antiquities (Smith 1886, 103–6). Again Smith's influence with the Faussett family is evident.

Chaffers submitted his valuation on 20 September. It provides details of how the collection was arranged. The bulk was ordered by object type in nineteen numbered drawers. Other items were held in two boxes, a basket and a small glazed cabinet. The mantelpiece was arrayed with curiosities, including fourteen Roman lamps, eight Egyptian porcelain mummy figures, and a bust with stone eyes. The collection was valued at £665, excluding the notebooks,[32] which the executors thought rather low.[33] They had not seen the notebooks, which in recent years had been kept by Dr Faussett at Oxford,[34] and decided to ask Hawkins to dispatch them for examination, before deciding whether or not to sell.[35] By 30 September they had determined to proceed, and to include the manuscripts in the valuation price.[36]

The BM's trustees considered the offer on 8 October. Chaffers' valuation was tabled with Faussett's notebooks, and a report from Hawkins was read. This commended the collection as 'probably the most instructive and interesting ever formed of such objects'. It emphasized the importance of the documentation and that every item was 'ticketed with the name of the place where it was found', but the trustees were unmoved, and 'declined to give so large a sum as there were no sufficient funds'. The matter was back on their agenda for 12 November, when a letter from the Archaeological Institute's Central Committee was read. Clearly Franks had canvassed support. The letter stated that the Institute contemplated making valuable donations of British materials to the Museum, but looked for the formation of a national series to which the Faussett Collection would be a valuable asset. The trustees response was unaltered (BM 1854). Meanwhile, Smith waited anxiously for news: 'although each party consults me in turn, both take care not to let me know where the matter stands'.[37]

As it became known that the purchase might fall through, various private collectors expressed an interest. The Derbyshire barrow digger, Thomas Bateman, was eager to buy, so too was Albert Way.[38] Smith had visited Mayer in early September,[39] and had doubtless discussed with him what might happen if the trustees refused. Some of the correspondence relating to this period has yet to be traced, but there are strong hints that Wright, Mayer and perhaps Smith met in Liverpool in October to discuss tactics. Shortly afterwards, Wright was planning a lecture on Saxon antiquities, and in early November, a second(?) 'Faussett Club' dinner, this time in London, was being talked about.[40] Mayer was probably unknown to the British Museum's officers, but tactfully placed them in his debt by making a gift to the Museum of twenty-five Wedgwood medallions, and a rare and valuable fourteenth-century astrolabe (Franks 1854, 30).[41] He expressed his interest in the Faussett Collection to the executors, who promised that he should have the first refusal.[42] Doubtless Smith had been in contact, and Mayer's undertaking not to split the Collection would have proven attractive to them.[43] The motive behind these moves is revealed in a letter from Smith to Bateman. Mayer was considering a bold philanthropic gesture on behalf of British Archaeology: 'to *buy* the collection and after I, at his expense, had printed an account of it, *to give* it to the British Museum!!!'[44]

With this prospect, Smith became anxious to see Bryan Faussett's notebooks, which he had never been able to examine closely. These were still with Hawkins at the British Museum. Accordingly, at the end of November, Smith wrote to ask Godfrey Faussett if he might borrow them for a day or two.[45] Permission was granted immediately. Nevertheless, when Smith applied to Hawkins, the latter refused to hand them over, and informed Mr Faussett that he strongly objected to Smith having them.[46] A strong supporter of Albert Way, Hawkins was not one to forget old scores. However, since it was by Smith's advice that the Collection was on offer to the Museum, the snub was particularly inappropriate. Mayer was disgusted at Hawkins' attitude, and immediately withdrew his plan of giving the collection to the Museum.[47]

When the Archaeological Institute met on 2 December, they heard that a continental museum had registered its interest in the collection, and voted unanimously to petition the BM's trustees (Archaeol. Inst. 1854, 52–3; Smith 1853, 189–91). Hawkins had exhibited the Faussett notebooks to the Society of Antiquaries in November (Evans 1956, 274). Its officers now wrote to advise the trustees that if they accepted Faussett, W.M. Wylie, author of the *Fairford Graves*, would make a gift of his own collection (BM 1854, 7). The matter was considered anew on 10 December, and on 14 January, but the reply was always the same, and the full significance of the refusal became clear. The trustees would not even try to raise the money. Finance was not the problem; the trustees did not want the antiquities – probably they did not want *any* British antiquities!

If there were any doubts that lack of finance was merely an excuse, these were dispelled on 11 February, when the Board considered estimates for the coming financial year. The finance sub-committee had recommended that they should seek a purchase fund of £4,000 if the Faussett Collection were to be bought, and £3,500 if it were not. The trustees submitted a request for £3,500 (BM 1854, 9). In a last desperate measure, the Antiquaries and the Institute wrote directly to the Lords of the Treasury (Anon. 1854a). This was unlikely to succeed, and in any case, Godfrey Faussett's patience was at an end. On 18 February, he wrote to Mayer saying that he and Hawkins had agreed that if the treasury had not responded by then, he would withdraw the offer.[48] The following week, Mayer visited Heppington with Chaffers (whom he knew through the Chester congress) and bought the collection for £700. With characteristic generosity, Mayer paid the full cost of the valuation;[49] the Museum would have paid only one half.

This was not quite the end of the matter, for Mayer had declined to buy the coins and seals, which were immediately sold at Sotheby's along with Faussett's papers.[50] Smith was anxious to know if there was anything else relating to the Saxon antiquities and, indeed, the papers had included important correspondence between Douglas and Godfrey Faussett. Fortunately, Chaffers had managed to purchase these for Mayer.[51] The coins were another question, and Smith was obliged to contact the purchasers directly. His efforts were rewarded by the discovery of six Saxon weights made from Roman coins, which had previously escaped attention (Smith 1856, xliii).

News of Mayer's acquisition was greeted, by societies and the press alike, with praise for the purchaser and condemnation of the BM's trustees. Smith wrote a tract on the subject, and included a list of the board members, partly to shame them and partly to demonstrate that they comprised the great and the good, most of whom had no specialist knowledge (Smith 1854a). On 1 June the outcry reached Parliament, and the trustees were ordered to supply the House of Commons with copies of all communications relating to the Faussett Collection, which were published for public scrutiny (Hansard 1854a, 283; BM 1854). Smith was frustrated to find that the trustee's minutes did not record who had attended the crucial board meetings (Smith 1854b). However, by remarkable good fortune, a private letter survives, which points to the individuals concerned. This was written by William Vaux, one of Hawkins' assistants, to the archaeologist, Henry Layard, who was concerned to know why his Assyrian antiquities were confined to the museum basement.[52]

The problems created by what Smith called the 'monstrous anomaly' of the board were every bit as bad as they appeared to outsiders (Smith 1854a, 186). Of the forty-seven trustees, twenty-seven held post by reason of their position – including the Archbishop of Canterbury, the Speaker of the House of Commons and the First Lord of the Admiralty! Needless to say, very few of these officials attended meetings, and the same applied to the nine family trustees. The remaining fifteen places were elected by the board – in practice the other elected members of the board – who were thereby able to introduce persons of their own taste and outlook. These elected members formed the majority at board meetings, but altogether no more than seven or eight attended, and numbers were often as low as four or five. In Vaux's words: 'Practically this is the greatest evil – it throws all the arrangements in the hands of two or three men, who if they stick together (as Hamilton, Dundas and the Duke of Somerset for instance) can carry or reject what they like.' What they liked were *Greek* antiquities. When the Faussett antiquities were finally rejected on 11 February only five trustees were present. One is known to have been Viscount Mahon, President of the Society of Antiquaries, who was in favour of the purchase (BM 1854, 9). Another was the Duke of Somerset, who was against it. Hamilton and Dundas were united in opposition, and would have made every effort to attend. Clearly, the gang of three had voted together.

The views of Edward Seymour, Duke of Somerset (1804–85), were expressed in a Commons answer about the Faussett Collection on 3 July. In his opinion, the job of the trustees was:

> to consider how, with the limited funds available, they could best secure those antiquities, which, if they did not purchase, the country would not possess. This was the case with regard to classical antiquities, although British antiquities would very likely find a place in some provincial museum (Hansard 1854b, 1054–8; Smith 1854b, 267).

This last suggestion was impracticable. As late as 1870, when Roach Smith advised William Gibbs about bequeathing his collection, it proved impossible to find a suitable local museum (Smith 1891, 52). For the Faussett Collection, the only realistic alternative to the BM was a private collection, with the attendant risk that the collection might be split up when the owner died. Lord Seymour's next comment shows an even greater lack of insight: the Museum was for ever being offered expensive collections which were reputedly unique, for example a recent offer of some Pacific shells. Smith lost no time in printing a scathing reply, underlining the stupidity of comparing Faussett's antiquities with shells, 'as if the one grew like the other, and was re-produced yearly' (Smith 1854b, 267).

The former MP, Sir David Dundas (1799–1877), regarded by many as being 'not quite, quite right',[53] was no better informed than Lord Seymour. Vaux actually heard him remark that he 'did not think we wanted a heap of Saxon antiquities in the Museum!' The third member of the club, William Hamilton (1777–1859), unlike the others, had at least some claims as an antiquary (Plate 6). As Lord Elgin's secretary in Constantinople he had assisted in obtaining the Rosetta stone and the Elgin marbles. A co-founder of the Royal Geographical Society (Anderson 1890) and former Vice-President of the Society of Antiquaries, Hamilton (although not there) had even been named as President of the Primeval Section at the BAA's Canterbury Congress. Nevertheless, in Hamilton's opinion museums should be 'rather for the improvement of fine arts than merely as an historical collection of objects' (Parliamentary Commission 1850, 781). In a period dominated by historicizing styles, the need to display well-designed historical objects had already been recognized by the government, and in 1852 had given rise to a new Museum of Ornamental Art in Marlborough House (Wilson 1985b, 71). Unfortunately, Hamilton's definition of fine art was Greek art. Such was his bias against other civilizations, that he had vehemently opposed plans to display Layard's Nineveh sculptures. According to Vaux: 'Hamilton would not see with any but Greek eyes, they were not Greek. He wished them at the bottom of the sea . . .' Even in the 1850s such views were preposterously conservative. In France, medieval art

PLATE 6   W.R. HAMILTON IN 1850; engraving
(British Museum Dept. Prints and Drawings)

had been fashionable since the early 1830s. In Russia, Denmark, Germany, and elsewhere, museums of national art and antiquities had already opened or were about to open (Basin 1967, 218 ff.; Sklenář 1983, 78–82). This is not to say that Saxon or Merovingian art was universally appreciated, since a tendency to view through 'Greek eyes' naturally persisted. Even the German archaeologist, Ludwig Lindenschmit, had been reluctant to accept that the Selzen graves belonged to early Germanic tribes, since the jewellery found among the grave-goods did not match his grandiose preconceptions. Trained in the classical school, Lindenschmit could not appreciate the style of decoration, which seemed bewildering, fantastic and adventurous (Lindenschmit 1848, 23–4; Kühn 1976, 218). However, he and others were willing to respect their historical interest and to learn, whereas Hamilton was not. In Vaux's words: 'I say such prejudices are not only wrong but disgraceful and that a man who is so narrow minded, is not fit to be a trustee of any miscellaneous collection.' Matters were made even worse because the trustees refused to allow Museum officers to attend their meetings. All communications had to be in writing, and there were no opportunities for discussion or for questions to be asked. Because of this, the poor attendance, and the bias of Hamilton's clique, decisions were made almost arbitrarily. Faussett was refused, yet less than two years previously, at the end of 1851, the trustees had agreed to spend £200 on Professor J.K. Bähr's collection of Latvian grave-goods. Ironically the collection was regarded as being of special scientific value because it was well documented, with details of find spots (Franks 1852, 14).

Ultimately, the blame for the mismanagement lay with Parliament. The composition of the board had been recognized as problematic by the 1850 Parliamentary Commission on the Museum's government, as was the board's involvement in decisions about acquisitions – which should have been left to curatorial staff. However, the Commission's recommendations in this area had been ignored. Smith (a man of Liberal political sympathies) saw this as further evidence of the need for parliamentary reform: 'When our Government shall be composed of statesmen instead of placemen . . . then, and then only, may it be expected that our national antiquities will be cared for and protected . . .' (Smith 1856, vi). In this respect, Smith may have been somewhat naive. We may note that the extraordinary composition of the Board of Trustees remained unaltered until the British Museum Act of 1963 – despite a long series of Parliamentary reforms between 1858 and 1949.[54]

Whether or not the trustees were in any way embarrassed by their public denunciation is not known. Certainly, an anti-British bias was still evident in 1855–6 when they received another genuinely unrepeatable offer in Roach Smith's own important collection of London antiquities. After an initial refusal, however, when it became clear that there would be another public outcry, the trustees backed down and made a bid, albeit at well below the price of an independent valuation. This Smith accepted, making a financial sacrifice in order to preserve the integrity and scientific value of his collection (Kidd 1977).

Franks' pleasure at succeeding on this occasion must have been short-lived, for in almost the same week Anthony Panizzi, a man of Greek tastes, was appointed as Principal Librarian. Franks consequently had a difficult time at the Museum for several years to come (Wilson 1985a, 12–14). Even so, after Hamilton's death in 1859 the quality of decision-making seems to have improved, and following the 1860 Select Committee's report on the Museum, neither the trustees nor Panizzi could ignore the need to collect British antiquities (Parliamentary Committee 1860, vii–ix). Meanwhile, slowly but surely, Franks had been developing the British and medieval European collections into a museum resource of major international importance. In 1866, having failed to attain his goal of purging the Museum of British material, Panizzi relented, and accepted its permanence by creating the Department of British and Medieval antiquities (Miller 1973, 299, 213 and 313).

Antiquarian ill-feeling towards the Museum persisted for some time. Hillier refused even to offer the BM his collection of Saxon grave-goods from the Isle of Wight and sold them to Lord Londesborough.[55] Wylie stuck to his word, withheld his collection, and eventually gave it to the Ashmolean Museum. Akerman donated or sold his collection to Mayer, even though it was promised to the BM, and Mayer purchased Rolfe's museum (White 1988, 122). The idea of creating a national archaeological collection at Liverpool instead of London arose immediately after the Faussett purchase. Fairholt wrote to Mayer to say that:

> . . . this would give that town a character of a peculiar kind and one worth obtaining . . . I should urge it strongly, and be equally strong in hoping that the grand *nucleus* you possess in the Faussett Collection be never allowed to leave the City of Liverpool now it has reached it.[56]

Fortunately for Liverpool, Mayer took heed of this advice, and in 1867 donated his Egyptian museum, including the Faussett Collection, to Liverpool Town Council. Although the archaeological collections did not expand to become a national series, their national significance is indisputable, and in the year of Mayer's centenary, it is appropriate that this has, almost inadvertently, been recognized by the government's new funding arrangements for the museum.

THE PUBLICATION OF *INVENTORIUM SEPULCHRALE*

On receiving the Faussett antiquities, Mayer lost no time in displaying them to the public. He was also anxious to publish the manuscripts, partly out of respect for the Revd Bryan Faussett, and partly because he wished to underline the philanthropic nature of his purchase (Smith 1856, i). He asked Smith to edit the work, and his illustrator friend, F.W. Fairholt, to prepare the plates. The prospectus appeared at the beginning of April.[57] Meanwhile Wright completed a 'nice popular paper on Anglo-Saxon antiquities',[58] which he read on 27 September before members of the Historic Society of Lancashire and Cheshire and the British Association for the Advancement of Science. Mayer's new acquisitions were exhibited at the same event, and were reported in *The Illustrated London News* (Anon. 1854b; Wright 1855, 8). Mayer was delighted by his new public profile and told Smith: 'How much I owe you you are the best judge, for with me the debt has become so large that I am affrighted when I think of it.'[59] The *Inventorium* was in proof form by December 1855, and was submitted to Akerman, Kemble and Wright for comment.[60] In general, Smith's editorial work was of very high quality.[61] Apart from the addition of some helpful footnotes, Faussett's text was left virtually unaltered. Whilst some might consider that it included unnecessary detail, Smith held that the work's authenticity and fidelity would be adversely affected by abridgement. So keen was Smith to preserve the integrity of the text that he not only included, but actually illustrated, two post-medieval sword pommels and knife handle, even though he believed that they had been placed in the graves by Faussett's friends as a joke (Smith 1856, 29–30; 82). His only substantial alteration was to place the Crundale antiquities last since, unlike the other finds, these were Roman (which Faussett had not recognized). A preface summarized the history of the Collection, and was supported by an appendix comprising transcripts of relevant correspondence (Smith and Mayer were both ardent collectors of autograph letters). An introduction, supplemented by a full bibliography, discussed Faussett's discoveries in the light of contemporary knowledge; its value as a synthesis of recent discoveries was underlined by the cuts, which had been borrowed from many previous works on Dark-Age cemetery finds. Other aspects of the format show the influence of continental publications, particularly Bähr's *Gräber der Liven*.[62]

Fairholt's illustrations were unsurpassed in an English publication.[63] Recent works, notably Akerman's *Remains of Pagan Saxondom* (1855), had demonstrated the potential of high quality tinted engravings in the illustration of Saxon jewellery, and Mayer provided no less than seven coloured plates (Plate 7). But the plates alone cost over ten shillings per set,[64] and Mayer became worried about rising costs. Smith wrote to

PLATE 7   TINTED ENGRAVING from *Inventorium Sepulchrale* (Plate II) by F.W. Fairholt (Museum of
London)

PLATE 8 ENGRAVING OF JOSEPH MAYER from
Inventorium Sepulchrale (Museum of London)

reassure him, saying that the work would bring: 'great returns in honourable fame . . .
There are chances, my dear Sir, which occur only once in an age; and the Faussett
Collection was a *chance of chances*. In a month or so you will see the effect.'[65] Even so,
Mayer was concerned that his beneficence should not go unnoticed and proposed that his
portrait should be included in the volume. Smith had doubts, and suggested that it
should be circulated separately to friends,[66] but when the *Inventorium* finally appeared
during the third week of April, 1856,[67] Mayer's portrait was firmly bound in every copy
(Plate 8). This was not inappropriate, for in normal circumstances the volume would
have sold for three guineas, whereas Mayer set the price at only two (Smith 1883, 69).

Although not widely reviewed, both the *Inventorium* and Mayer were highly
commended, and it was generally recognized that no such volume would have appeared if
the Faussett Collection had gone to the British Museum (Anon. 1856a–c; Wright 1856).
Franks wrote saying that: 'The publication of the work is the only thing which in any
measure reconciles me to the loss of the collection to the National Museum.'[68] Smith,
Wright and Mayer, were justly proud of their achievements, and for some years their
'Faussett Club dinners' became a feature of the social life which was attendant upon
meetings of the British Association.[69] The *Inventorium* provided Mayer with the
recognition he so earnestly sought, and led directly to membership of, or high office in
some prestigious societies.[70] He was delighted and in the latter part of 1856 commissioned
two marble portrait medallions of Smith, keeping one (Plate 9), and presenting the other
to Smith with a cast of his own portrait and a bust.[71] He also paid Smith 200 guineas
(Smith 1883, 69), a sum so large that Mayer may perhaps have wanted to compensate him
for losses which he incurred by selling his collection to the British Museum.

Smith now retired to Kent, remarking: '[I] leave London anything but a rich man;
and I intend following up my publication with a view to adding to my scanty income.'[72]

PLATE 9   PORTRAIT MEDALLION of C.R. Smith by
G. Fontana, 1856 (Walker Art Gallery, Liverpool)

Mayer talked of funding him to write ambitious new works; a 'general review of our
Saxon antiquities', a collection of Roman inscriptions from Britain, and an illustrated
catalogue of Mayer's museum were discussed.[73] Unfortunately, Smith had several
publications in progress, and by the time they were completed, the impetus had gone
and his output greatly declined. Mayer, nevertheless, did finance a few of Smith's
smaller papers. He also assisted the publication of several historical works by Wright,
and others. Sponsorship of this kind was highly unusual, and is regarded as one of his
most important contributions to scholarship (White 1989). However, nothing else that
Mayer sponsored evoked the praise which he received for the *Inventorium*: 'To edit and
illustrate a book like this requires peculiar powers, and we congratulate Mr. Mayer on
having so judiciously secured them . . . There can be no better monument to his
memory than this beautiful volume' (Anon. 1856c).

The influence which the *Inventorium* may have had on the course of Anglo-Saxon
cemetery studies is difficult to determine. Probably it did no more than to reinforce the
best contemporary practices of observation and documentation. Whilst Faussett's
standard of excavation and recording had not been surpassed in 1856, it had been
equalled, if with no great consistency, by Akerman and by others. Moreover, the
method of presentation of a dated inventory of graves, favoured by Faussett, had already
almost superseded the less satisfactory general discussion and excavation diary formats.
The importance of the *Inventorium*, both then and now, lay primarily in the information
which it contained. Smith's introduction, although now long obsolete, was also
acclaimed as a notable achievement:

For the first time he has enabled us to classify the somewhat chaotic mass of Saxon antiquities
discovered at home and abroad; and by the careful comparison of their peculiarities, and the

thoughtful testing of the historic record, made one illustrate the other so completely, that we may safely refer certain ornaments to certain tribes, who had settled in various parts of England . . .. (Anon. 1856c).

Clearly, Smith had gone a long way towards achieving the goal he had set in his paper of 1842. The means by which he accomplished this will now be considered in the second part of this paper.

ROACH SMITH'S CONTRIBUTION TO ANGLO-SAXON ARCHAEOLOGY

The *Inventorium Sepulchrale* appeared two thirds of the way through what might be described as the second period of Saxon cemetery exploration, which began in 1842 and tailed off sharply in the early 1860s. Although some important excavations were still to be published in 1856, the two most significant reports of this period – by Wylie (1852) and Neville (1852) – had appeared, and Smith had already drawn his principal conclusions, most of which feature in his introduction to the *Inventorium*. The following summary of Smith's contribution to Anglo-Saxon studies may therefore also be regarded as a discussion of the various themes which appear in his introduction.

That so many of Smith's deductions remain valid is due to the care with which he recorded data, his wide reading and clarity of thought, and his cautious approach to interpretation. Whereas earlier writers on sepulchral remains – Douglas (1793), Colt Hoare (1812; 1819) and Bloxham (1834) – had centred their efforts on classifying entire burials, grave-goods included, according to broad characteristics, Smith and his contemporaries concentrated on the description and classification of the artifacts. Individual burials remained important, not only as evidence of funeral rites, but because they provided a context for the finds. Cemetery layouts were generally not studied, despite signs of interest in the subject by Douglas (1793, Pls. XXVIII–XXVIV etc.), Dryden (1852) and Troyon (1841).

The validity of Smith's work rested upon the principle of dating by association with objects of known date, first propounded by Douglas. In 1843 he published an article which gently corrected some errors in a book on sepulchral remains by Bloxham (1834; Smith 1843b). The most important amendment concerned a coiled(?) Saxon pot from Churchover, Warwickshire (Plate 10a).[74] The author had considered this to be probably Roman (Bloxham 1834, 34), but Smith thought otherwise on the basis of associated weapons and shield bosses (Smith 1843b, 41). To support his interpretation, Smith illustrated a stamped hand-made globular urn from another mixed cemetery recently identified at Marston St Lawrence, Northamptonshire (Plate 10b; ibid., 44; both vessels are reproduced in Smith 1856, xv). Whilst Douglas had suggested in a footnote that urns of this variety were Saxon (Douglas 1793, 131, fn.), his idea seems to have been overlooked, and Smith here became the first to illustrate correctly-identified hand-made

PLATE 10   ANGLO-SAXON POTS from Smith's *Collectanea Antiqua* Vol. I (1843); (a) coiled(?) vessel from Churchover, Warwickshire; (b) hand-made vessel from Marston St Lawrence, Northamptonshire (Museum of London)

Saxon urns. Four years later, in a JBAA article on finds from Kingston-upon-Soar, Derbyshire, the range of published forms was extended to include what are now called bossed urns, biconical urns and *Buckelurne* (Henslow 1847). The writer maintained that these belonged to the 'Ancient Britains', although Smith knew better, and a tactful note to this effect was inserted by Wright (1847, 58). Such errors of basic identification became much less frequent after the publication that year of Akerman's *Index* (Akerman 1847). The Kingston urns were eventually republished with a correct identification by Smith (1852a, 228–34). When Kemble later published his important article on mortuary urns recently found in Lower Saxony, their identification rested upon their similarity to these and other Saxon urns from the Midlands, and it was the striking English parallels which convinced some of Kemble's German colleagues that his urns were Saxon, not Slavonic, which had been the prevailing wisdom (Kemble 1855a).

Having ascertained the means of dating Saxon burials, Smith set about to identify and describe the varieties of objects which they contained. His early classificatory work on brooches has already been mentioned, and his introduction is noteworthy for his tripartite classification of Kentish circular brooches, based on construction (Smith 1856, xx–xxiv). This has served as the basis of more recent classifications by Leeds (1936, 115–24) and Avent (1975, 1), although Smith's first and third classes are transposed in their schemes.

Smith's limited experience of excavation taught him that: 'It is important to note the position of things *in situ* to determine their use' (Smith 1847, 237). This remark arose from the 1847 excavations at Ozingell (Osengal), Kent, by Rolfe, assisted by Smith, Wright, Fairholt and others. Here, in a grave, an object interpreted by Douglas as a bow brace was found, hollow side up, immediately beneath the umbo of a shield. Clearly this was the shield's handle (Smith 1853, 3, 11 and Plate II, Nos. 5–6). To record the fact, a drawing was made showing the skeleton and grave-goods *in situ* – a rarity in English publications of this period (Plate 11). In 1851, Smith published two puzzling objects, hoping that similar items might be found in position as buried (Smith 1851b, 165). A few months later, his network of correspondents had sent in their observations, and

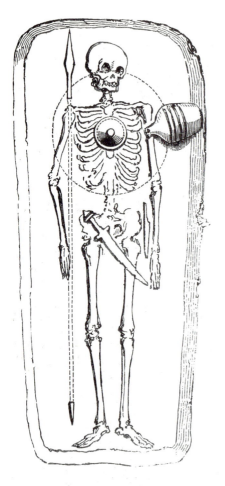

PLATE 11   SKETCH BY F.W. FAIRHOLT of a grave at Ozingell,
Kent, from Smith's *Collectanea Antiqua* Vol. III (Museum
of London)

Smith was able to pronounce them to be 'pendant girdle-ornaments, somewhat analogous to the modern châtelaine' – another interpretation which has stood the test of time (Meaney 1981, 247–8). All were incomplete but, by combining evidence of finds in different degrees of completeness, Smith was able to build up a picture of the entire artifact (Plate 12; Smith 1852a, 234–5). The same inductive methods were used in his discussion of Saxon shields.

Other writers did not compare and weigh evidence with the same degree of care. In 1850 a skeleton at Little Wilbraham had been found upon which: 'partly upon the occipital portion of the cranium, and the circular vertebrae, was placed a curious and apparently unique object . . . a headpiece or kind of crown' (Deck 1851). The accompanying illustration depicts a wooden bucket with bronze hoops, decorated with vandykes. The same mistake had already occurred in France and Germany (Oberlin 1773, 159 and Table XVI; Houben and Fiedler 1839, 67 and Table XLVIII). Until Smith had convinced him otherwise, even Cochet adopted this interpretation for a bucket hoop from Dieppe (Smith 1851b, 160–1, 169 and Plate XLV; 1875, 466–7; Cochet 1854, 310–6; 1857, 279–98).

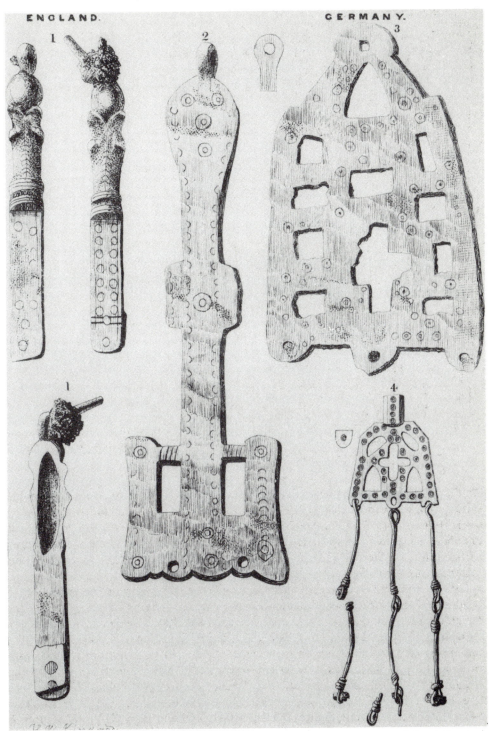

PLATE 12   THE INDENTIFICATION OF THE *CHATELAINE* was achieved by comparing English and German discoveries. Plate LVI from Vol. II of Smith's *Collectanea Antiqua* (Museum of London)

Smith's caution in the interpretation of artifacts actually led him into error by his refusal to accept the amuletic usage of certain grave-goods. Here he over-reacted to Douglas, who saw amulets and magical practices everywhere, even supposing that glass tumblers had held the *aqua magica* and that iron shears and mirrors had been used in divination (Douglas 1793, 44–46, 22, and 80–81 resp.; Meaney 1981, 269–71). In his discussion of crystal balls, Douglas had discoursed at enormous length on the use of gems in divination, from Zoroaster and the *Druidical speculum* to the 'celebrated vision and mysterious operations of Dr Dee and Mr Kelly' (op. cit., 14–19). Smith may perhaps be forgiven for suggesting that they were merely ornaments for attachment to the dress (Smith 1864, 150). However, even where an amuletic use was well-established, as in the contemporary Neapolitan use of cowrie shells, Smith would not accept it for the Anglo-Saxons (Smith 1856, 68). His prejudice led also to the incorrect identification of certain objects; for example model weapons were interpreted as 'tooth, ear and nail picks' (Smith 1856, xxviii; cf. Meaney 1981, 149). Nevertheless, in seeking to redress this imbalance, Audrey Meaney has commented that:

> Roach Smith's views . . . have had a profound effect upon Anglo-Saxon archaeology virtually up to the present day. Not that this was altogether a bad thing . . . a sceptical attitude in scholarship is always to be preferred to a too ready credulity (Meaney 1981, 271).

Despite his scepticism about amulets, Smith wrote to great effect on the significance of the boar on the helmet from Benty Grange, Derbyshire, citing historical sources (Smith 1852a, 238–42). The use of literary evidence in the interpretation and naming of Saxon artifacts had been demonstrated by Douglas (1793), and became a feature of antiquarian study during the mid-nineteenth century. It was greatly assisted by the fashion for publishing Anglo-Saxon texts in English translation, notably *Beowulf* (Kemble 1835–7). In 1847, Smith arranged a scientific examination of wood adhering to weapons from the mixed cemetery at Northfleet, Kent. The shaft of the spear proved to be ash, which was seen as a confirmation of Beowulf, where the spear-shaft was termed *aesc*, meaning ash (Smith 1847, 239). Although not in the same scholastic league as Kemble's *Beowulf*, a discussion of continental Dark-Age sources by Rigollot (1850) was also influential. It was his comments upon Agathios' angon which led to the successful search for the weapon in France by Wylie (1853a). The latter's paper on this subject drew attention on both sides of the channel, and became a celebrated instance of the use of historical sources in naming archaeological artifacts (Akerman and Linden-schmit 1855; Wylie 1855; Smith 1860, 131).

It was literary sources also which first made it clear that cremation was the traditional rite of Germanic peoples, and, by inference, that where inhumation was practised, it probably represented a subsequent development. Mixed cemeteries could be explained in terms of length of use. This notion was challenged when Neville found Saxon cremation urns buried above Saxon inhumations at Little Wilbraham, Cambridgeshire, and Smith made an ingenious attempt to reconcile the discovery with conventional wisdom by suggesting that the urns, having been exhumed when the graves were dug, were carefully replaced after they had been infilled (Smith 1855, 146; 1886, 51). Even today it is doubtful that this problem may be satisfactorily resolved, although Akerman and Neville were probably nearer the truth in suggesting that the two rites could have been in contemporaneous use (Akerman 1855, xvi; Neville 1852, 11).

Having studied the written sources, the historian Kemble concluded that urn-burials were always pagan, and that inhumations were always Christian (Kemble 1855b). Smith was unconvinced, but having submitted the proofs of *Inventorium Sepulchrale* to Kemble, was obliged to include his views in the introduction.[75] Wylie subsequently suggested that the rite probably changed to inhumation as a result of contact with Christian customs, and was not necessarily used solely by Christians (Wylie 1857). Smith ultimately accepted the force of Wylie's argument (Smith 1871, x), and had already adopted a similar argument to explain cruciform brooches (Smith 1850, 89). This was unfortunate because, in their earliest form, cruciform brooches are now known to have lacked the cross bar, being inspired by Roman bow brooches (Aberg 1926, 28–56).

The possibility of interaction between early Saxons and Roman civilization fascinated both Smith and Wright. The latter noted that Saxon burials had been found adjacent to Roman cemeteries at Canterbury, Strood and Colchester (Wright 1847, 51), and Smith pointed to the burial of money with the dead, and the Romanizing style of some brooches as further evidence of such contacts (Smith 1850, 88 and 220). His search for evidence of continuity received false encouragement from a hand-made biconical Saxon urn in the Faussett Collection, with an incised Latin inscription (Smith 1855; 1856, xvi; 1858b). Whilst recognizing that the urn was an East Anglian type (he later found evidence to show that it came from North Elmham, Norfolk), Smith understandably failed to realize that the inscription followed an early Roman formula, and must therefore have been a relatively recent forgery (Haverfield 1901, 312).

Perhaps Smith's greatest contribution to Saxon cemetery studies lies in his recognition of the regional differences in Saxon brooches and other grave-goods. Until 1847 most of the known Saxon material had come from Kent, and hopes of distinguishing regional tribal characteristics depended upon new discoveries outside the county. The only other substantial groups of finds were from the Isle of Wight, and had aroused a comment from Smith about their close affinity to the Kentish finds (Smith 1846, 461). In 1847, however, a substantial Saxon cemetery was excavated at Fairford in Gloucestershire, and Wright immediately noticed that the two shield bosses were of a form not hitherto found in Kent (Wright 1847, 52). Three years later, in 1850, the Marston St Lawrence finds were exhibited to the Society of Antiquaries, and Smith commented that unlike the Kentish burials, these did not include swords, and the brooches were of different forms (Dryden 1852; Smith 1852d). On museum visits he had found parallels to the concave (saucer) brooches in the Upper Thames Valley (although their distribution is now known to be wider). Other (small long) brooches were similar to examples from Warwickshire, Leicestershire, Northamptonshire and Suffolk. The large (great square-headed) fibula was of a class found also on the continent. During the following year, Smith identified as a class what are now termed Anglian cruciform brooches, giving their distribution as East Anglia and the Midlands (Smith 1851b, 166 and Plate XL), and in 1860 he noted the distinctive character of Kentish buckles (Smith 1860, 143). Smith likened these regional variations to English dialects, suggesting that both indicated a descent from tribes of common origin, language and customs. He was particularly struck by similarities between the provincial dialects of Kent and the Isle of Wight, which as an Isle of Wight man living in Kent he was well qualified to comment upon (Smith 1871, vi–vii; Smith and Smith 1881–2).

In 1850, Smith linked the regional differences in artifact types which he had so recently recognized to Bede's account of the territories settled by Jutes, Angles and Saxons (Smith 1850, 88– 9). This seeming confirmation of Bede appeared just one year after Kemble's highly acclaimed history of the Anglo-Saxons, which had cast serious doubts on Bede's reliability (Kemble 1849, eg. 1–3). Smith's observation, although of far-reaching importance, was made almost in passing. It was left to Wright, always the more fluent writer, to explain in detail the distinctive features in the artifacts of the three tribal groups, based on information compiled by Smith (Wright 1852, 399–431; 1855). Wright made an original and important contribution to this topic in 1854, when he charted the first distribution map of the British Isles, pointing the way for more detailed studies by Leeds (1913). This shows the eighty-one Saxon cemeteries then known in relation to Roman roads, rivers, towns (Wright 1855; republished by Smith 1856). Wright believed, perhaps correctly, that the various clusters of cemeteries indicated those areas which had been occupied by the different tribal groups. He hoped too that the map would stimulate investigations leading to further discoveries; he was particularly keen to discover a Saxon cemetery on the borders of Wales, presumably because this might help to indicate the extent of Anglo-Saxon penetration.[76]

Smith was obviously pleased to find apparent correlations between archaeological and historical sources, but sounded a note of caution in his introduction: 'It is not a slight analogy in some instances only that will establish this theory; it must spring from the remains themselves, and be palpable and convincing, or it must be rejected' (Smith 1856, xii). To Roach Smith archaeology was no longer subservient to history. In this and in other aspects of methodology, his approach had acquired a consistency and coherence which distinguished him from many of his contemporaries. Akerman for example, had no hesitation in freely mixing current conceptions and 'facts'. As a result, his conclusions are more often seen to be erroneous, and even at the time of writing were sometimes at variance with one another (Francis 1984, 19).

Smith's comparative work on Dark-Age antiquities was by no means confined to England, and his importance rests to no small extent on his achievements in placing Anglo-Saxon remains in their European setting. Smith became aware of close parallels between English and continental discoveries almost from the beginning of his Anglo-Saxon research. In the late summer of 1843, he paid his third visit to France, calling on M. Ferét, of Dieppe, who showed him Merovingian artifacts recently found at Ste-Marguerite (Seine-Maritime). These were later published by Wylie, along with Ferét's opinion that they were Saxon (Wylie 1853b). This interpretation rested in part on the similarity of the pottery to 'Saxon' material (from Kent?), and of the buckles to finds from Strood. Since Smith recorded Ferét's discoveries as Saxon in his journal for 1843, it is quite possible that this interpretation originated with his visit.[77] Unfortunately, since Wylie did not illustrate the pottery, its identification may now not be verified.

The potential value of studying continental parallels to Saxon materials was underlined at the Canterbury Congress of 1844. During a discussion of the Bourne Park finds, someone commented that an unidentified Danish gentleman (this must have been Thomsen), had found Saxon remains in Canterbury museum, and from their similarity to relics in Copenhagen Museum had suggested that they belonged to Germanic invaders from Jutland. Bede's remarks about the Jutish origins of the Kentish settlers were footnoted in the proceedings (Dunkin 1845, 187–9). Worsaae's visit of 1846–7 might have encouraged further thoughts on this subject (Wilkins 1961), but it was not until 1850 that Smith fully recognized the potential. In that year he made an antiquarian excursion to North Germany, and was particularly struck by the 'Frankish' grave-finds in Wiesbaden Museum (Smith 1851a, 129–31; 1851c). Not only were these arranged in burial-groups – to Smith a novel method of display (Smith 1868, vii; 1886, 295), but they were described in detail in a publication. This was none other than the Lindenschmit brothers' *Germanischen Todtenlager von Selzen* (1848), which laid the corner-stone for the interpretation of German Dark-Age materials (Böhner 1969). Smith purchased a copy himself and on returning to England recommended it excitedly to others.[78] Similarities between the Selzen and English discoveries were immediately apparent to him: 'The general analogy is very striking, but at the same time there seem to be some peculiarities in each' (Smith 1851b, 160).

Smith's growing conviction that English and continental materials should be studied together received a boost during the following year. Not only did the Great Exhibition bring many continental archaeologists to London – including Troyon of Lausanne and Rigollot of Amiens (Smith 1886, 223) – but Smith paid a further visit to France, where Cochet brought him up to date with recent Frankish cemetery excavations near Dieppe – at Londinières, Douvrend and Envermeu.[79] In the spring of 1852 he published his notes on Selzen and Dieppe in the *Collectanea*, aiming to demonstrate the relationship between English and Frankish remains (Smith 1852a). To this end, he used a novel technique of juxtaposing illustrations of parallels. Four plates of German and English remains demonstrated the close similarity of what are now termed radiate brooches, iron knives, glass-claw beakers, and ceramic jugs, biconical bowls, and bottles (see Plate 12). Having discovered an angon in a grave in Strood, Smith later went so far as to suggest that its owner might have been a Frank (Smith 1860, 135); Frankish settlement in Kent during the sixth century is now widely accepted (Hawkes 1982, 72). Elsewhere, Smith remarked on some of the differences between English and continental finds, for example the comparative rarity in England of *franciscas* (Smith 1851c), and the superiority of Kentish composite brooches over their continental counterparts, which led Smith to suggest that they were probably made in this country (Smith 1856, xxiii).

Further research was necessary to confirm such points, especially '. . . on an extended scale in the countries north of the Rhine' (Smith 1852a, 204). Apart from Smith, however, few English archaeologists had established useful contacts with continental antiquaries; Worsaae alone was widely known. 'There is *no such thing* as *correspondence* between English and Foreign societies' complained Smith in 1851.[80] Nevertheless, by the time *Inventorium Sepulchrale* had been published in 1856 all this had changed. Whether by design or opportunity, Smith's plea for excavations north of the Rhine had been answered by Kemble, who had published an article on mortuary urns, some excavated by himself, from Stade and Lüneburg, in Lower Saxony (Kemble 1855a). These urns were of immense importance, for they provided unequivocal evidence for the region of departure of Saxon migrants who occupied the Midlands and East Anglia.

More direct evidence of Smith's influence is seen in the activities of W.M. Wylie. The men first met in 1851 when Wylie sent Smith some of the Fairford brooches for comment (Smith 1891, 119; 1852c). Wylie's first publication, *The Fairford Graves*, bears evidence of Smith's advice in matters of interpretation. Immediately after its appearance in 1852, again doubtless following Smith's counsel, Wylie traced his footsteps to Dieppe, where he met Ferét and assisted the Abbé Cochet in making excavations (Wylie 1853a; 1853b; Webster 1978). Referring to Wylie and Smith, Cochet later remarked that English help was the most important outside influence on his study (Kidd 1978, 63). Wylie's interest in funereal remains subsequently took him to Germany, Italy and back to France in 1855. The results of these excursions were published in *Archaeologia*. In so doing, Wylie achieved no more than Smith, albeit in novel areas of research. Where he exceeded Smith was in attracting articles on Dark-Age remains for *Archaeologia* from eminent continental archaeologists. These included Ludwig Lindenschmit, Menzel and Cochet. Several became FSAs. Together with Akerman's papers on Saxon cemetery excavations (which included the first excavations of any kind sponsored by the Society of Antiquaries), the *Archaeologia*s for 1855–60 contain no less than nine papers on continental Dark-Age antiquities, six on Saxon, and three on medieval French burials by Cochet. The latter were of interest because they demonstrated the continuation of pagan burial superstitions well into the Christian era. This international approach bore fruit in 1863, with the publication of Kemble's *Horae Ferales*. With Franks' copiously illustrated discussion of artifact types, this became in effect the first European-wide survey of prehistoric and Dark-Age burial customs and antiquities (Kemble, Latham and Franks 1863).

Although the *Horae Ferales* extended beyond even Smith's horizons, it necessarily relied upon foundations which he had laid with respect to the Anglo-Saxon materials. Whilst he did little in the way of cemetery excavation, for which Akerman rightly holds most of the credit (Francis 1984), Smith was responsible for most of the conceptual strides in the study of Saxon artifacts during this period. The careful identification and publication of artifacts, which he had done so much to encourage, was an essential precursor of more detailed studies by others, notably Baldwin Brown (1915). His fundamentally important work on the classification and regional distribution of brooch types and other finds, with his recognition of the links between such regional differences and Bede's account of the Anglo-Saxon migrations, stand among the most significant achievements of Victorian archaeology. It was probably this which gave rise to Cochet's remark that: 'Il est une justice que j'aime à rendre à M. Roach Smith, c'est que seul, et presque avec l'unique secours de son intelligence, il a parfaitement deviné l'archéologie saxonne' (Cochet 1857, 264).

The potential which this approach revealed pointed the way for Leeds (1913), and indeed for all future artifact distribution studies. But it was perhaps in his international approach to the subject that Smith's greatest influence on his contemporaries may be seen. Through just one article of cardinal significance, Smith had demonstrated in a lucid and novel manner that the solution to certain archaeological problems lay beyond the confines of this island (Smith 1852a). In England, as on the continent, the interest in Teutonic remains had arisen from a search for the roots of nationhood (Levine 1986, 79–82, 98; Sklenář 1983, 62–7). It is ironic that the problems which emerged from this nationalistic aim were the first to excite cross-channel co-operation between antiquarians, in what came to be perceived as a mutual archaeological problem.

EPILOGUE

It is with Smith's German visit of 1850 that we conclude. Having returned home with the Selzen volume carefully stowed in his baggage, still excited by the Merovingian remains which he had seen in Wiesbaden, Smith wrote to his friend Bateman in terms which, with hindsight, have a strangely prophetic significance:

> You must give us some little notices of your more recent Saxon discoveries. I have some remarkable materials at hand for a paper making comparison between the *continental* and the English, but the expense is too much for me . . . I wish I could find some liberal man of humble birth and humble pretentions who would take us by the hand firmly and freely. We would raise a statue of him in the temple of archaeology.[81]

Unknown to Smith, he had already met such a man in the person of Joseph Mayer. By our conference and this collection of papers we have raised another small monument in his honour. Nothing would have given greater delight to Charles Roach Smith.

Acknowledgements

I should like to express my very deep gratitude to Dafydd Kidd of the British Museum and Roger White for much encouragement, some fascinating conversations on nineteenth-century archaeology, and for assistance on numerous points concerning Saxon and Merovingian archaeology. Special thanks are due to Diana Harford for chauffeuring me around Faussett's Saxon cemetery sites. Arising from my visit to Lower Heppington, Mr G. Finn and Mrs Elizabeth Blaxland very generously donated two rare photographs of Heppington to Liverpool Museum, one of which is reproduced here (Plate 3). Thanks for assistance and advice are due also to: John Francis; Francis Grew of the Museum of London; John Giles; Frank Jenkins; Mrs Parker of Heppington; Judy Rudoe and Leslie Webster of the British Museum, Edmund Southworth of Liverpool Museum, and the staff of Liverpool City Library Record Office. I am indebted to Trevor Hurst and Maggie Cox of the Museum of London for photographic services, to the British Museum's Department of Prints and Drawings for permission to reproduce photographs, and to Tony Dyson of the Museum who kindly commented on my typescript. I acknowledge with particular gratitude grants from the Society of Antiquaries of London and from the University of London Central Research Fund in support of my research on Charles Roach Smith, which have enabled me to examine a number of relevant manuscript collections.

Abbreviations

Archaeol. Inst.: Archaeological Institute
Archaeol. J.: The Archaeological Journal
BAA: British Archaeological Association
B.A.R.: British Archaeological Reports British Series
BL: British Library

BM: British Museum
BM:DMLA: British Museum, Department of Medieval and Later Antiquities
BM:DWAA: British Museum, Department of Western Asiatic Antiquities
Collect. Antiq.: *Collectanea Antiqua*, printed for the subscribers, London.
DNMC:MA: Danish National Museum, Copenhagen, Museum Archives
FSA: Fellow of the Society of Antiquaries of London
HSL&C: Historic Society of Lancashire and Cheshire
JBAA: *Journal of the British Archaeological Association*
J. Brit. Archaeol. Assoc.: *Journal of the British Archaeological Association*
LCLRO: Liverpool Central Library Record Office
LM: Liverpool Museum
PRO: Public Record Office
SAL: Society of Antiquaries of London
SM:BAC: Sheffield Museum, Bateman Antiquarian Correspondence
Trans. Hist. Soc. Lancs. & Chesh.: *Transactions of the Historical Society of Lancashire and Cheshire*

Notes

1. PRO, Prerogative Court of Canterbury, Quire 64, proved February 1776.
2. The story of these years is told in a letter from T.G. Faussett to J. Mayer, 5 August 1854, Bebington Central Library, Joseph Mayer Papers; published by Smith (1856) 201–7.
3. Now in the possession of LM.
4. Ex. Mayer collection, now SAL, MS. 723. Letters from Revd J. Douglas to G. Faussett. These are published by Jessup (1975), and in part by Smith (1856).
5. On a visit to Bridge in preparation for this paper, the writer was told by a local resident that there had been battles all about the locality which accounted for the Bourne Park tumuli.
6. C.R. Smith, untitled manuscript diary for 1827. Private Coll.
7. Most of the known notebooks are held by the BM:DMLA.
8. BM:DMLA, C.R. Smith, unpublished manuscript journal, "Vol. IIII. 1840 & 1841", entry for 25 January 1841.
9. The house has been demolished, although it survived until the early 1950s (Jessup 1953). The photograph reproduced as Plate 3 (one of a pair) was in the possession of a local resident, but has since been donated to LM (see Acknowledgements).
10. T.G. Faussett to J. Mayer, 5 August 1854, see Note 2.
11. BM:DMLA, C.R. Smith, unpublished manuscript journal "Journal 1842, Vol. V", entry for 17 October 1842.
12. Loc. cit. Note 11.
13. LCLRO, Ref. 920 MAY, C.R. Smith's *Retrospections* Portfolio 2, C.R. Smith to W.H. Rolfe, 20 October, 1842.
14. BM:DMLA, C.R. Smith, unpublished manuscript notebook, "Notes 1842, 1851 etc.", 48–9.
15. As for Note 11. The pavilion survived largely unaltered until the early 1950s, see Jessup (1953).
16. Smith: LCLRO, Ref. 920 MAY, W. Chaffers to C.R. Smith, 2 March 1854; Faussett: Douglas (1793, 37). Reference was made to the French Benedictine, Bernard de Montfauçon (1655–1741), whose great study of classical antiquities (Montfauçon 1719), became the principal text-book in the study of Romano-British antiquities during the mid-18th to early 19th centuries.
17. SAL, MS. 590, Scrap-book compiled by C.R. Smith entitled "British Archaeological Association, First Congress 1844", letter of 5 August 1844, loose between pp. 26–7.
18. Loc. cit. Note 17, G. Faussett to C.R. Smith, affixed to p. 36; BAA (1845b) 267.

19. Smith (1883) 64–5. It seems that the men first met some months earlier when Mayer visited Smith's museum (Mayer 1849, 121).

20. SM:BAC, Vol. III, C.R. Smith to T. Bateman, 28 June 1849.

21. Loc. cit., C.R. Smith to T. Bateman, 20 September 1849.

22. SAL, election records, 10 January 1850. His other sponsors included W. Chaffers (see above).

23. Notably the Soc. Antiqs. de l'Ouest: LCLRO, 920 MAY, Mayer Papers, C.R. Smith to J. Mayer, 11 November 1852; NLW 5118D, M. Dupres to C.R. Smith, 24 May 1853.

24. HSL&C (1850, 2, 183, 212; 1851, 1); SM:BAC, Vol. III, C.R. Smith to T. Bateman, 19 September 1851.

25. LM, Acc. No. 30.131, item 2, C.R. Smith to J. Mayer, 26 August 1852.

26. BL, Add. MS. 36653, Diary of Sir Henry Ellis, entry for 2 May 1839.

27. Corporation of London Record Office, Library Journal, 1837–1844.

28. The importance of the Danish model is suggested in many places, eg. the report of the Parliamentary Commission (1850, 38–9), and Franks (1853), who also organized the British collection according to the Danish three-age system (Daniel 1950, 82).

29. DNMC:MA, C.R. Smith to J.A.A. Worsaae, 3 December 1853.

30. PRO, Prerogative Court of Canterbury, Quire 606, proved 9 August 1853.

31. BM:DWAA, Museum Archive, 1st. Ser. f. 1733, G. Faussett to E. Hawkins(?), undated, but prior to Chaffers' visit to value the collection.

32. Two copies of the valuation are extant: BM:DWAA, Museum Archive, 2nd Ser. f. 1957; LCLRO, 920 MAY, Mayer Papers, Correspondence of W. Chaffers. Published (BM 1854, 1–3).

33. BM:DWAA, Museum Archive, 2nd. Ser. f. 1956, G. Faussett to E. Hawkins, 30 September 1853.

34. Loc. cit. Note 30.

35. Loc. cit. Note 33, 1st Ser. f. 1734, G. Faussett to E. Hawkins, 22 September 1853.

36. As for Note 33.

37. SM:BAC, Vol. V, C.R. Smith to T. Bateman, 17 November 1853; Smith 1854, 184.

38. Loc. cit., C.R. Smith to T. Bateman, 28 November 1853.

39. Bebington Central Library, Joseph Mayer's "Autographs" book, p. 57.

40. BL, Add. MS. 33346, f. 4, T. Wright to J. Mayer, 31 October 1853; f. 5, T. Wright to J. Mayer, 6 November 1853.

41. BM:DMLA, Acc. Nos. 1853.11–4.1 etc. The number indicates that they were accessioned in November, and must have been donated not long before then.

42. As for Note 38.

43. On 24 November Mayer wrote to Franks saying: 'if you refuse them they shall not be separated if I can help it'. BM, Dept. Medieval and Later Antiquities, Correspondence files.

44. SM:BAC, Vol. V, C.R. Smith to T. Bateman, 26 December 1853.

45. SM:BAC, Vol. V, C.R. Smith to T. Bateman, 28 November 1853.

46. As for Note 29.

47. DNMC:MA, C.R. Smith to J.A.A. Worsaae, 1 February 1854, and ref. cited in Note 44.

48. LCLRO, 920 MAY, Mayer Papers, Revd G. Faussett to J. Mayer, 18 February 1854.

49. Loc. cit., W. Chaffers to J. Mayer, 18 February 1854; BM, Dept. Medieval and Later Antiquities, Correspondence Files, J. Mayer to A.W. Franks, 26 February 1854.

50. Loc. cit. Note 48, G. Faussett to C.R. Smith, 2 March 1854.

51. LCLRO, 920 MAY, Mayer Papers, W. Chaffers to C.R. Smith, 2 March 1854.

52. BL, Add. MS. 38984, ff. 374–8, W. Vaux to H. Layard, April 1856.

53. BL, Add. MS. 52009, f. 66, A. Panizzi to Lord Holland.

54. Namely, the Abolition of Property Qualifications of M.P.s – 1858, The Second Reform Act – 1867, The Third Reform Act – 1884, and the Representation of the People Acts of 1918, 1928 and 1949.

55. DNMC:MA, C.R. Smith to J.A.A. Worsaae, 5 June 1855.

56. LCLRO, 920 MAY, Mayer Papers, F.W. Fairholt to J. Mayer, n.d.

57. LCLRO, 920 MAY, Mayer Papers, C.R. Smith to J. Mayer, 6 April 1854.

58. BL, Add. MS. 33346, f. 8, T. Wright to J. Mayer, 28 March 1854.

59. LCLRO, Acc. No. 1207, J. Mayer to C.R. Smith, 18 September 1854.

60. LCLRO, Ref. Hg 0695, proof edition of *Inventorium Sepulchrale*, dated 1855, and annotated by C.R. Smith, J.M. Kemble, J.Y. Akerman, Thomas Wright and F.W. Fairholt.

61. There are some errors in the numbering of the artifacts (pers. comm., R. White).

62. Both the *Inventorium* and Bähr (1850) use quarto paper. Both have an introduction in which the circumstances of discovery are summarized, followed by a separate discussion of each class of find, and then of the ethnological origins of the antiquities. Both provide tables, of coins only in Bähr and of all the finds in *Inventorium Sepulchrale*. Both locate the plates at the end and use indices to link items shown on the plates with individual graves. Some of these features are found also in Lindenschmit (1848).

63. LCLRO, 920 MAY, Mayer Papers, A.W. Franks to J. Mayer, 22 April 1856. If he had seen anything of equivalent quality in a continental publication, it cannot have been in the field of Dark-Age studies.

64. Loc. cit., Invoice by T. Brooker, Christmas 1856.

65. Loc. cit., C.R. Smith to J. Mayer, 20 February 1856.

66. Loc. cit., C.R. Smith to J. Mayer, 4 April 1856.

67. It had not appeared by 15 April 1856, on the evidence of a letter of that date: Swiss Cottage Library, London Borough of Camden, Autograph Letter File, E. Meteyard to C.R. Smith. It had been published by 22 April: letter cited in Note 63.

68. Loc. cit. Note 63.

69. LCLRO, 920 MAY, Mayer Papers, various letters from J. Clarke to J. Mayer; BL, Add. MS. 33346–7, Letters from T. Wright to J. Mayer.

70. A copy was sent to the Soc. Antiqs. de France just before his election (BL, Add. MS 33346, f. 257, T. Wright to J. Mayer, 16 June 1858). He was elected to the Royal Society of Northern Antiquaries on 15 December 1855 (LCLRO, Acc. No. 2528a, C.R. Smith's *Retrospections* Portfolio II, C.C. Rafn to J. Mayer, 16 April 1856), and in 1858 to the Council of the Ethnological Society (BL, Add. MS. 33346, f. 252, T. Wright to J. Mayer, 1 July 1858).

71. LCLRO, 920 MAY, Mayer Papers, G. Fontana to C.R. Smith, 3 February 1857.

72. SM:BAC, Vol. V, C.R. Smith to T. Bateman, 1 September 1856.

73. Loc. cit., C.R. Smith to T. Bateman, 7 January 1857.

74. Smith called it 'turned', but it is more likely to have been coiled (pers. comm., R. White).

75. Two of Kemble's letters to Smith on this subject have survived: BM:DMLA, 11 December 1855; Maidstone Museum & Art Gallery, in Charles Warne's copy of *Inventorium Sepulchrale*, undated.

76. BL, Add. Ms. 33346, f. 4, T. Wright to J. Mayer, 31 October 1853; f. 52, T. Wright to J. Mayer, 23 October 1855.

77. Loc. cit. Note 11, entry for 4 September 1843.

78. Bibliothèque Municipale d'Abbeville, MS.682 D11. C.R. Smith to Boucher de Perthes, 27 September 1850; South Shields, Arbeia Roman Fort and Museum, 48.154(145), C. Kroll to C.R. Smith, 22 April 1851.

79. Evidence for this visit is provided by a letter written by C.R. Smith to the Abbé Cochet whilst the former was at Rouen. Although no date is given, this may be determined by internal evidence (Kidd 1978, 71). Gifts from Cochet to Smith, made probably on this occasion, include the Londinières *francisca* and a pot from Envermeu (BM:DMLA Acc. Nos 56,7–1,1416 and 5187, respectively; D. Kidd, pers. comm.).

80. Society of Antiquaries of Newcastle upon Tyne, Correspondence Vol. VI, C.R. Smith to J. Adamson, 7 February 1851.

81. SM:BAC, Vol. III, C.R. Smith to T. Bateman, 15 September 1850.

82. This part of *Collectanea Antiqua* had been distributed by July 1845 since it is mentioned in a letter from Revd B. Poste to C.R. Smith of 18 July 1845: SAL, C.R. Smith scrap-book entitled "British Archaeological Association Second Congress 1845".

83. This part had been distributed by August 1851, as it is mentioned in the Journal of Revd J. Woodruff, Kent Archives Office, entry for 22 August 1851,

84. Stated to be Wright's work in a letter from T. Wright to J. Mayer, 29 August 1856: BL, Add. Ms. 33346, f. 80.

Bibliography

Aberg, N. 1926: *The Anglo-Saxons in England* . . . Cambridge

Åkerman, J.Y. 1843: in "December 22, 1842", *Proceedings of the Numismatic Society.*, 88.

Akerman, J.Y. 1847: *An Archaeological Index to Remains of Antiquity in the Celtic, Romano-British and Anglo-Saxon Periods*, London.

Akerman, J.Y. 1855: *Remains of Pagan Saxondom*, London.

Akerman, J.Y. and Lindenschmit, L. 1855: "Note on the Angon of Agathias . . .", *Archaeologia* 36, 78–9.

Anderson, R.E. 1890: "Hamilton, William Richard (1777–1859)" in Stephen, L. and Lee, S. (Eds.) *Dictionary of National Biography* XXIV, 234–5, London.

Anon., 1845a: "Museum of National Antiquities", *The Builder* III, No. CXXVI, 5 July 313–4.

Anon., 1845b: "Museum of National Antiquities", *The Builder* III, No. CXLIV, 8 November 537.

Anon., 1845c: "Museum of National Antiquities", *The Builder* III, No. CXLVI, 22 November 557.

Anon., 1854a: "The Faussett Collection", *The Athenaeum* 1373, 18 February 213.

Anon 1854b: "The Faussett Collection of Antiquities" *The Illustrated London News* XXV, No. 706, 7 October 345–6.

Anon., 1856a: "[Review of *Inventorium Sepulchrale*]", *The Literary Gazette*, 16 August 581–2.

Anon., 1856b: "Notes on Books", *Daily Telegraph*, 4 October.

Anon., 1856c: "The Faussett Collection", *The Art Journal.*, October

Archaeol. Inst. 1854: "Proceedings of the Meetings of the Archaeological Institute" in *Archaeol. J.* XI.

Avent, R. 1975: *Anglo-Saxon Disc and Composite Brooches* B.A.R. 11, Oxford.

BAA, 1845a: "Proceedings of the Central Committee" in *Archaeol. J.* I.

BAA, 1845b: "British Archaeological Association. First Annual Meeting, Canterbury, September, 1844", *Archaeol. J.* I, 267–83.

BAA, 1846a: "British Archaeological Association", *J. Brit. Archaeol. Assoc.* I, i–xiii.

BAA, 1846b: *Transactions of the British Archaeological Association, at its Second Annual Congress, held at Winchester, August 1845* . . ., London.

Bähr, J.K. 1850: *Die Gräber der Liven*, Dresden.

Bazin, G. 1967: *The Museum Age*, Brussels.

Bloxham, M.H. 1834: *A Glimpse at the Monumental Architecture and Sculpture of Great Britain* . . ., London.

Böhner, K. 1969: "Vorwort zum Neudruck" in Lindenschmit (1848), Mainz, reprinted.

BM, 1854: *Copies of Reports, Memorials, or other Communications to or from the Trustees of the British Museum, on the subject of the Faussett Collection of Anglo-Saxon Antiquities*, London.

Brown, G.B. 1915: *The Arts in Early England*, III–IV, London.

"C.C." 1843: "Original Correspondence. City of London Antiquities", *The Literary Gazette* 1387, 19 August 545–6.

Cochet, L'Abbé J.B.D. 1854: *La Normandie Souteraine*, Rouen.

Cochet, L'Abbé J.B.D. 1857: *Sépultures Gauloises, Romaines, Franques et Normandes* . . ., Paris.

Conyngham, Lord A. and Akerman, J.Y. 1844: "An Account of the opening and examination of a considerable number of Tumuli on Breach Downs, in the County of Kent . . .", *Archaeologia* XXX, 47–56.

Daniel, G.E. 1950: *A Hundred Years of Archaeology*, London.

Deck, I. 1851: "Anglo-Saxon Remains, found at Little Wilbraham, Cambridgeshire", *Archaeol. J.* 8, 172–8.

Douglas, Revd J. 1793: *Nenia Britannica: Or, an Account of Some Hundred Sepulchres, of the Ancient Inhabitants of Britain*, London.

Dryden, Sir H. 1852: "An Account of a Discovery of early Saxon remains at Barrow Furlong, on the Hill Farm, in the parish of Marston St. Laurence . . . Northampton[shire] . . .", *Archaeologia* 34, 326–34.

Dunkin, A.J. (Ed.) 1845: *A Report of the Proceedings of the British Archaeological Association, at the First General Meeting, held at Canterbury, in . . . 1844*, London.

"E. H." 1845: "Preservation of National Antiquities", *The Builder* III, No. CXV, 19 April 181–2.

Evans, J. 1956: *A History of the Society of Antiquaries*, Oxford.

Evison, V.I. 1979: *A Corpus of Wheel-Thrown Pottery in Anglo-Saxon Graves*, Monograph of the Royal Archaeological Institute.

Faussett, Revd B., edited by Smith, C.R. 1856: *Inventorium Sepulchrale: An account of some antiquities dug up at Gilton, Kingston, Sibertswold, Barfriston, Beakesbourne, Chartham, and Crundale . . . Kent, from A.D. 1757 to A.D. 1773*, printed for the subscribers, London.

Fox, Col. A. Lane 1872: "Address to the Department of Anthropology" in *Report of the British Association for the Advancement of Science* 42, 157–74.

Francis, J.C. 1984: *The Development of the Study of Pagan Anglo-Saxon Remains to 1913 with Particular Reference to the Mid-Nineteenth Century and the Works of J.Y. Akerman*, unpublished BA Dissertation, University of York.

Franks, A.W. 1852: "The Collection of British Antiquities in the British Museum", *Archaeol. J.* IX, 9–15.

Franks, A.W. 1853: "On the Additions to the Collection of National Antiquities in the British Museum", *Archaeol. J.* X, 1– 13.

Franks, A.W. 1854: "The Additions to the Collection of National Antiquities in the British Museum", *Archaeol. J.* XI (1854) 23–32.

Gibson, M. 1988: "Joseph Mayer" in Gibson, M. (Ed.) 1988, 1–27.

Gibson, M. (Ed.) 1988: *Joseph Mayer of Liverpool 1803–1886* Soc. Antiqs. London 1988.

Hansard, 1845: *Hansard's Parliamentary Debates* 3rd Ser. LXXXI, London.

Hansard, 1854a: *Journal House of Commons* 109, 283.

Hansard, 1854b: *Hansard's Parliamentary Debates* 3rd Ser. CXXIV, London.

Hasted, E. 1790: *The History and Topographical Survey of the County of Kent* III, Canterbury.

Haverfield, F. 1901: "Romano-British Norfolk" in H.A. Doubleday (Ed.) *A History of Norfolk Vol. 1 The Victoria History of the Counties of England*, Westminster.

Hawkes, S.C. 1982: "Anglo-Saxon Kent *c* 425–725" in Leach, P.E. (Ed.), *Archaeology in Kent to AD 1500* Council for British Archaeology Research Report 48, 64–78.

Henslow, Revd J.S. 1847: "On Supposed British Cinerary Urns, Found at the village of Kingston, near Derby, in 1844" *J. Brit. Archaeol. Assoc.* II, 60–63.

Hoare, Sir R. Colt 1812: *The Ancient History of South Wiltshire*, London.

Hoare, Sir R. Colt 1819: *The Ancient History of North Wiltshire*, London.

Houben, P. and Fiedler, F. 1839: *Denkmaeler von Castra Vetera und Colonia Traiana in Ph. Houben's Antiquarium zu Xanten*, Xanten.

HSL&C 1850: "Proceedings" in *Trans. Hist. Soc. Lancs. & Chesh.*, II.

HSL&C 1851: "Proceedings" in *Trans. Hist. Soc. Lancs. & Chesh.*, III.

Jessup, R.F. 1953: in Jessup, R.F. and Zarnecki, G. "The Faussett Pavilion" *Archaeologia Cantiana* LXVI, 1–8.

Jessup, R. 1975: *Man of Many Talents. An Informal Biography of James Douglas, 1753–1819*, Chichester.

Kemble, J.M. (Ed.) 1835–7: *The Anglo-Saxon Poems of Beowulf, The Traveller's Song and the Battle of Finnesburh*, 2nd Edition with translation, London.

Kemble, J.M. 1849: *The Saxons in England*, London.

Kemble, J.M. 1855a: "On Mortuary Urns found at Stade-on-the-Elbe, and other parts of North Germany, now in the Museum of the Historical Society of Hanover . . .", *Archaeologia* XXXVI, 270–83.

Kemble, J.M. 1855b (for 1856): "Burial and Cremation", *Archaeol. J.* 12, 309–37.

Kemble, J.M., Edited by Latham, R.G. and Franks, A.W. 1863: *Horae Ferales – Studies in the Archaeology of the Northern Nations*, London.

Kidd, D. 1977: "Charles Roach Smith and his Museum of London Antiquities" in Camber, R. (Ed.) *Collectors and Collections* British Museum Yearbook 2, London, 105–35.

Kidd, D. 1978: "Charles Roach Smith and the Abbé Cochet" *Centenaire de l'Abbé Cochet – 1975. Actes du Colloque International d'Archéologie*, Rouen, 63–77.

Kühn, H. 1976: *Geschichte der Vorgeschichtsforschung*, Berlin.

Lee, Sir S. 1900: "Wright, Thomas (1810–1877)" in *The Dictionary of National Biography* XXI, 130–3, Oxford.

Leeds, E.T. 1913: *The Archaeology of the Anglo-Saxon Settlements*, Oxford.

Leeds, E.T. 1936: *Early Anglo-Saxon Art and Archaeology*, Oxford.

Levine, P. 1986: *The Amateur and the Professional. Antiquarians, Historians and Archaeologists in Victorian England, 1838–1886*, Cambridge.

Lindenschmit, W. and L. 1848: *Das Germanische Todtenlager bei Selzen in der Provinz Rheinhessen*, Mainz.

Matson, C. 1961: "William Rolfe, A Noted Sandwich Antiquarian", *Archaeologia Cantiana* LXXXVI, 180–5.

Mayer, J. 1849: J. Mayer "On Ancient Shoes, as used in this and other parts of the Country" *Trans. Hist. Soc. Lancs. Chesh. I* (1849) 117–21.

Meaney, A. 1981: *Anglo-Saxon Amulets*, B.A.R. 96, Oxford.

Miller, E. 1973: *That Noble Cabinet*, London.

Montfauçon, B. de 1719 (supplement 1724): *L'Antiquité Expliquée*, Paris.

Neville, Hon. R.C. 1852: *Saxon Obsequies illustrated by Ornaments and Weapons: discovered . . . in a Cemetery near Little Wilbraham, Cambridgeshire, during the autumn of 1851 . . .*, London.

Oberlin, J.J. 1773: *Museum Schoepflini*, Argentorati.

Parliamentary Commission, 1850: *Report of the Commissioners appointed to Inquire into the Constitution and Government of the British Museum; with Minutes of Evidence*, London.

Parliamentary Committee, 1835–6: *Report from the Select Committee on the Condition, Management and Affaires of the British Museum; together with the Minutes of Evidence, Appendix and Index*.

Parliamentary Committee, 1860: *Report from the Select Committee on the British Museum; together with the Proceedings of the Committee, Minutes of Evidence, and Appendix*, London.

Pettigrew, T.J. 1846: "Introductory Paper. On the Objects and Pursuit of Antiquarian Researches", in BAA (1846b) 1–15.

Rhodes, M. forthcoming: *The Contribution to British Archaeology of Charles Roach Smith (1806–90)*, University of London Ph.D. thesis, in preparation.

Rigollot, J. 1850: "Recherches historiques sur les peuples de la race teutonique qui envahirent les Gaules au Ve siècle . . ..", *Mémoires de la Societé des Antiquaries de Picardie* X, 122–227.

Sklenář, K. 1983: *Archaeology in Central Europe: the First 500 Years*, Leicester 1983.

Smith, C.R. 1837: "Observations on the Roman Remains found in various parts of London in the years 1834, 1835, 1836 . . ." *Archaeologia* XXVII, 140–52.

Smith, C.R. 1843a (for 1848): "Coins Found in Kent" *Collect. Antiq.* I, Pt. 1, 5–8.

Smith, C.R. 1843b (for 1848): "Warwickshire Antiquities in the Collection of Matthew Holbeche Bloxham, Esq., Rugby", *Collect. Antiq.* I, Pt. III, 33–48.

Smith, C.R. 1844a: "Account of Some Antiquities Found in the Neighbourhood of Sandwich . . . Kent . . .", *Archaeologia* XXX (1844) 132–6.

Smith, C.R. 1844b: "To the Editor of the Times", *The Times*, June 22, 8.

Smith, C.R. 1845 (for 1848)[82]: in Revd W. Vallance "Anglo-Saxon Antiquities discovered at Sittingbourne, Kent, from 1825 to 1828" *Collect. Antiq.* I, Pt. VII, London.

Smith, C.R. 1846: in "Abstract of the Proceedings of the Second Congress" in BAA (1846b).

Smith, C.R. 1847: "Discovery of Anglo-Saxon Remains at Northfleet, Kent", *J. Brit. Archaeol. Assoc.* III, for 1848, 235–40.

Smith, C.R. 1848: "Preface", in *Collect. Antiq.* I, v–xi, London.

Smith, C.R. 1849 (for 1852): "Roman Villa at Hartlip, Kent", *Collect. Antiq.* II, Pt. 1, 1–24.

Smith, C.R. 1850a: *The Antiquities of Richborough, Reculver, and Lymne, in Kent*, printed for the subscribers, London.

Smith, C.R. 1851a: "Notes on Some of the Antiquities of Trèves, Mayence, and other places on the Moselle and Rhine" *Collect. Antiq.* II, Pts. III–IV, 65–152; reprinted, London.

Smith, C.R. 1851b (for 1852)[83]: "Anglo-Saxon Remains found in Kent, Suffolk, and Leicestershire" *Collect. Antiq.* II, Pt. VI, 155–70.

Smith, C.R. 1851c "Notes from a Journal of a Fortnight's Tour on the Rhine", *The Gentleman's Magazine*, 2nd Ser. XXXV, 42–9.

Smith, C.R. 1852a: "Anglo-Saxon and Frankish Remains", *Collect. Antiq.* II, Pts. VIII–IX, 203–48.

Smith, C.R. 1852b: with J. Elliott *Report on Excavations Made on the Site of the Roman Castrum at Lymne, in Kent, in 1850*, printed for the subscribers to the excavations, London.

Smith, C.R. 1852c: "Notes on Saxon Sepulchral Remains found at Fairford, Gloucestershire . . ." *Archaeologia* XXXIV, 77–82.

Smith, C.R. 1852d: in Dryden (1852, 326–8).

Smith, C.R. 1853 (for 1854): "Anglo-Saxon Remains discovered at Ozingell, Kent", *Collect. Antiq.* III, Pt. 1, 1–18.

Smith, C.R. 1854a: "The Faussett Collection of Anglo-Saxon Antiquities" *Collect. Antiq.* III, London, 179–92; reprinted.

Smith, C.R. 1854b: "The National Antiquities. (Appendix to p. 192)", *Collect. Antiq.* III, London, 266–9.

Smith, C.R. 1855: "On a Roman Sepulchral Inscription on an Anglo-Saxon Urn in the Faussett Collection . . ." *Report of the British Association for the Advancement of Science* 25, 145–6.

Smith, C.R. 1856: in Faussett (1856).

Smith, C.R. 1858a: *Report on Excavations Made Upon the Site of the Roman Castrum at Pevensey, in Sussex, in 1852 . . .* printed for the subscribers to the excavations, London.

Smith, C.R. 1858b (for 1861): "Inscribed Funereal Urn in the Museum of Joseph Mayer, Esq.", *Collect. Antiq.* V, Pt. II, 115–21.

Smith, C.R. 1859: *Illustrations of Roman London*, printed for the subscribers, London.

Smith, C.R. 1860 (for 1861): "Anglo-Saxon Remains found in Kent and Lincolnshire", *Collect. Antiq.* V, Pt. III, 129–40.

Smith, C.R. 1864 (for 1868): "Anglo-Saxon Remains discovered in Kent, in Cambridgeshire, and in some other Counties", *Collect. Antiq.* VI, Pt. II, 136–72.

Smith, C.R. 1868: "Preface" in *Collect. Antiq.* VI, v–viii.

Smith, C.R. 1871: *A Catalogue of Anglo-Saxon and Other Antiquities discovered at Faversham, in Kent, and Bequeathed by William Gibbs Esq. . . . to the South Kensington Museum . . .* London.

Smith, C.R. 1875: "The Abbé Cochet" *Archaeol. J.* XXXII, 462–70.

Smith, Major H. and Smith, C.R. 1881–2: "Isle of Wight Words" in "Series C. Original Glossaries", *Glossaries of Words used in the Isle of Wight, North Lincoln, Radnor, West Worcester, Cumberland, and Oxford . . .* English Dialect Society 12, ix–xii and 1–64, reprinted.

Smith, C.R. 1883: *Retrospections, Social and Archaeological* I, printed for the subscribers, London.

Smith, C.R. 1886: *Retrospections, Social and Archaeological* II, printed for the subscribers, London.

Smith, C.R. 1891: Waller J.G. (Ed.), *Retrospections, Social and Archaeological* III, printed for the subscribers, London.

Taylor, E.R. 1932: "The Humours of Archaeology, or, The Canterbury Congress of 1844 and the Early Days of the Association" *J. Brit. Archaeol. Assoc. 2nd Ser.* XXXVIII, 183–234.

Troyon, F. 1841: *Description des Tombeaux de Bel-Air près Cheseaux sur Lausanne*, Lausanne.

Webster, L. 1978: "The Abbé Cochet and W.M. Wylie" in *Centenaire de L'Abbé Cochet, 1975. Actes du Colloque International d'Archéologie. Rouen 3–4–5 Juillet 1975*, Rouen 1978, 155–9.

White, R. 1988: "Mayer and British Archaeology" in Gibson, M. (Ed.) 1988, 118–36.

Wilkins, J. 1961: "Worsaae and British Antiquities", *Antiquity* XXXV, 214–20.

Wilson, D.M. 1985a: *The Forgotten Collector. Augustus Wollaston Franks of the British Museum*, London.

Wilson, T. 1985b: "The Origins of the Maiolica Collections of the British Museum and the Victoria and Albert Museum 1851–55" *Estralto della Rivista "Faenza". Bolletino del Museo Internazionale delle Ceramiche di Faenza Annata* LXXI, No. 1–3, 68–81.

Wright, T. 1845: *The Archaeological Album; or, Museum of National Antiquities*, London.

Wright, T. 1847: "On Recent Discoveries of Anglo-Saxon Antiquities" *J. Brit. Archaeol. Assoc.* II, 50–59.

Wright, T. 1852: *The Celt, the Roman, and the Saxon*, London.

Wright, T. 1855: "On Anglo-Saxon Antiquities, with a particular reference to the Faussett Collection", *Trans. Hist. Soc. Lancs. & Chesh.* 7, 1–39.

Wright, T. 1856: "The Faussett Collection of Anglo-Saxon Antiquities", *The Gentleman's Magazine*, 3rd Ser. I, 277–82.(84)

Wylie, W.M. 1852: *The Fairford Graves*, Oxford.

Wylie, W.M. 1853a: "Remarks on the Angon, or Barbed Javelin of the Franks, described by Agathius" *Archaeologia* XXXV, 48–55.

Wylie, W.M. 1853b: "Account of Teutonic Remains, apparently Saxon, found near Dieppe . . ." *Archaeologia* XXXV, 100–13.

Wylie, W.M. 1855: "Remarks on the Angon of the Franks and the Pilum of Vegetius . . ." *Archaeologia* XXXVI, 80–84.

Wylie, W.M. 1857: "The Burning and Burial of the Dead", *Archaeologia* XXXVII, 455–78.

CHAPTER THREE

ANGLO-SAXON BURIAL: THE COMPUTER AT WORK

Jeremy Huggett and Julian Richards

INTRODUCTION

This paper is about the application of computers to the study of Anglo-Saxon cemeteries. It is not about how computers work; nor does it seek to provide an instruction manual on computerized cemetery analysis. It is not even a report on work, either completed or in progress, although examples will be given as appropriate.

Instead, it concerns the present and possible future impact of computers on the theory and practice of mortuary studies in general, and Anglo-Saxon cemetery studies in particular. It will be argued that Anglo-Saxon cemetery analysis is at a moment of crisis, but it will be suggested that computerized approaches offer a means by which that crisis may be resolved.

The paper is in three parts. First, we shall survey the recent background, and describe why we are at a critical time for cemetery analysis; secondly, we shall examine how computers can currently assist in the re-analysis of old data; and thirdly, we shall suggest some ways in which computers might be used in the future.

THE BACKGROUND

The last major conference to be held on Anglo-Saxon cemeteries was held in Oxford in 1979, a decade ago (Rahtz, Dickinson and Watts 1980). It seemed to be an exciting time. A host of new theoretical approaches were challenging traditonal cultural history. Lecture halls, at least in one university, were resounding to several rival '—isms': functionalism, structuralism and marxism. The prospect was offered of removing Anglo-Saxon archaeology from its incestuous relationship with history, and establishing it, with its ally, prehistory, firmly in the Social Sciences.

Hope-Taylor had delivered a challenge in the Yeavering report:

> our so-called Anglo-Saxon archaeology is today still blinkered by antiquarian pre-occupation with grave-goods. Every year we see Anglo-Saxon cemeteries used as convenient quarries to provide raw material for the perpetuation of an habitual and unquestioning academic activity (itself not without a curiously ritual aspect). The Anglo-Saxon cemetery in Britain has never been studied as a complete phenomenon, as the deeply revealing local entity it certainly is. It ought by now to have been recognised as an unwritten form of historical document roughly equivalent . . . to the parish register of later times. Hope-Taylor 1977.

At the Oxford Conference, papers delivered by prehistorians seemed to point the way forward (Bradley 1980, Hodder 1980), and there were a few brave Anglo-Saxon examples to follow (Arnold 1980, Pader 1980).

At the same time computers were already beginning to have an impact upon archaeology, although there had been few forays into the Anglo-Saxon period. A doctoral thesis by M.E.Wilson had used the statistical package CLUSTAN to classify several Anglo-Saxon artefact categories within a cultural-historical framework (Wilson 1972), but this was an isolated exception. Indeed, the paper at that Oxford Conference on the possibilities of computer usage was given by an archaeologist whose speciality lay in the Roman period (Jones 1980). Computers, like theory, were being more warmly embraced by our colleagues in other periods, particularly prehistory, where both were seen as having a certain glamour.

Yet many Anglo-Saxonists were aware of the potential of computer applications. Tania Dickinson, in her opening address to the Oxford Conference noted that:

> The varieties of quantitative analysis, which include types utilising computer programmes (sic), have been current in archaeology for well over a decade (Doran and Hodson 1975), but they have not yet been made the explicit basis for the classification of a major group of Anglo-Saxon artefacts. (1980, 18)

What, then, is the current situation?

Developments in Information Technology

Certainly, information technology has developed at a rapid, and accelerating, pace. First, no one can ignore the widespread availablity of micro-computers. Decreasing prices coupled with increasing processing power and storage capacity have put serious computing within everyone's reach. Secondly, the impact of word processing should not be underestimated. Word processing is most people's introduction to computing and proves that modest investments of time and money can provide reasonable returns. Thirdly, the distinction between programmer and non-programmer has become blurred. In 1979 to make serious use of a computer one really had to be able to program, often in 'serious' languages such as FORTRAN or Algol. Today commercially available applications packages provide for most needs, including databases, graphics, and statistical spreadsheets. Programming is confined to 'high-level' English language type instructions. Programs even exist which will write other programs once the user has defined the task required.

Finally, mention should also be made of the increasing interest in archaeology of computer specialists, who are attracted to archaeology because of its data, and problems, and the publicity it may provide. Computer manufacturers, such as IBM and Olivetti, are now involved in sponsoring archaeological research. Connected with this has been the increase over the last few years of archaeologists trained to use computers, although formal training is still inadequate (Richards 1985, 1986a, 1987a).

Developments in Cemetery Studies

There can be no doubt, therefore, that computers are now more widely available than in 1979. How has this availability affected Anglo-Saxon cemetery analysis? On the whole there really seems to have been little change. To an optimist this may be regarded as a period of consolidation; to a pessimist it has been one of stagnation.

The 1979 Conference computing paper described the use of computers to carry out a complex multivariate statistical analysis of cemetery data (Jones ibid.). The link between computing and statistics was symptomatic of early archaeological computing, and was responsible for frightening many archaeologists away from them. The use of computers in Anglo-Saxon cemetery research has generally been tied to individual research projects where computers have been used to test a specific theory, as in the work of Pader (1980, 1982), Shepard (1979), and Richards (1982, 1984, 1987b). In mortuary studies in general, computers have frequently been utilized for wealth score approaches (e.g. Shennan 1975). For the Anglo-Saxon period both Alcock (1981) and Arnold (1980) have attempted manual wealth score analyses and Brenan (1984–85) has used a computerized wealth score analysis package to examine the Anglo-Saxon cemetery at Sleaford. However, there has been no widespread theoretical acceptance of this kind of analysis, and Orton and Hodson (1981) have pointed out some of the statistical pitfalls stemming from small sample size. Yet, there is a danger that the tools may become tarnished by the purpose to which they have been applied. Many have associated computers with systems theory, and a rigid application of functionalist dogma, with explicit inputs and outputs (Doran 1970, and see Richards 1986b).

The most significant developments have perhaps come about as incidental to other applications. Two areas, in particular, offer great potential.

First, on-site computer recording has been employed on at least two Anglo-Saxon cemetery sites: West Heslerton (Powlesland 1985), and Sutton Hoo (Carver 1987). In both cases, this extends the quantity of data that can be recovered, and breaks down the division between excavation and post-excavation work. At Mucking the computing was done at a post-excavation stage (Catton, Jones and Moffett 1982), and the equipment employed was found to be inappropriate to the size of the problem (Moffett 1986).

Secondly, the computerization of county sites and monuments records for cultural resource management has almost by accident provided us with a tremendously valuable research tool (Allden 1986). No longer will it be possible for doctorates to be awarded for the gathering of corpuses of data when the same outcome can be achieved by a three parameter query to a computerized data bank. Academic access to Sites and Monuments Records creates tremendous potential for spatial studies, and allows the archaeologist to concentrate on the analysis, rather than data gathering.

But developments in computerized cemetery studies have lagged behind. The hesitancy to use computers for routine cemetery post-excavation analysis must largely be due to uncertainty over what that analysis should consist of.

Certainly a few more nails have been banged into the coffin of culture history, although the corpse seems reluctant to lie down. The approach was appropriate to the post-war decades, but its continued relevance must be questioned. Several problems have been raised. First, as Dickinson pointed out in 1979, chronologies and distributions have been revised, but remain incomplete (Dickinson ibid.). Secondly, the implicit assumptions of the 'Adventus hypothesis' have been questioned (Arnold 1984, Hills 1979). Was it an invasion? How many invaders were there? What really happened to the native population? Thirdly, doubts have been cast about using archaeological data to respond to an agenda set by historians (Hills ibid.), particularly when many historians now seem themselves to be more interested in broader economic and social problems.

But the demise of culture history has left a vacuum. In particular it has left a hole in cemetery reports where previously there used to be a section of discussion or interpretation. For previous generations a cemetery report was incomplete without a section on the cultural affinities and dating of the material. For pottery the bible would be Myres (1969, 1977), for metalwork it would be Leeds (1913, 1949) and others. But the days have gone when a single individual could hold all the information – all those continental parallels – in a human brain. And the new generation has questioned the traditional wisdom. They want hypotheses to be testable, and how does one test if a cremation urn is Anglian of the early sixth century?

The consequence has been that excavators are no longer sure what is expected of a cemetery report. They are uncertain whether it is still adequate to cite Myres (ibid.), and wonder whether they should instead be saying something about society. But the excursions into social analysis have not yet established a standard procedure which can be followed, although the recent Sewerby report suggests a number of analyses which such a procedure should include (Hirst 1985). Is this the reason why our awful publication record, highlighted by Dickinson in 1979 (ibid.), is still so bad? Even the specialists cannot agree. A few years ago, the Early Anglo-Saxon Pottery Group tried to define what it thought should constitute a cremation cemetery report. It could not even agree what scale the pot drawings should be at (Early Anglo-Saxon Pottery Group 1984).

The problem is not one unique to Anglo-Saxon cemeteries. The Cunliffe report (1982) tried to address the problem of protracted post-excavation work in British

Archaeology as a whole. The committee's solution was to minimize the amount of secondary research that should be undertaken as part of the publication of primary evidence. The Scole Committee for East Anglia had, in a sense, already anticipated that policy. By publishing straightforward catalogues of material divorced from interpretation, as in the Bergh Apton (Green and Rogerson 1978) and Spong Hill reports (Hills 1977, Hills and Penn 1981, Hills, Penn and Rickett 1984, Hills, Penn and Rickett 1987), they have ensured the rapid availability of material for other scholars. Yet one must still wonder if that is a satisfactory long term solution. Sites are always excavated within a theoretical framework (see, for example, Carver 1989). Hopefully the questions to be answered will be explicitly stated. Presenting raw data, without a theoretical context, denies that there are theoretical biases in data collection and recording, and ultimately reduces the archaeology to a mechanical data logging procedure. It is notable that in their recommendations to the Historic Buildings and Monuments Commission (English Heritage) the Society for Medieval Archaeology (1987) has welcomed recent trends in early Anglo-Saxon cemetery studies in enlarging the scope of interpretation from mere artefact cataloguing.

We do not claim to know the answer. No one really seems to know what we should be saying from Anglo-Saxon cemeteries. We would suggest, however, that computers could offer a systematized post-excavation cemetery analysis package, which would streamline publication, and make sites comparable. But first archaeologists must agree what that package must consist of, and those are archaeological problems, not computing ones.

RE-ANALYSING OLD DATA

There appears to be a feeling amongst some Anglo-Saxon archaeologists that the problems connected with attempts to use old excavation reports are so great that perhaps the attempt should not be made at all. This belief is particularly prevalent when computers are brought into the discussion: the application of twentieth-century technology to nineteenth-century excavation reports is seen to be in some way more problematic than its application to more modern reports. For example, a recently published excavation report stated that the new computer-aided methods of research and analysis were considerably hampered by the lack of recently excavated, readily accessible data (Cook and Dacre 1985, 52). Whilst there is indeed a considerable backlog in terms of incomplete, unpublished, and inaccessible cemetery excavation reports which presents a major barrier to research, this viewpoint would seem to suggest that most of the last hundred years or so of Anglo-Saxon archaeology should be discarded in favour of the (few) more recent and (fewer still) accessible cemetery reports, if taken to its logical conclusion. However, the introduction of a computer does not somehow make old cemetery data any less suitable for analysis – rather, a computer may actively assist the process by forcing a clear, logical, and explicit approach to the extraction of data from old reports.

There are many problems associated with old cemetery data, although it should be emphasised that they are common to any attempts to use old data and not specific to cemetery studies. Paramount amongst these is what is perceived to be its overall low quality, with poor recording compared with modern standards perhaps being the main culprit. In some instances, the excavator was not even present at the opening of some graves and depended on descriptions given by the workmen, and most Anglo-Saxon archaeologists are familiar with the problems of attempting to reconstruct a series of graves from a sketchy description in a diary. In most cases, it is not known whether the complete cemetery was excavated, though in fact it is generally safe to assume that it was not. In addition, old reports are often difficult to trace and are often found in obscure local journals. However, it should be stressed that some of these problems are not peculiar to old cemetery reports. There still are recent cases of unpublished and inaccessible cemetery excavations. Nor is the problem of incompletely excavated cemeteries restricted to the nineteenth and early twentieth centuries – there are many instances of more recent cemetery investigations which for one reason or another have not been fully excavated. Indeed, there is a growing conflict here between the need for total excavation of a site in order to allow more reliability in any social analysis for instance, and the desire to preserve part of the cemetery for future archaeologists.

Publication standards, as well as excavation standards, raise difficulties. These may range from selective publication to reports which consist simply of catalogues of grave-goods unrelated to the graves they came from. For as long as interests in Anglo-Saxon archaeology focused primarily on the artefacts, and particularly on those 'diagnostic' pieces which could be arranged in elaborate typological sequences, items which did not appear to fit in with any current scheme were often not considered worth publishing or were even discarded on site. As recently as 1951 it was possible for Lethbridge to write in the Lackford report:

> It seems quite unnecessary to give a detailed description of each pot. Not only would this be tedious to read and costly to publish, but when there is nothing in the contents of a particular vessel to give any information as to its possible date, its description appears to be of small importance. (1951, 7).

All cemeteries are excavated with an eye to the theories and concepts relating to burials that are current at the time. One of the main objectives of early cemetery excavations was the recovery of objects, and this is perhaps most apparent in those reports which simply list a catalogue of artefacts. Even with the development of the culture-historical approach the recovery of artefacts continued to play a major role in order to create distribution maps and establish typologies. Questions asked of cemetery evidence today have shifted to the examination of social structure, economy and ritual through the burial evidence. Such aspects are reflected in modern cemetery recording just as much as the artefact-orientated approach which was current earlier in this century. Simply to abandon a set of data because it was collected under a different conceptual regime makes little sense. On that basis, evidence produced during one phase of investigations would be inapplicable to a later phase. Thus modern excavation reports, which may be out of date in perhaps twenty-five years, will be just as useless then as some might claim old excavation reports are today, once the investigation of cemetery evidence has moved on again into a new phase.

However, allowances can be made for biases in the record introduced as a result of the questions that were being asked of the data at the time. It should be possible to remove the filter from data collected under a different paradigm, or to at least quantify any biases that may have resulted. To take Lackford again as an example, Lethbridge (1951, 14) said that he had drawn only:

1. Early pots which might have a bearing on the origins of the settlers
2. Pots which contained a recognizable object
3. Pots associated with another pot
4. Groups of vessels produced by the same hand
5. Pots of a late date

As a result, the assumptions and reasoning behind Lethbridge's recording are known, and can be taken into account as a kind of 'bias correction factor'. Indeed, it could even be argued that using data for a purpose for which it was not originally recorded is more likely to produce reliable results. There is a tendency for excavation evidence to be shaped not only by the recovery techniques, but also by the questions in the mind of the excavator. Breaking that mould and applying new ideas and techniques to old data may in fact help to circumvent any bias inherent in the old excavation reports.

Much is said about the poor quality of old cemetery reports, but criticisms are rarely backed up with more than one or two concrete examples. In an attempt to assess the overall level of information that could be derived from old cemetery reports sixty-five cemeteries from central England ranging from Derbyshire and Staffordshire through Oxfordshire and Gloucestershire to Wiltshire and Hampshire and consisting of around 2,500 burials were selected and subjectively ranked. The cemeteries range in size from three or four individuals to over two hundred. Thirty-one cemeteries from the sample contained more than twenty-five individuals of which fifteen cemeteries are larger than fifty burials. The selection procedure was based on Meaney's definition of a cemetery as consisting of three or more individuals (Meaney 1964, 29), and any cemetery report which did not distinguish between individual burials or identify which artefacts came from which grave was rejected.

The criteria used to assess the level of recording were whether information concerning the age, sex, orientation, body position and type, quantity and position of grave-goods was given for each burial. A cemetery report with all of these classes of information present was classed as 'Very Good', those with all but one present were 'Good' while those with all but two or three present were rated 'Fair', the remainder being rated 'Poor'. While this assessment is clearly subjective, the classes are weighted in favour of the lower categories of recording, since the criteria are more strictly defined at the higher levels. The results were:

Very Good	9 cemeteries (14 per cent)
Good	23 cemeteries (35 per cent)
Fair	25 cemeteries (38 per cent)
Poor	8 cemeteries (12 per cent)

From this it can be seen that 87 per cent of cemeteries from the sample (fifty-seven out of sixty-five) were considered on this basis to have a generally reasonable level of recording. Of the remaining eight cemeteries, two contain twelve burials each, one nine burials, and the remainder less than five burials each, so that the number of poorly recorded burials is apparently very small – forty-five out of 2,500. Nor are all of the cemeteries rated as 'Very Good' or 'Good' recently excavated: for example, while Collingbourne Ducis is included (Gingell 1976), so also is Brighthampton (Akerman 1857, 1860).

Taking the criteria used above, the number of cemeteries where each class of information was absent is as follows:

No orientation	21
No sex	11
No body position	17
No age	28
No grave-goods	0
No grave-goods position	16

Thus, the information most often missing was the age of the individual, followed by the orientation of the body. Not surprisingly, grave-goods, where present, are always recorded, although the actual position in which they were found may be absent.

It should be recognized that this survey ignores a number of problems. No attempt has been made to assess the reliability of the recording. Nor has any allowance been made for the absence or otherwise of cemetery or grave-plans, for example. To take a more specific instance, the assignment of age or sex cannot be relied on in many instances even though it has been given in the report. Burials in early reports were often sexed on the basis of simple assumptions rather than skeletal evidence – weapons with males, jewellery with females. The problem is that reports rarely state whether the assigned sex was arrived at through skeletal identification or through the association of grave-goods.

More recently, computer-based statistical analyses have been applied in order to assess the reliability of the sexing of burials, although the results are not always consistent. For example, Pader (1982) discovered a good fit between burials sexed by skeleton and those sexed by artefacts in the cemeteries in her study, which might suggest that the intuitive sexing by grave-goods is quite reliable. On the other hand, analysis of the sex-links of grave-goods from 188 cremation burials with adequate skeletal identifications and grave-goods present indicate many of these assumptions to be unwarranted. Few grave-goods appear to be sex-linked – miniatures are mainly associated with males, and ivory with females, but no other objects, including brooches and beads, are significantly linked one way or the other (Richards 1987b).

Given these limitations, the sample data set of sixty-five cemeteries has been shown to have a reasonable level of recording overall, indeed, perhaps better than might have been expected. This reservoir of information should not be abandoned simply because there are problems with the recording, if only because old data constitutes such a high proportion of the total sample available. Nor is this situation likely to change greatly, with cemetery excavations becoming increasingly rare, and a general moratorium on Anglo-Saxon cemetery excavations has been proposed (Society for Medieval Archaeology

1987). Indeed, it is this very depth of available data that makes Anglo-Saxon studies unusual. Rather, means need to be sought by which the problems associated with this data might be overcome or at least reduced.

Of course, some data are more reliable than others. One approach to this would be to attempt to weigh the information according to its reliability. It is a common misapprehension that once information is stored on computer it is given an undesirable and undeserved permanency, and this is often the reason for qualms about computerized excavation recording since in some cases an honest answer might well be an uncertain one. However, this problem can be largely overcome by using a second linked variable to indicate the degree of belief in the identification of the first variable. These degrees of belief or confidence in a variable are obviously subjective and open to discussion, but the principle that the reliability of data can be graded remains.

For instance, the reliability of the identification of a site as an Anglo-Saxon cemetery will be directly related to the date of discovery. Confidence factors may therefore range from 75 per cent of those graves with weapons recorded in Meaney's gazetteer (1964) to 99 per cent of those discovered today. Certainty as to site location may be as high as 90 per cent, but confidence that a site has been completely excavated may be as low as 25 per cent since the information is usually not recorded for old excavations. Confidence in the number of graves recorded will vary: perhaps 90 per cent of those with grave-goods will have been recorded, falling to 25 per cent for those without. The reliability of the number of objects found within a grave will be very low for organic objects in old cemeteries, say 5 per cent, rising to only 25 per cent for modern excavations. Figures for inorganic objects will be considerably higher – perhaps 90 per cent for rich items, and 75 per cent for poorer items such as rusty blades. Descriptions of the objects recorded tend to be reliable and may be assigned a figure of *c.* 90 per cent. There may be argument about the actual numbers used here, but the overall range is fairly accurate, and serves to quantify the reliabilty or otherwise of cemetery data in an albeit subjective way. The conclusion from this sort of exercise is that the most reliable information is the presence of a cemetery (which can then be used in spatial analysis) and the description of grave-goods, particularly those which are drawn. Therefore, in terms of the three levels of cemetery analysis, inter-site work and intra-grave analysis may be more reliable than intra-site studies.

How then can the computer assist in re-analysing old data? Using a computer does not suddenly make the data more objective, and it certainly does not make it any more reliable. Nor can the computer make a poorly recorded cemetery better. Why then bother to computerize old cemeteries? The most obvious answer is that they are there – such a large body of data should not be ignored. To avoid the question by stating that the level of recording is inadequate is not sufficient – new approaches and techniques need to be developed which take account the recording standards which, in many cases, may be demonstrated to be better than is often assumed. Given that there is so much data, it makes a lot of sense to put it onto a computer in order to manipulate it. A computerized version of Meaney's gazetteer, expanded to include details of each individual grave, could be a valuable jumping off point for any research project. It would not be a straightforward matter to computerize, if only because of the size of the data set. The ability to retrieve the data rapidly and manipulate it efficiently once it is on the machine will to a large extent depend on the efficiency of the data storage and the system that controls it, and will almost inevitably mean that the data will need to be coded. The system would also have to be sufficiently flexible to handle the multitude of possible descriptions and terms and yet remain extremely efficient in storing the data. One such computer system is currently under development and has been used to record many of the the sixty-five cemeteries referred to earlier. It has a highly efficient storage system and uses a uniquely flexible coding system which allows the computer to 'learn' new categories of information as they arise (Huggett 1987, 1988).

Some of the cemeteries on such a system will be capable of sustaining the sort of concentrated and minute analyses that one would wish to apply to the more recently excavated cemeteries. For the majority, however, it would be unrealistic to expect that such methods would be of much use. However, the strength of using old cemetery data lies more in the quantity then the quality. There are far more old excavation reports than new, and while they may cover the same sort of geographical area, there is a much higher density of cemeteries excavated during the nineteenth and early twentieth centuries. One of the major shortcomings of social analyses based upon archaeological mortuary data which has become appreciated increasingly is the absence of a regional perspective (for example, Chapman and Randsborg 1981, 23). The use of an efficient and flexible computer system which can be used to interactively record and analyse a large number of Anglo-Saxon burials from a wide range of cemeteries would go some way to enabling such a regional approach, but in order to accomplish this, the assembled data set relies heavily on old reports. Indeed, the geographical area covered by the cemetery sample referred to above allows not only the facility to study mortuary evidence within a regional context, but also has the potential to enable a comparison of adjacent regions and an examination of their interfaces. The scale of such a project makes the use of a computer imperative, and the development of a computer system along such lines would enable the rapid development, testing, and modification of hypotheses concerning the nature and interpretation of Anglo-Saxon burial ritual (Huggett 1988).

The role of the computer in analysing old data lies especially in areas where it can offer new approaches to that data. Two overlapping themes may be distinguished: the use of a generalizing rather than a particular approach, and the use of hypothesis testing.

First, the use of the computer has been linked with a shift in emphasis in cemetery studies from the individual rich grave and beautiful artefact to the overall context and underlying pattern.

In fact, this is something of a false division in computing terms, as the computer is equally applicable to both types of approach, though the actual application may be different. The computer in its database role can still be of considerable help in the more traditional studies of material culture through the grave-goods, perhaps acting as no more than a convenient filing system.

Computers are ideally suited for studying large numbers of comparable units. This facility is necessary in both the general and the particular, where information on large quantities of other material will still be important for comparative purposes.

New information, which may previously have been buried in a mass of data, may become apparent. This may include the recognition of patterns in the data, such as associations. This is simply a result of having the information literally at one's fingertips. A database consisting of all Anglo-Saxon burials from a particular region might, for example, be used to discover patterning in the grave-goods or their layout without any immediate recourse to statistics. A multi-dimensional examination of burial ritual using a computer database as an integral part of the study will enable the interactive generation and testing of hypotheses arising from the recognition of pattern in the data in addition to the testing of pre-existing hypotheses (Huggett 1987).

A good database system allows the user to simply browse through the data, perhaps checking an idea out before submitting it to some form of statistical test. The retrieval system should be reasonably flexible, able to select records which match a combination of criteria so that quite complex questions can be asked. Even relatively straightforward questions, such as identifying the different ways brooches might be worn, or the different sets of brooches that appear with burials, would be extremely time-consuming using even an extensively cross-referenced manual card index, and quite basic database systems can provide something of a quantum leap in terms of ease and speed of data retrieval. One basic facility might be a graphics element to allow the automatic production of distribution plans. It would be relatively simple to produce individual plans for each class of object found in a cemetery (see Alvey and Moffett 1985).

A variety of commercial database packages are available. Most of these are simple to use for straightforward input and retrieval of small data sets without the need for a great knowledge of computing. Larger data sets may require purpose-built systems incorporating efficient storage and retrieval techniques: factors which become increasingly important as the quantity of data increases.

The second approach linked with computer usage is the hypothetico-deductive method. The traditional approach to Anglo-Saxon archaeology has been dominated by the human expert. The discipline developed through individuals who became expert about a particular category of material, whether square-headed brooches, or pots. Their scholarship consisted of comprehensive knowledge of all the material within their field. On that basis they were able to pronounce on where any fresh material fitted into the established pattern. The fact that they had studied the material for x number of years was considered to be sufficient qualification by which to assess their judgement. Unfortunately, the rules which they applied in reaching judgements, whilst obvious to them, were rarely explicitly stated, and remained obscure to others. For example, even for those who are specialists in the field of Anglo-Saxon pottery it is extremely difficult to say, with any degree of confidence, that a particular vessel belongs to one of Myres' categories in preference to another.

There are three apparent consequences. First, knowledge which was not set down was limited to the life span of the individual concerned. Secondly, where others tried to apply the same criteria in classifying other objects they may have applied the criteria differently, through lack of knowledge of the rules. Thirdly, rival typologies and explanations could be propounded, but since the assumptions were unstated, there was no means of choosing between them, other than by an examination of the credentials of the individuals putting forward the rival views.

It is essential to emphasise that the use of the computer does not make this process any more objective. Even the rules employed by an expert system have to be written by the human programmer, although they will then at least be rigorously applied. Using a computer does require that rules and assumptions should be explicitly stated. In order to classify a pot the attributes to be used must be clearly defined. The choice of which attributes are significant is as subjective as before, but the reasons for placing Pot X in Group A rather than Group B become readily apparent, and the exercise may be repeated by others. In this way statements adopt the status of hypotheses which may be tested.

In this it seems to us that it may be easier to computerize the study of inhumation than cremation. When an inhumation burial is recorded interest tends to be focused upon a finite number of grave-goods and their position. Although position can cause some descriptive problems, in general the human perception has a number of clearly defined categories, both for general types of object which may be either present or absent, and where they are laid in the grave. Whilst these distinctions may have little significance, at least they can be precisely recorded. For cremation, on the other hand, interest tends to focus upon one object in the burial, namely the cremation vessel. We are taking one object in the grave, and elevating its status. This means that analysis becomes linked with the study of artefact typology. Here one enters a minefield of ethnographic and experimental work on the cognition of pottery types (see for example, Birmingham 1975, Hardin 1979, Kempton 1981). Anglo-Saxon pottery offers no clearly definable types, and the human brain is inadequate at coping with the fine gradation between classes. Computers may help to clarify the issues, but do not offer an easy solution.

A CASE STUDY

An example may help to illustrate a number of the points which we have been trying to make. First, it may demonstrate the role of the computer as a means of hypothetico-deductive testing. Secondly, it will show how interest focuses on the general, rather than the particular. Thirdly, it may reveal some of the problems of dealing with artefact classification, and one possible means of overcoming them, and finally, it may show how information may be extracted from new data which allows us to view old data in a fresh light.

The study starts with a general theory about material culture and mortuary behaviour which it is proposed to apply to Anglo-Saxon cremation burial. The theory leads to a number of hypotheses about Anglo-Saxon burial, which may be refined into testable hypotheses. A method is defined and then a test is applied, supporting the original hypothesis.

1. The general theory is that of structuralism, as derived from anthropology and the works of archaeologists interested in that area (see Hodder 1982), in particular those working on mortuary symbolism (e.g. Van de Velde 1979, Shanks and Tilley 1982).
2. The hypothesis proposed is that the Anglo-Saxons used symbols to make statement about the identity of their dead, in particular, that the form and decoration of a cremation urn is related to the identity of the occupant, and may be read like a memorial gravestone, if only we can understand the code.

3. This may be translated into a testable hypothesis which says that grave-goods and skeletal types will not be randomly distributed through types of pots, but that particular grave-good classes, and particular age and sex groupings will be found to be associated with particular styles of pottery.
4. The method used was to define types of pot and types of grave-good, and record skeletal information where available. Of the three, classifying the pottery was the most difficult. The process could never be completely objective, but subjectivity could be reduced by describing form and decoration at as fine a level as possible, rather than pre-selecting attributes. The help of the computer could then be enlisted in deciding which were significant, that is, meaningful to the Anglo-Saxons. A pilot sample of *c.* 500 vessels from three recent excavations was recorded at as detailed a level as possible, and then the computer was used to test which attributes of form and decoration were correlated with either grave-goods or skeletal groupings.
5. On this basis the method could then be re-defined for the full sample of 2,440 vessels from eighteen sites, including old and new excavations. Only those attributes which had been found to be correlated with other features were now recorded. The initial hypotheses could then be tested against the total sample.
6. This is not the place to describe the results in any detail (see Richards 1987b), but it may be helpful to give a few examples.

First, for burials where the age of the deceased could be identified from skeletal remains, it was demonstrated that the size of a cremation vessel was directly in proportion to the age of the occupant, although the relative status of the deceased also has to be taken into account. Adult females, for example, are not generally buried in such tall vessels as adult males. From this it should be possible to provide a rough age, within a definable margin of error, for the occupant of vessels where no skeletal remains survive, or where none were recorded, with those from older excavations in particular falling into this category.

Secondly, the use of incised decoration was demonstrated to be closely tied to the identity of the deceased. Every motif, with the exception of hanging arches, is significantly correlated (using the chi-square significance test) with at least one class of grave-good. Again then, aspects of the decoration of a pot can be used to predict details of the social identity of the deceased, even when the presence or absence of grave-goods has not been recorded.

The arrangement of the incised decoration, including both the number of motifs, and their layout, appears to be less important as an indicator of the identity of the deceased. Similarly, the average number of lines used in a motif also appears to be irrelevant in marking the occupant. All these attributes seem to be related to the identity of the potter, rather than that of the deceased. They are communicating to a local audience, familiar with the styles of individual potters.

The use of stamped and plastic decoration was also found to be correlated with the inclusion of some grave-goods, but there are few links between individual stamp types and particular objects, or skeletal groups. The links appear to be rather with the general form and layout of the stamp. The individual designs may, however perform an 'heraldic' or totemic function (see Arnold 1983).

Thirdly, grave-goods do not appear to be directly related to age and sex groupings, although there are several correlations with the form and decoration of vessels. Objects which were found to be especially associated with particular classes of vessel could now be identified to be deliberate grave-goods, rather than objects which had fallen into the cremation by accident from the surrounding soil. Worked flints, for example, were demonstrated to be common in narrow-necked vessels. Miniature toilet implements, were also correlated with this vessel form. A few grave-goods, particularly brooches, exhibited no significant associations, and if they do have a communicative role, they must be marking something not signified in the pottery.

The overall conclusion was that there were different levels of stylistic variability in Anglo-Saxon cremation vessels, and that there was support both for Myres' approach, and for an approach based on the symbolism of social identity. In fact both were right. Some attributes, such as the proportion of decorated vessels in the assemblage, marked an assemblage as Anglian or Saxon, whilst finer differences distinguished between regional groupings at a sub-kingdom level (Richards 1988). Specific decorative motifs appeared to mark age, sex, and other social groupings. Thus cremation urns must have been manufactured for a known person, or type of person; or less probably, selected from a large range. The use of incised standing arches, for example, also signifies a group who are represented by the inclusion of miniature iron shears on the pyre. Some of these miniatures may be marking the burial as that of a child, but others may be representing other aspects of identity, and not all children will be accompanied by shears. The actual number of arches, however, and the number of lines per arch, may be used to distinguish vessels produced by particular potters, and would have no significance to a wider audience. One cannot fully explain the stylistic variability in Anglo-Saxon funerary ceramics by examining one level alone. A composite model is needed, incorporating several levels of differentiation, and offering reconciliation between the culture historical and more recent schools of thought. The overall impression is of society with a highly complex iconography and finely divided but well-defined social roles. In order to disentangle that complexity, the use of the computer is seen as being essential.

This case study serves to illustrate the point that while the large quantities of available data are often of questionable quality, new information may be derived from the old data by use of hypotheses generated and tested with new data. The computer can play a vital role throughout.

THE FUTURE

M oving on from the application of computers to old data, it remains to be seen how the computer can provide assistance with modern cemetery data. In one particular area, the application of a computer may provide substantial help which it cannot do with old cemetery data – that of the excavation and post-excavation (pre-publication) process (Richards 1989).

In the commercial world generalized packages are available which perform tasks common to many people: these include word processing packages, database packages, statistical packages and graphics packages. Using any one of these packages means that there is no need to start from scratch each time – there is usually a software package somewhere which has been designed to carry out a specific process. Linking a number of these packages together enables quite complex and elaborate work to be carried out with some ease. Using commercially available off-the-shelf packages rather than purpose-built software means that the development time of a system from its inception to full implementation is reduced considerably. However, commercial packages always carry their own limitations and compromises, and since they are not designed with archaeologists in mind, these may result in undesirable restrictions being placed on any would-be archaeological application. Consequently, it is important that time is spent both analysing the problem and examining the available software before any decision is made concerning either the development of a purpose-built system or the purchase of a commercial system. However, a package need not necessarily impose a strait-jacket: a graphics package will not determine the picture that is produced using it, although there may be restrictions in other respects, such as the degree of resolution or the size of picture available, for instance.

In the archaeological world, generalized software packages are gradually becoming available in the form of excavation recording systems. As in the commercial world, there are variations on the same theme, each of which has its own proponents and detractors. However, there does at present appear to be a gap for archaeological software to assist with the post-excavation process. In fact, the distinction made between the excavation and post-excavation process is no longer valid, particularly when a computer is used, since an on-site computer allows the traditional post-excavation process to start while the excavation is still in progress. As a result, a post-excavation package should not be seen as a separate entity, but as an integral part of an excavation system.

If the various stages of post-excavation cemetery analysis can be identified and broken down into a number of clearly definable and manageable tasks, it should be possible to develop a computer package to perform them. This process is perhaps easier with cemeteries than with other classes of site because of the degree of uniformity in the data – graves are fairly predictable – and this in turn makes it worthwhile to establish such a system because it could have a wide application. A number of core analyses that need to be performed could be identified. For example, a cemetery could be broken down in terms of age, sex, orientation of graves, along with various spatial analyses such as distributions of graves and grave-goods, and tests for associations of grave-goods.

A package produced along these lines would be particularly useful for non-specialists. Increasingly, cemeteries are excavated and written up by professional units with responsibility for a particular region, but non-Anglo-Saxon specialists are often responsible for post-excavation work. The development of a package by specialists for use by non-specialists would help them to produce the type of information which will be of interest to specialists and provide a framework for that section of the report. One result of this would be that it would become possible for cemetery reports to be compared with much less difficulty. In addition, such a package would ease and assist publication, particularly if the cemetery was recorded on computer to start with. A system on similar lines has been developed at the University of London Institute of

-Archaeology, which is intended to provide a comprehensive suite of computer programs for cemetery analysis (Hodson and Tyers 1988).

It ought to be possible for a computer to give substantially more assistance than simply acting as a rapid filing system. To date, however, number-crunching in the form of SPSS or similar statistical packages seems to be the traditional application for computers in archaeology, and Anglo-Saxon archaeology is no exception. There is no doubt that such work is of considerable value, but computers offer more than simply the facility to handle large quantities of data. Computers still have the aura of a black art: the preserve of scientists and mathematicians. Yet the latest advertising ploys designed to entice people to introduce computers into their offices or even their homes is to call computers 'information processors' rather than adding machines. Processing archaeological information on computer should involve far more than storing and retrieving data more rapidly than before. They might potentially be used to provide active assistance in the analytical as well as the storage and retrieval process.

So how might the Anglo-Saxon archaeologist move on from the artefact or excavation database? Recent developments in the computing world offer the potential of computer systems that do more than simply store data or crunch numbers, but which provide substantial help in solving archaeological problems.

Computer modelling is one such area. Hardware and software are now becoming available which enable the archaeologist to reconstruct a site in three dimensions. These may be applied to entire areas, reproducing the set of surfaces which constitute the site, or to individual contexts or artefacts. The modelling may represent the site as it was found and recorded during the excavation process, or the computer can be used in attempts to reconstruct the site as it might once have appeared.

For example, Paul Reilly, at IBM UK, is currently collaborating on a project developing three-dimensional representations of Sutton Hoo. The use of a three-dimensional digitizer in the field has been used to survey the 'sandmen' burials for computer display (Reilly and Walter 1987), and work has been carried out modelling the ship buried in Mound 1 using a computer. Further work will include attempts to model and understand the collapse of the Mound 1 burial chamber (Reilly and Richards 1987).

The rapidly developing field of expert systems may also have some application in archaeology although, as if to balance the problems they might help to solve, there are a variety of problems which might be raised by their use.

An expert system may be defined as a computer model of a domain or a problem area: a model which allows the computer to reason about information presented to it and come to conclusions, make decisions, or offer forecasts, just as a human expert would. The major difference between a database system and an expert system is that the expert system actually has some knowledge about the problem domain it was set up to handle in order to improve the reliability of the results produced by the system.

James Doran was the first archaeologist using computers to point out the need for advanced archaeological computer systems to have some knowledge of their application area (Doran 1977). He saw the reason for the poor behaviour of his computer-based cemetery simulation, SOLCEM, as a combination of the lack of knowledge contained within the system of what a cemetery actually was, and no means of applying such knowledge to the data it was working on. To answer this problem, Doran proposed the development of what, in essence, is an expert system. Since 1977 no one has taken up this challenge in either Anglo-Saxon or general cemetery studies, although a number of small expert systems have been produced in other areas. These include systems for ageing animal teeth (Brough and Parfitt 1984), and classifying Roman amphorae (Bourelly and Chouraqui 1984), Beaker pottery (Bishop and Thomas 1984), or Sassanid iconography (Lagrange and Renaud 1985). Several other systems are currently under development (for example, Baker (1986) on bird bones).

Perhaps the first thing to note about such systems is that all the applications listed above are very limited problems that can be broken down systematically into their component parts with the various methods and approaches being easily identified. For example, particular characteristics in a class of pottery can be identified and used in a recognized and repeatable manner in order to classify groups of vessels. Such classificatory systems basically diagnose the type of object (it might be a disease or mechanical fault for that matter) from a number of characteristics and assign it to one group or other on the basis of its findings. The potential use of such a system as an aid to establishing corpuses of material should be obvious. Indeed, expert systems techniques are currently being applied to a corpus of Anglo-Saxon dress pins (Ross 1990).

There are problems with the application of these systems, however, and these are also beginning to be recognized in the computing world which has tended to throw expert systems techniques at any and every problem, regardless of suitability. Paramount among these problems is the question of uncertainty – how does the system cope with situations where the data is uncertain or ambiguous? How does it handle missing data, or deal with borderline cases and resolve conflicts? The honest answer is not very well – expert systems work best in situations where there is no need to make allowances for uncertainty and simply rely on logical reasoning. More philosophical problems remain to be addressed: is archaeological theory to do with the study and analysis of burials sufficiently well-structured to allow its encapsulation in a series of rules? What about the danger that once such formalization is carried out, the knowledge encapsulated in an expert system will stagnate and fossilize? After all, formalization is carried out by a process of abstraction according to the current conceptual and theoretical framework. Is the formal deductive reasoning mechanism used in an expert system equally applicable to all problems? How reliable a model of human reasoning is the expert system? Human experts tend to apply a combination of experience and common sense in order to focus the problem-solving process on a likely approach, and apply it again to assess the validity or otherwise of a solution. No computer system can yet emulate this facility. Whose expertise should be captured in a system – things produced by committees generally consist of compromises. How will an expert system be updated, if at all? Even if such systems are used by non-specialists, what happens to the experts whose knowledge was elicited?

This is not to deny that expert systems may have their place. In Anglo-Saxon archaeology they may perhaps be most obviously applied to artefact studies, classifying objects according to set criteria, for example. Any problem that is restricted and well-defined is a potential expert system application. Packages and tools to create expert systems exist, although problems may result from forcing data into unsuitable data structures and using inapplicable search strategies or methods of handling uncertainty. However, the design, implementation and development of an expert system may prove beneficial to a particular subject area in that it requires clarity of thought and a logical and explicit approach to a problem area. Thus the process of eliciting knowledge which was previously implicit and unstated may result in a more rigorous approach to a subject or domain (Huggett and Baker 1985, Baker 1986).

One other possibility for the application of expert systems is for archaeologists to use them not as 'experts' – replacements for human specialists – but as models for testing hypotheses. Computer-based simulations are already used to model and test, for example, hypotheses concerning settlement patterns, social development, economic patterning, and these use rigorously defined, well-bounded model worlds which could be reproduced as a series of rules in an expert system. Such a development would help to answer Doran's criticism that simulations have no knowledge of the domain they operate in (1977, 444). Changes in conditions, redefinition of methods, reassessment of hypotheses and general fine-tuning of such 'expert simulation systems' would be relatively easily achieved by the alteration of one or more of the explicitly defined rules governing the performance of the system. Some of the objections raised above need no longer apply: the expert system is a model, simulating a hypothesis or set of hypotheses rather than emulating a human expert. No usurpation of function takes place and the computer remains a powerful tool in the hands of a human expert.

The belief that computers should not be used for doing things we do already, only better, but for doing things we cannot do at all (but can only dream about) may be slightly extreme, but it serves to suggest that there is more to using computers than simply using them as storage systems. The challenge is to use computers for processing our information in new and exciting ways, rather than just doing the same things faster. The computer has the potential to provide substantial assistance to the archaeologist and the development of 'learning' computer systems offer new possibilities in all areas. It is a challenge that is only now beginning to be taken up.

Bibliography

Akerman, J.Y. 1857: "Researches in a cemetery of the Anglo-Saxon period at Brighthampton, Oxon.", *Archaeologia* 37, 391–8.

Akerman, J.Y. 1860: "A cemetery of the Anglo-Saxon period at Brighthampton, Oxon.", *Archaeologia* 38, 84–97.

Alcock, L. 1981: "Quantity or quality: the Anglian graves of Bernicia", in Evison, V.I. (Ed.), 1981, 168–83.

Allden, A.J. 1986: "The use of computers for sites and monuments records", in Richards, J.D. (Ed.), 1986, 33–7.

Alvey, B.A.P. and Moffett, J.C. 1985: "Hard copy graphics displays for archaeologists", *The London Archaeologist* 9, 5, 40–6.

Arnold, C.J. 1980: "Wealth and social structure: a matter of life and death", in Rahtz, P., Dickinson, T. and Watts, L. (Eds.), 1980, 81–142.

Arnold, C.J. 1983: "The Sancton-Baston potter", *Scottish Archaeological Review*, 2(1), 17–30.

Arnold, C.J. 1984: Roman Britain to Saxon England. London.

Baker, K.G. 1986: "Archaeology and Expert Systems: some problems encountered during practical work", *Proceedings of the Second International Expert Systems Conference*, London, 211–219.

Bishop, M.C. and Thomas, J. 1984: "BEAKER – an expert system for the BBC micro", *Computer Applications in Archaeology 1984*, 56–62.

Birmingham, J. 1975: "Traditional potters of the Kathmandu valley: an ethno-archaeological study", *Man 10* (New series), 370–86.

Bourelly, L. and Chouraqui, E. 1984: "Systeme Experte et simulation d'un raisonnement en Archeologie", *Informatique et Gestion 151*, 46–51.

Bradley, R. 1980: "Anglo-Saxon cemeteries: some suggestions for future research", in Rahtz, P., Dickinson, T. and Watts, L. (Eds.), 1980, 171–6.

Brenan, J. 1984–85: "Assessing social status in the Anglo-Saxon cemetery at Sleaford", *Bulletin of the Institute of Archaeology 21–22*, 125–31.

Brough, D.R. and Parfitt, N. 1984: "An expert system for the ageing of a domestic animal", *Computer Applications in Archaeology 1984*, 49–55.

Burnham, B.C. and Kingsbury, J. (Eds.) 1979: Space, hierarchy and society: interdisciplinary studies in social area analysis. B. A. R. 59.

Carver, M.O.H. 1987: "Graphic Recording at Sutton Hoo", *The Field Archaeologist 7*, 102–3.

Carver, M.O.H. 1989: "Digging for ideas", *Antiquity 63*, 666–74.

Catton, J.P.J., Jones, M.U. and Moffett, J.C. 1982: "The 1965–1978 Mucking excavation computer database", in *Computer Applications in Archaeology 1981*, 36–43.

Chapman, R.W., Kinnes, I. and Randsborg, K. (Eds.) 1981: The archaeology of death. Cambridge.

Chapman, R.W. and Randsborg, K. 1981: "Approaches to the archaeology of death", in Chapman, R.W., Kinnes, I. and Randsborg, K. (Eds.), 1981, 1–24.

Cook, A.M. and Dacre, M.W. 1985: Excavations at Portway, Andover 1973–1975. *Oxford University Committee for Archaeology Monograph No. 4.*

Cooper, M.A. and Richards, J.D. (Eds.) 1985: Current issues in archaeological computing. B.A.R. International Series 271.

Cunliffe, B.W. et al. 1982: The publication of archaeological excavations. *The report of a joint working party of the Council for British Archaeology and the Department of the Environment.*

Dickinson, T. 1980: "The present state of Anglo-Saxon cemetery studies", in Rahtz, P., Dickinson, T. and Watts, L. (Eds.), 1980, 11–34.

Doran, J.E. 1970: "Systems theory, computer simulations and archaeology", *World Archaeology 1*, 289–98.

Doran, J.E. 1977: "Knowledge representation for archaeological inference", Elcock, D.W. and Michie, D. (Eds.) *Machine Intelligence 8*, 433–54.

Doran, J.E. and Hodson, F.R. 1975: Mathematics and computers in archaeology. Edinburgh.

Early Anglo-Saxon Pottery Group 1984: Principles of publication of Anglo-Saxon cremation cemeteries.

Gingell, C. 1976: "The excavation of an early Anglo-Saxon cemetery at Collingbourne Ducis", *Wiltshire Archaeological Magazine 70/1*, 61–98.

Green, B. and Rogerson, A. 1978: The Anglo-Saxon cemetery at Bergh Apton, Norfolk. *East Anglian Archaeology Report No. 7.*

Hardin, M.A. 1979: "The cognitive basis of productivity in a decorative art style: implications of an ethnographic study for archaeologist's taxonomies", in Kramer, C. (Ed.) 1979, 75–101.

Hills, C.M. 1977: The Anglo-Saxon cemetery at Spong Hill, North Elmham, Part I. *East Anglian Archaeology Report No. 6.*

Hills, C.M. 1979: "The archaeology of Anglo-Saxon England in the pagan period: a review", *Anglo-Saxon England 8*, 297–329.

Hills, C.M. and Penn, K. 1981: The Anglo-Saxon cemetery at Spong Hill, North Elmham, Part II. *East Anglian Archaeology Report No. 11.*

Hills, C.M., Penn, K. and Rickett, R. 1984: The Anglo-Saxon cemetery at Spong Hill, North Elmham, Part III. *East Anglian Archaeology Report No. 21.*

Hills, C.M., Penn, K. and Rickett, R. 1987: The Anglo-Saxon cemetery at Spong Hill, North Elmham, Part IV. *East Anglian Archaeology Report No. 34.*

Hirst, S.M. 1985: An Anglo-Saxon inhumation cemetery at Sewerby, East Yorkshire. *York University Archaeological Publications No. 4.*

Hodder, I. 1980: "Social structure and cemeteries: a critical appraisal", in Rahtz, P., Dickinson, T. and Watts, L. (Eds.), 1980, 161–70.

Hodder, I. (Ed.) 1982: Symbolic and structural archaeology. Cambridge.

Hodson, F.R. and Tyers, P.A. 1988: "Data analysis for archaeologists: the Institute of Archaeology packages", in Rahtz, S.P.Q. (Ed.) *Computer and Quantitative Methods in Archaeology 1988*. B.A.R. International Series 446, 31–41.

Hope-Taylor, B. 1977: Yeavering: an Anglo-British centre in early Northumbria. *DoE Archaeological Report No. 7*, HMSO, London.

Huggett, J. 1987: "Recording Early Anglo-Saxon Burials – a Computer-Based Approach", *Science and Archaeology*, 29, 3–13.

Huggett, J. 1988: "Compacting Anglo-Saxon cemetery data", *Computer and Quantative Methods in Archaeology 1987*. B.A.R. International Series 393, Oxford.

Huggett, J. and Baker, K.G. 1985: "The computerised archaeologist: the development of expert systems", *Science and Archaeology 27*, 3–7.

Humphreys, S.C. and King, H. (Eds.) 1981: Mortality and immortality: the anthropology and archaeology of death. London.

Jones, R. 1980: "Computers and cemeteries: opportunities and limitations", in Rahtz, P., Dickinson, T. and Watts, L. (Eds.), 1980, 179–95.

Kempton, W. 1981: The folk classification of ceramics: a study of cognitive prototypes. New York.

Kramer, C. (Ed.) 1979: Ethnoarchaeology. New York.

Lagrange, M.S. and Renaud, M. 1985: "Intelligent knowledge-based systems in archaeology: a computerized simulation of reasoning by means of an expert system", *Computers and the Humanities 19*, 1, 37–52.

Leeds, E.T. 1913: The archaeology of the Anglo-Saxon settlements. Oxford.

Leeds, E.T. 1949: A corpus of early Anglo-Saxon great square-headed brooches. Oxford.

Lethbridge, T.C. 1951: A cemetery at Lackford, Suffolk: report of the excavation of a cemetery of the Pagan Anglo-Saxon period in 1947. *Cambridge Antiquarian Society*. New Series, No. VI.

Meaney, A.L. 1964: A gazetteer of Early Anglo-Saxon burial sites. London.

Moffett, J.C. 1986: "Archaeological databases and microcomputers", *Computer Applications in Archaeology 1985*, 109–13.

Myres, J.N.L. 1969: Anglo-Saxon pottery and the settlement of England. Oxford.

Myres, J.N.L. 1977: A corpus of Anglo-Saxon pottery of the Pagan period. Cambridge.

Orton, C.R. and Hodson, F.R. 1981. "Rank and class: interpreting the evidence from prehistoric cemeteries", in Humphreys, S.C. and King, H. (Eds.), 1981, 103–15.

Pader, E.-J. 1980: "Material symbolism and social relations in mortuary studies", in Rahtz, P., Dickinson, T. and Watts, L. (Eds.), 1980, 143–59.

Pader, E.-J. 1982: Symbolism, social relations and the interpretation of mortuary remains. B. A. R. International Series 130.

Powlesland, D.J. 1985: "Random access and data compression with reference to remote data collection: 1 and 1 = 1", in Cooper, M.A. and Richards, J.D. (Eds.), 1985, 23–33.

Rahtz, P., Dickinson, T. and Watts, L. (Eds.) 1980: Anglo-Saxon cemeteries 1979. B. A. R. 82.

Rahtz, S. (Ed.) 1987: Information technology in the humanities: tools, techniques and applications. Chicester.

Reilly, P and Richards, J.D. 1988: "New perspectives on Sutton Hoo: the potential of 3-D graphics", in Ruggles, C.L.N. and Rahtz, S.P.Q. (eds.) *Computer and Quantitative Methods in Archaeology 1987* B.A.R. International Series 393, 173–185.

Reilly, P. and Walker, A. 1987: "Three-dimensional digital recording in the field: preliminary experiments", *Archaeological Computing Newsletter 10*, 7–12.

Richards, J.D. 1982: "Anglo-Saxon pot shapes: cognitive investigations", *Science and Archaeology 24*, 33–46.

Richards, J.D. 1984: "Funerary symbolism in Anglo-Saxon England: further social dimensions of mortuary practices", *Scottish Archaeological Review 3*, 42–55.

Richards, J.D. 1985: "Training archaeologists to use computers", *Archaeological Computing Newsletter 2*, 2–5.

Richards, J.D. 1986a: "Into the black art: achieving computer literacy in archaeology", *Computer Applications in Archaeology 1985*, 121–5.

Richards, J.D. 1986b: "Computers in archaeological theory and practice", *Science and Archaeology 28*, 51–55.

Richards, J.D. 1987a: "Archaeologists and the computer", in Rahtz, S. (Ed.), 1987, 159–69.

Richards, J.D. 1987b: The significance of form and decoration of Anglo-Saxon cremation urns. B.A.R. 166.

Richards, J.D. 1988: "Style and symbol: explaining variability in Anglo-Saxon cremation burials", in Driscoll, D. & Nieke, M. (Eds.), *Power and Politics in Early Medieval Britain and Ireland*, Edinburgh, 145–61.

Richards, J.D. 1989: "Computers and burial archaeology", in Roberts, C.A., Lee, F. and Butliff J. (Eds.) Burial Archaeology: *Current Research, Methods and Developments* B.A.R. 211, 105–11.

Richards, J.D. (Ed.) 1986: Computer usage in British archaeology. *Institute of Field Archaeologists Occasional Paper No. 1.* Birmingham.

Ross, S. 1990: "Expert systems for databases", in Cacaly, S. and Larfield, G. (Eds.), *Sciences historiques, sciences du passe et nouvelles technologies d'information: Bilan et évaluation.* Lille.

Shanks, M. and Tilley, C. 1982: "Ideology, symbolic power and ritual communication: a reinterpretation of Neolithic mortuary practices", in Hodder, I. (Ed.), 1982, 129–54.

Shennan, S. 1975: "The social organisation at Branc", *Antiquity 49*, 279–88.

Shepard, J.F. 1979: "The social identity of the individual in isolated barrows and barrow cemeteries in Anglo-Saxon England", in Burnham, B.C. and Kingsbury, J. (Eds.), 1979, 47–79.

Society for Medieval Archaeology 1987: Archaeology and the Middle Ages.

van de Velde. 1979: "The social anthropology of a Neolithic cemetery in the Netherlands", *Current Anthropology 20*, 37–58.

Wilson, M.E. 1972: The archaeological evidence of the Hwiccian area. Unpublished doctoral thesis. Durham University.

Chapter Four

Resurrecting the Dead: The Potential of Palaeopathology

Keith Manchester

The pathology of a group of people is never randomly produced. It reflects the environment in which they live, the geographical and climatic influences which bear on them, the pressure of competing or coexisting forms of life, and their behaviour in the environment. Dr Calvin Wells

Palaeopathology is defined, following the original designation of the term by Sir Marc Armand Ruffer, as the scientific study of the corporeal remains of earlier peoples. As an antiquarian medical interest, its roots go back to the nineteenth century and beyond. In these early days of Virchow and his colleagues, the intellectually diverse study encompassed animal and human remains, both fossilized and unfossilized. The integration of findings, essentially pathological, into the wider interests of archaeology and medical history was not attempted. It was not until the early years of the twentieth century, and the work of Ruffer, Elliot Smith, Wood Jones, and others, that palaeopathology achieved recognition as an academic discipline. But, even in those formative years, palaeopathology was almost exclusively descriptive and diagnostic, although the relevance of the study to archaeology and medical history was becoming realized. Sir Mortimer Wheeler wrote that archaeology must be seasoned with humanity, that dead archaeology is the dried dust that blows. Calvin Wells was probably the first to exploit the interpretative potential of palaeopathology. It was he who first showed that the study may be used to extend clinical medicine into former times, to add a time dimension to illness, and to attribute symptoms and physical signs to the diagnoses made from osteoarchaeological remains. Calvin Wells was a Norfolk general practitioner whose intense and indefatigable interest made him a household name within the rather esoteric world of palaeopathology.

Palaeopathology must be interpretative and reconstructive, in order to fulfil its integral role in archaeology, and in order to understand the whole being of antiquity. Of course, the scientific analysis of corporeal remains is basic. Equally, the description, both technical and lay, of pathological lesions and the diagnoses made from them, are germane. Left at this point, however, palaeopathology too joins the driest dust that blows. It is not the intention in this present paper to discuss the nature of palaeopathological lesions, nor to consider diagnostic criteria of diseases, nor to argue differential diagnoses. Such discussion, vital to the advancement and enhancement of palaeopathology, is the realm of the specialist audience. The present paper's purpose is instead to consider what interpretations may be made of this basic data. The interpretations of palaeopathology are threefold, each capable of separate consideration, but all three coming together for a total understanding of disease in its archaic environment.

The first interpretation is at a very individual, personal, and subjective level. It is vital to the understanding of man, but of little importance in the understanding of mankind. It consists of a clinical assessment of the diagnosis, in which an illness is reconstructed. It is an attempt, drawing analogy from modern clinical practice, to understand the suffering of the afflicted person of antiquity and to try to recall the natural, often untreated, course of disease from its beginning to its end, which may have been resolution, healing, even death. Illness, however, is rarely totally self-centred. The morbidity usually affects the patient's kinsmen, if not economically then certainly emotionally. A few specific examples of injury and disease serve to illustrate the above aspects.

Osteoarthritis, or, to be pedantic, osteoarthrosis, is a relentless degenerative accompaniment of ageing joints. It is an abnormality readily recognizable, through various degrees of severity, in osteoarchaeological remains. It is ubiquitous and, let us not mistake, it will, given enough time, affect us all. It is characterized by pain, joint-deformity, and increasing restriction of function. Osteoarthrosis of the knee and hip may be accompanied by a degree of instability of the joint and by a gradual and progressive restriction of movement. The practising clinician and the layman are both equally familiar with this problem. Today however, the pain can be assuaged by analgesics, and the deformity and disfunction may, ultimately, be relieved by artificial joint replacement. The sufferer of antiquity was not so fortunate. Whilst we accept the presence of laudanum and other herbal preparations, long-term relief of pain was probably not available. Prosthetic surgery was certainly not available. Constant pain and increasing immobility must surely have increased the sufferer's dependence upon kinsmen, and perhaps because of, as it were, early retirement on medical grounds, placed a strain upon the economy of the society.

Consider now an acute disability for which the sufferer and society was unprepared and ill-adapted for. A man of Romano-British date from Baldock sustained lower leg fractures, either from a direct blow or falling from some height (Plate 1). Immediate and intense pain occurred, and immobility was total. We also know that this was a compound fracture, with open communication between skin surface and the fractured bones with, in consequence, the great potential for bacterial infection. That such infection did occur is manifest in this dry specimen. The surrounding pitting and the large cloaca or sinus to the interior of the bone are indications that osteomyelitis developed. In addition then to this horrific injury, the victim suffered from a chronic pus-discharging, foul-smelling wound on the lower leg. His social acceptance is questionable. Furthermore, the gross malunion indicates that he started to weight-bear on his legs long before he should have done, and effective splinting was not practised.

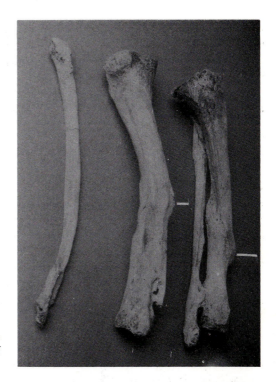

PLATE 1 MALUNITED FRACTURES OF TIBIAE AND
FIBULAE. Romano-British. Baldock. (Courtesy of
Charlotte Roberts; Calvin Wells Laboratory)

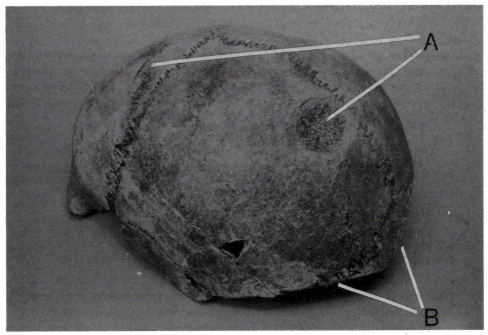

PLATE 2 CRANIUM. A tangential injuries. B linear decapitating injuries. Anglo-Saxon. Eccles, Kent.
(Calvin Wells Laboratory)

Considerable tolerance must have been shown to this cripple for the rest of his life, for he did indeed survive for some time.

The next example was not so fortunate. The specimen demonstrates a frenzied brutality in Anglo-Saxon Kent. This man sustained antemortem or rather perimortem, tangential blows to the cranium (Plate 2). These were not, however, fatal. There followed three posterior cranial decapitating blows, possibly preceded by a blade thrust through the left eye. It does not require great forensic acumen to predict that these were fatal blows. With the victim felled, the assailant then opened both sides of the chest by slashing the ribs, thrust the blade into the spine, and opened the abdomen by a posterior incision which was not of surgical precision or motivation. Perhaps this skeleton tells as much about the psychopathic victor as about the mutilated victim. Of course, we know nothing of the consequences for the victim's family from this evidence.

The second interpretation is, when considering separate representative specimens, of equal individual significance but, collectively, of greater overall archaeological relevance. In this second set of examples, it is the cause of the lesion rather than its effect which is of interest to us. Through the recognition of specific pathological lesions in skeletal remains, and by analogy with modern clinicopathological or epidemiological data, the responsible diseases and their causes may be deduced. There are many such diseases, the causes of which are related to the organization of society, the type of work undertaken, and nutritional deprivation or even excess.

The first example bridges the gap between the subject interpretation which we have

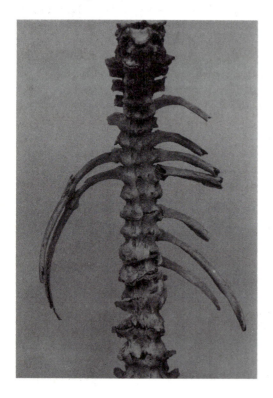

PLATE 3   SPINE AND RIBS. Anterior view. Diffuse idiopathic skeletal hyperostosis, showing ossification of anterior longitudinal ligament and of costovertebral joints. Romano-British. Droitwich. (Calvin Wells Laboratory)

already considered and this second archaeologically relevant interpretation. There is a disease, the elements of which were first described in clinical context within the past twenty years by Forestier, and which is today termed Diffuse Idiopathic Skeletal Hyperostosis. The features of this disease are becoming increasingly recognized in palaeopathological work. One of the earliest and most florid examples that I have seen is of Romano-British date from Droitwich. This man had a gradual and relentlessly progressive ossification of ligaments principally of the spine (Plate 3), but also around other joints. Even arteries became ossified. This poor petrified man had gross limitation of movement and possibly symptoms of circulatory deficiency. It is the cause, or rather the associations, of this disease which are, however, of interest in the present context. This disease has been noted predominantly in men beyond fifty years of age, with a frequent association with diabetes. Now, we know today, and the same conditions doubtless applied in antiquity, that maturity-onset diabetes is associated with obesity, and that this obesity may be a consequence of dietary excess. Clearly in antiquity insulin-dependent diabetes is a non-entity. Prior to Banting and Best and the discovery of insulin, such a disease was invariably fatal. Not so with maturity-onset diabetes which appears to be of relevance in the present context. Although, as yet, no prevalence studies of this disease in antiquity have been carried out, there is an impression that the disease was relatively common in medieval monastic communities. Even St William of York probably suffered from the disease. Detailed analysis has yet to be done, but the inference for nutritional status, and thereby economic well-being, for these communities is clear.

The second example too concerns nutritional problems, and demonstrates very clearly that palaeopathology has a very real and significant input in archaeological interpretation. There is a lesion which is observable in the roof of the orbits and is aetiologically related to a similar lesion of the outer surface of the cranium. These lesions, termed *cribra orbitalia* (Plate 4) and porotic hyperostosis (Plate 5), present a progressive gradation from small surface pitting to a somewhat porous overgrowth of bone. The lesions are caused through an expansion of the red blood cell forming tissues in the marrow in response to anaemia. First recognized in the Mediterranean and Tropical anaemia of Thallasaemia and Sickle cell anaemia, it is now recognized as a sequel to iron deficiency anaemia in temperate Europe. Very careful and diligent research by Patty Stuart MacAdam, using both archaic and modern clinical specimens and X-radiographs, has shown that these lesions develop only in young children as a sequel to anaemia at that age. The lesions, developed in childhood may however persist throughout adult life. Professor Moller-Christensen has now demonstrated the orbital lesion in about 69 per cent of the leprous skeletons excavated from Naestved leprosarium and dated between AD 1250 and 1550. Moller-Christensen also excavated and examined contemporaneous skeletons from Aebelholt monastic site, a site only a few miles from Naestved in Denmark. In this series of non-leprous skeletons, he found only 23 per cent with the orbital lesions. Not unreasonably therefore at that time, Moller-Christensen concluded that *cribra orbitalia*, or *usura orbitae* as he termed the lesion, was due directly to the leprosy bacillus. As I have stated, this is now known not to be so, and that lesion is of anaemic aetiology. Although anaemia is likely to be due to nutritional deficiency in early childhood, we should not forget the possibility of chronic intestinal parasite infestation as a cause of chronic blood loss and consequent anaemia. Perhaps some

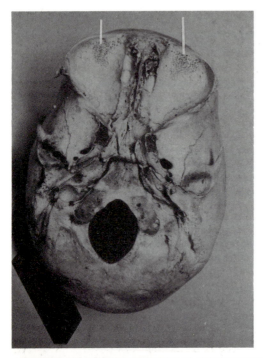

PLATE 4 SKULL BASE. Modern. Africa. (Manchester Museum) Cribra orbitalia. Cribriform perforations of roof of orbits

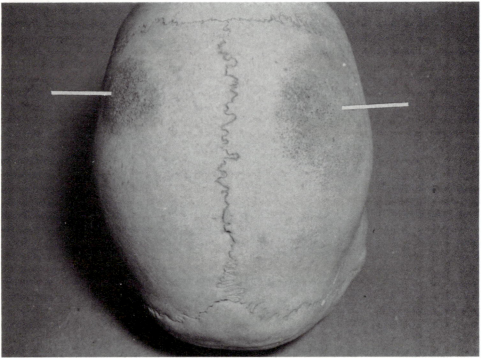

PLATE 5 CRANIUM. Superior view. Modern. Africa. (Calvin Wells Laboratory)
Porotic hyperostosis. Raised cribriform perforations of outer surface of parietal bones.

correlation of the palaeopathological observations with the environmental researches of Andrew Jones at York and workers elsewhere may be profitable in the future.

However, the implications for Naestved and Aebelholt are clear. The leprous inmates at medieval Naestved were almost certainly nutritionally deprived in early childhood in comparison with the non-leprosy sufferers buried at Aebelholt. The lepers were therefore from a socially and economically disadvantaged section of society. Examination and interpretation of this sort could certainly be advanced in future studies by trace-element analysis for palaeonutritional studies, by correlation of other skeletal indicators, gross and X-radiographic, of general-health status and by co-ordination of research with environmentalists.

The third example is mentioned only in passing, to show how palaeopathological findings may be related to ethnographic parallels. Charles Merbs observed a high frequency of temporomandibular, or jaw joint, osteoarthritis in skeletons of Inuit Indians which he interpreted as due to the known practice of leather working with the teeth by these people.

Epidemiology is the study of disease in relation to environment in all its facets. Clearly disease should not be studied in isolation because the origin, course, and termination of all disease is related to the being and the person's place in the environment. But some diseases, particularly those of infective aetiology, lend themselves to archaic epidemiology, or what we may term palaeoepidemiology. The malignant diseases of cancer, sarcoma, myeloma and the like comprise a similar group for profitable study, but I wish to consider the two infective diseases of leprosy and tuberculosis, diseases of such immense social, economic and medical significance in antiquity, and still today, and diseases which are very dear to my own palaeopathological heart.

Palaeoepidemiology is my third interpretative section, leading to an interpretation of disease in the environment, to the changing pattern of disease through time, and to the inter-relationship of diseases with each other and with immunological changes within the host. Both tuberculosis and leprosy are diseases caused by highly infective bacteria of the genus *Mycobacterium*. It is said that bacteria of this genus are responsible for more human suffering and misery than any other bacteria. This statement applies equally to the past. Discussion here of these two diseases in history can only be brief and cannot be examined in the depth which their importance and interest deserves.

Both tuberculosis and leprosy are relative newcomers to the scene of human disease. Tuberculosis, on skeletal and iconographic evidence (Plate 6), appeared sometime before the fourth millenium BC, the date of the earliest specimen. The disease seems first to have appeared in the Near East, and because this earliest phase was probably the result of bacterial transfer from infected tuberculous cattle, the archaeological evidence for the origins of domestication in the Near East may be significant. Thus, the Neolithic Revolution, if this term is still in vogue, may not have been entirely beneficial to mankind, but may also have been welcomed by opportunist *Mycobacteria*. Now, in these early days, the human infection was primarily of the gut, from milk and cattle flesh contamination. This is merely hypothesis because at present, proof lacks palaeopathological evidence. In palaeopathological terms the disease in man was probably sporadic and dependent upon cattle herd size and infection. If this assumption is correct, it seems that the *Mycobacterium* seized an opportunity when human population density increased

PLATE 6   THORACO-LUMBAR SPINE. Lateral view. Tuberculosis. Potts disease. (Courtesy Charlotte Roberts; Portsmouth Museum) Destruction and collapse of vertebral bodies, with acute angular curvature.

with urbanization. The biological objective of species survival was obtained by human transference of bacteria through infected exhaled breath. Thus, the terrible scourge of tuberculosis became a population-density-dependent disease increasing dramatically in incidence. The evidence, skeletal, and particularly pictorial and documentary, through the Middle Ages is in accord with this hypothesis.

The earliest irrefutable evidence of leprosy is skeletal and of second century BC date, although an Indian document of some 400 years before, is highly suggestive of the existence of the disease. The early skeletal evidence is from Egypt. Documentary and iconographic evidence, and now palaeopathological research (Plate 7, Figure 1) is demonstrating that leprosy gradually increased in prevalence throughout Europe at least until the thirteenth century AD. Thereafter, in Britain at least, leprosy declined fairly rapidly, and had disappeared as an endemic disease by the seventeenth century. There are several explanations for this decline, all, no doubt, of some significance. Segregation of the afflicted was widespread but, for many reasons, this cannot be the sole, or maybe even major, explanation. Doubtless too, the episodes of plague contributed to the decline by a reduction in overall population size, and a possible selective decimation of leprosaria inmates. Possibly of greater significance, however, is the coincident decline of leprosy and the increase in prevalence of tuberculosis during the advancing Middle Ages. There is a degree of cross-immunity, or shared immunological response, in the host to invasion by the bacilli of leprosy and tuberculosis. In some measure therefore, these two diseases are mutually exclusive, and tuberculosis being, as it were, the more

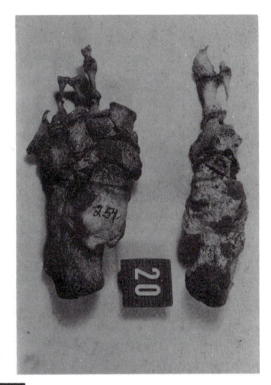

PLATE 7 FEET. Leprosy. Gross destruction and absorption of bones of feet, particularly meta-tarsals and phalanges. Medieval, Naestved, Denmark. (Leprosy Museum, Museum of Medical History, Copenhagen)

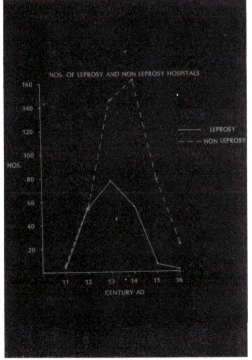

FIGURE 1   GRAPH OF LEPROSY AND NON-LEPROSY HOSPITALS in England, by foundation dates

virulent is dominant. In brief, the increase in prevalence of tuberculosis in mankind, consequent upon increasing population density associated with urbanization, stimulated an immune response in the community not only to the tubercle bacillus but also, by cross-immunity, to the leprosy bacillus. As a result, leprosy, as an endemic disease, declined and disappeared. It was, therefore, a developing social complexity, an increasing population density, and a bacterial inter-relationship which caused the demise of this most mutilating and pitiful disease of the soul, leprosy, in medieval Europe. The bacteriological and immunological basis for this hypothesis is sound. Historical and palaeopathological support is growing.

Finally, in the light of these observations and examples, whither palaeopathology? It is not an esoteric specialist backwater to be relegated to the appendix of a weighty excavation report. As a discipline, there is an interface with medical history, with clinical medicine, with ethnography, and with archaeology. The potential of palaeopathology will only be fully realized if this is exploited.

CHAPTER FIVE

CONSERVATION OF MATERIAL FROM ANGLO-SAXON CEMETERIES

Jacqui Watson and Glynis Edwards

Because of their complex associations, finds from Anglo-Saxon cemeteries can be studied from various viewpoints; for instance, to provide dating evidence, shed light on ritual practices, to indicate fashion, and reconstruct perished organic items. Such multidisciplinary involvement puts responsibility on the conservator to provide most of the basic information for the relevant specialists (Edwards 1989). Conservation will include X-radiography and the cleaning of objects to reveal their shape and decoration, so that they can be placed into typologies. Any associated fragments of straw, insects, pupa cases, or seeds preserved in the corrosion products should be noted as these will contribute to forensic evidence which might establish what time of year the body was buried, whether interment occurred soon after death, and whether, for example, there had been a covering of straw or rushes. Other mineral-preserved organic material should also be recorded, such as traces of a cloak or blanket covering the burial, or wood from a coffin which might be preserved on any object. The position of brooches together with associated textile evidence can indicate how the garments were worn and the position of beads can show if they were strung round the neck or fastened between brooches. All this information must be carefully recorded, and produced in a form which is compatible with the other records for the site.

Many metal grave-goods are found as assemblages corroded together with organic material which cannot be separated for conservation purposes, so that treatment and storage environments have to be tailor-made for individual groups. It is important to ensure that any conservation treatments which may interfere with the work of other scientists and specialists are not used.

The following is an outline of some of the conservation techniques that can be used to examine cemetery material, and some details of recent reconstruction work.

CONSERVATION AND EXAMINATION

M ost metal objects will be recovered as individual items, which should be left covered with a loose soil as this layer acts as a buffer, reducing the corrosion rate and the effects of rapid drying out. It will also protect any organic material preserved in the corrosion products, which can be extensive and extremely fragile. No consolidants should be used on site, as this makes later cleaning more difficult and can make identification on the scanning electron microscope (SEM) impossible. Where possible, objects should be lifted in sealed soil blocks so that they are not damaged in transit to the laboratory and so that they remain in a stable environment until they can be dealt with.

The confined space of a grave and the presence of a skeleton with closely associated artefacts may cause difficulties when lifting blocks of soil on cemetery sites. Different types of soil have their own problems, and as lifting may destroy details of features and stratigraphy, the ideal solution is for someone experienced in lifting techniques to work closely with the excavator who is familiar with his site. The blocks should be marked so that any plans made during excavation in the laboratory can be fitted into the site plan. Various means of lifting can be employed depending on the type of soil, the position of the block within the grave, and its size. Appropriately sized boxes may be used for small blocks while larger ones require the support of plaster bandages or polyurethane foam (this is a hazardous material and should not be used by anyone unfamiliar with its use or the precautions to be taken). It is difficult to give detailed instructions for lifting as there are so many differing sets of conditions on sites, but in each case it is important to think the whole process through to final excavation in the laboratory. The block must be supported securely by the lifting medium to prevent its collapse, and the underside must be supported to prevent the contents spilling out. It may need to be padded out to fit a box, and it is also important to protect its surface with a barrier if using plaster bandages or foam. Cling film may be used as the initial protection, and undercuts filled in with soil on top of this. Aluminium foil can then be used as the final barrier. The block can be separated from the ground by sliding something underneath, or, for larger blocks, by slowly undercutting and supporting the void with the lifting medium to leave a small soil pillar which can easily be broken.

In the laboratory the blocks can be examined using X-radiography to locate the position of metalwork and some dense organic materials such as ivory and bone. Other materials such as glass beads with a high metal content are also X-ray opaque and can clearly be seen on a X-radiograph, the different colours often represented by varying shades of grey. Plate 1 is a radiograph of a soil block which contains a fragment of an annular brooch and part of a necklace made up of glass and amber beads. The two glass beads probably have different compositions and maybe colour as they appear to have different densities on the radiograph. Amber, on the other hand, is X-ray transparent and in this example less dense than the surrounding soil, so that individual beads appear as black shapes. X-radiographs can only be used as a guide for the size and position of objects, because, since the X-ray beam is cone-shaped, items some distance from the film will be distorted and can appear to be as much as 15 per cent larger.

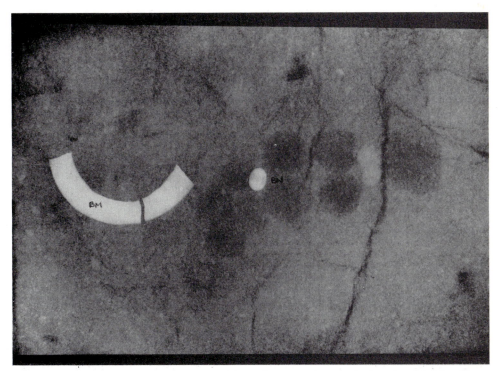

PLATE 1   X-RADIOGRAPH OF A SOIL BLOCK containing a fragment of an annular brooch and bead necklace
(English Heritage)

Excavation of soil blocks is just the same as excavating on site except that one is not exposed to the weather and can take more time over planning and photography. As the objects have been removed from their contexts it is very important that detailed plans of these micro-excavations are produced to record the position of individual objects and mineral preserved organic material. Plate 2 illustrates a purse complex from West Heslerton, North Yorkshire, in the process of being excavated; Figure 1 is the plan of the metal and organic objects it contained. Originally this was a leather purse with the neck held open by an ivory ring. Associated with it were two sets of girdle-hangers, one of copper alloy and the other of iron, a pair of leather laces with copper-alloy ends (possibly to close the bag), an iron knife in its leather scabbard and at least two different pieces of textile.

During excavation and subsequent cleaning the objects should be examined for evidence of manufacture and any organic material preserved in the corrosion products. Any isolated organic material should be left intact on an object until it has been examined by a specialist, and samples for identification should only be taken in consultation with them.

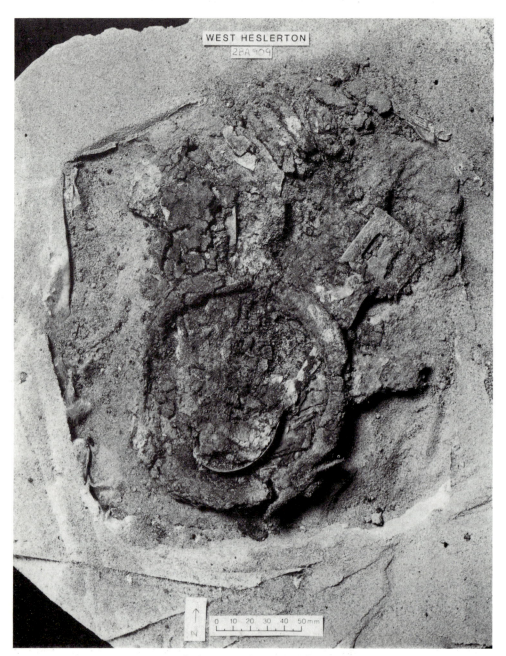

PLATE 2 PURSE GROUP during excavation in the laboratory (English Heritage)

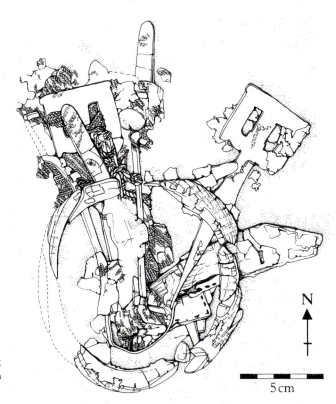

FIGURE 1 PLAN OF METALWORK
and preserved organic material in
purse complex

N

5 cm

IDENTIFICATION AND RECONSTRUCTION OF MINERAL-PRESERVED ORGANIC MATERIAL

In damp conditions most metals will corrode and the resulting corrosion products will stain any adjacent organic material. When buried, organic material impregnated with metal salts cannot readily be broken down by soil micro-organisms, and over long periods this material will become chemically altered by these minerals (Keepax, 1975). This process will affect all adjacent organic materials and it is important to establish what the preserved organic materials are related to before removing any samples.

Mineral-preserved organic material is more common on ironwork as this metal corrodes more rapidly than copper, lead or silver alloys. Ironically, a burial environment that is aggressive for metals will promote large-scale preservation of organic material by this phenomenon. Inhumations, particularly in sandy soil, appear to promote the rapid corrosion of ironwork and provide a valuable source of mineral-preserved organic material for study. For the Anglo-Saxon period this is especially important as there are few waterlogged sites where organic objects are preserved in abundance.

Fresh and waterlogged organic materials are identified by examining their micro-

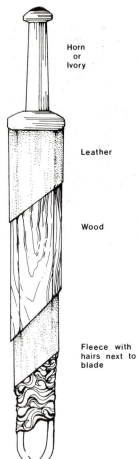

Horn
or
Ivory

Leather

Wood

Fleece with
hairs next to
blade

FIGURE 2 ANGLO-SAXON SWORD with cut away scabbard illustrating the
different organic components

scopic structure, and this is also possible for mineral-preserved examples. With some experience it is possible to distinguish between most organic materials, such as horn, bone, wood and leather, with the aid of a hand lens, or low-powered incident light microscope. The identification of wood species, however, often requires the use of a scanning electron microscope, along with access to microscope keys and a reference collection. In some cases the structure of the organic material has changed along with its chemical composition, and often large crystals of corrosion products obscure diagnostic features. Special preparation techniques have been developed to overcome such difficulties and again the scanning electron microscope enables the necessary detail to be seen without optical interference from the minerals (Watson 1988).

Mineral-preserved textiles are easily recognized and are frequently the only organic materials referred to in excavation reports. A good illustration of some of the other organic materials that may be preserved is given by a sword in its scabbard shown in Figure 2 and Plate 3. The hilt is made up of three separate pieces of horn which

(a)

(b)

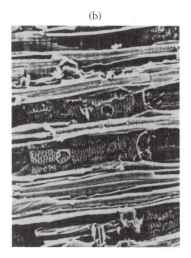

(c)

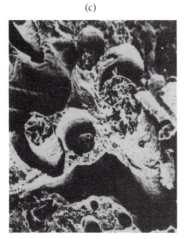

PLATE 3   ELECTRON MICROGRAPHS of organic material preserved by iron corrosion products (a) Horn (b) Wood (c) Fleece. All are approximately 300x magnification

correspond to the pommel, grip and guard sections distinguished by a change in grain direction. Mineral-preserved horn can be recognized by its ridged structure with fine laminations giving the impression of grain, and often misinterpreted as wood. Ivory was sometimes used for the hilt instead of horn, but this is usually only preserved as a fine orange powder where the diagnostic features are only visible at high magnifications in the region of 500–1000x. The scabbard is shown cut away to reveal the different layers. On the outside is leather which was used to hold all the layers together, but this is rarely preserved because it is furthest away from the corroding blade. Underneath the leather are thin layers of wood to keep the scabbard rigid. This is lined with fleece, the hairs next to the blade presumably so that the lanolin oiled the blade preventing it from rusting (Biek 1963, 103–4, 106, 108).

Providing accurate plans are made during the excavation of individual pieces of metalwork, either on site or in the laboratory, it is often possible to reconstruct large organic items such as clothing, coffins, caskets, and even furniture from traces of these materials in the corrosion products. A great deal of work has been done on mineral preserved textiles, where it has been possible to indicate the style of garments worn (Owen-Crocker, 1986) in addition to recording weave details (Walton & Eastwood, 1983). Occasionally fragments have been preserved by just a light coating of copper salts, and in such cases it is possible to analyse for dye residues.

When metal fittings have been used, wooden objects such as caskets and coffins can be reconstructed. Figure 3 shows two possible reconstructions of a small Anglo-Saxon casket based on the mineral-preserved wood on nine iron fittings. Unfortunately in this example none of the corner brackets had been placed so that the exact construction of the joints could be interpreted. Other examples have produced evidence for comb and tenoned mitre joints, indicating quite sophisticated carpentry in use at this early date. In Figure 4 the iron fittings provide evidence for the

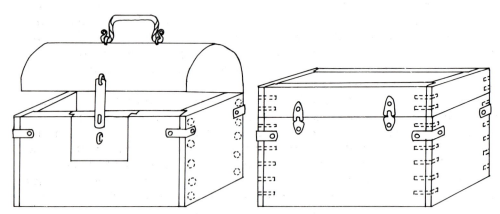

FIGURE 3   TWO POSSIBLE RECONSTRUCTIONS of an Anglo-Saxon casket, based on the wood preserved on the metal fittings

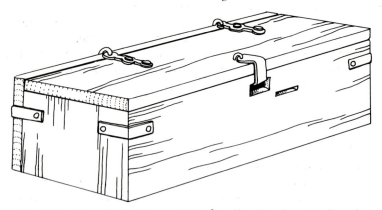

FIGURE 4   RECONSTRUCTION OF AN ANGLIAN COFFIN from the mineral-preserved wood on the iron fittings

complicated construction of an Anglian coffin. Here both butt and mitred joints were probably held together with wooden tenons or dowels, as no additional iron nails were found.

Other wooden objects represented solely by their metal fittings include shields, the construction of which is discussed by Harke (1981). Bowls are also usually only represented by decorative mounts or repairs, but these wood fragments are occasionally preserved where the orientation of the grain indicates that they had been lathe turned (Morris, 1982). Probably the most complicated carpentry to study is that of furniture, which was sometimes included in high status burials. Such pieces are rarely recognized as they are for the most part constructed of elements carefully joined together and held firm with wooden pegs or glue. When excavated only the decorative mounts are likely to remain along with small eyelets used to attach upholstery to the wooden frame as on the bed found at Swallowcliffe Down (Speake, 1989).

In addition to recording carpentry details, it is possible to suggest how the timber was reduced into planks – flat sawing, quarter sawing, radial or tangential splitting (Darrah, 1982). If oak has been used it may be possible in some instances to count the number of annual rings over a given distance. This information may give some indication whether the tree had been grown in forest or open land, but it is unlikely that a sufficient depth of wood would be preserved to confirm this or allow any valid tree-ring analysis to be undertaken. It is also worth noting the type of wood used as haftings, mature timber or coppiced poles, as such information will add to our knowledge of Anglo-Saxon woodland management.

Evidence for organic coatings such as resins can sometimes be implied by abnormal preservation of the impregnated material. Wood or textiles which have been soaked with pitch or oil to make them water repellant will tend not to absorb iron corrosion products when buried, at least initially, but at the same time will be protected from the normal decay processes. Over time the resin itself eventually breaks down, but high concentrations of metal salts locally continue to preserve this material. When examined microscopically the organic material originally impregnated with a resin can appear in almost pristine condition, while any untreated material will contain high amounts of metal salts. This type of preservation has been noted on clench nails from reused ship timbers where caulking had been used between the planks.

This paper is a brief introduction to some of the conservation and examination techniques used in the study of Anglo-Saxon cemetery material illustrating the information that can be obtained. Further advances in excavation, recording and examination will add to the information that can be retrieved and increase our appreciation and understanding of early craftsmanship.

Acknowledgements

We would like to thank Dominic Powlesland for allowing us to illustrate this paper with unpublished material from his excavations at West Heslerton, North Yorkshire. Photographs of the X-radiograph and the purse group were provided by Louise Woodman. We are grateful to English Heritage for its continuing support of this research.

Bibliography

Biek, L. 1963: *Archaeology and the Microscope*, Lutterworth Press, London.

Darrah, R. 1982: "Working Seasoned Oak", in *Woodworking Techniques Before AD 1500*, McGrail, S. (Ed.) B.A.R. International Series, No. 129, 219–229.

Edwards, G. 1989: "Guidelines for Dealing with Material from Sites where Organic Remains have been Preserved by Metal Corrosion Products", in *Evidence Preserved in Corrosion Products*, Janaway, R. (Ed.), UKIC Occasional Paper 8, 3–7.

Harke, H. 1981: "Anglo-Saxon Shields from Petersfinger – a Myth", *Medieval Archaeology*, 25, 141–144.

Keepax, C. 1975: "Scanning Electron Microscopy of Wood Replaced by Iron Corrosion Products", *Journal of Archaeological Science*, 2, 145–150.

Morris, C. 1982: "Aspects of Anglo-Saxon and Anglo-Scandinavian Lathe Turning", in *Woodworking Techniques Before AD 1500*, McGrail, S. (Ed.) B.A.R. International Series, No. 129, 245–261.

Owen-Crocker, G.R. 1986: *Dress in Anglo-Saxon England*, Manchester University Press.

Speake, G. 1989: *A Saxon Bed Burial on Swallowcliffe Down*, English Heritage Archaeological Report No. 10, 82–98.

Walton, P. and Eastwood, G. 1983: *A Brief Guide to the Cataloguing of Archaeological Textiles*, Wordplex, York.

Watson, J. 1988: "The Identification of Organic Materials preserved by Metal Corrosion Products", in *The Use of the Scanning Electron Microscope in Archaeology*, Olsen, S. (Ed.) B.A.R. International Series, No. 452, 65–76.

CHAPTER SIX

ASPECTS OF EARLY BROOCH DESIGN AND PRODUCTION

David Leigh

T he jewellery excavated from Anglo-Saxon cemeteries has evoked a fascination and provoked a stream of scholarship neither of which is difficult to explain. These glittering and exotic objects, especially the brooches, promise insights into a remote culture at many levels, from the spiritual, through the sociological and the chronological to the art-historical and the technological. Unfashionable though brooch studies may have become over recent years, this potential has by no means been exhausted, and I hope to demonstrate this by examining three kinds of evidence provided by the late fifth and early sixth-century Kentish square-headed brooches.

THE TOOLING OF DECORATIVE DEVICES

S quare-headed brooches were cast in two-part moulds from which they emerged with their chip-carved ornament in need of cleaning and decoration (Lamm 1973). There were two kinds of decoration. One resulted in *colouristic effects*; the other in *textural* effects. The former included niello, garnet inlay and mercury gilding; and on non-Kentish Anglo-Saxon brooches colour variation was also achieved by tinning and by the use of enamel or glass inlay. The textural effects consisted of repeated impressions which broke the otherwise smooth surface of the polished metal.

To produce either the indentations required for niello, or those for textural effects, such as notching and punching, it was necessary to use a hard-tipped tool, the character of which can be deduced from close inspection of the marks remaining on the brooches.

Niello Patterns

Niello is a black inlaying material which at this time was composed of either silver sulphide or a mixed copper silver sulphide (Oddy, Bimson and La Niece 1983). It was applied in either solid or molten form to indentations in the metal surface. In poorer quality work, and especially in brooches made of copper alloy, the indentations usually take the form of roughly engraved continuous lines. In higher quality objects of this period, and particularly on Kentish silver brooches, the indentations consist of rows of repeating triangles, and sometimes of two such rows in opposition, the triangles interlocking to greater or lesser extent (Figure 1a). The visual effect of rows of black triangles against a gilded silver background is quite startling, and gains in impact from the zig-zag metal lines seen in reserve between the pairs of triangles. Such glamorous effects are not achieved on copper alloy brooches.

The indentations were made by repeated blows of a triangular or sub-triangular punch directed onto the surface of the metal. The tip of the tool must have been sufficiently hard and durable to transmit each impact and to continue making repeated, consistent impressions in the silver alloy. A single brooch may have as many as four to five hundred such impressions; a pair up to a thousand.

Within any restricted group of brooches – such as those one hundred or so from Kent and the Isle of Wight, generally termed Kentish – there seems every likelihood that a limited number of tools would have been in use, especially on brooches which were

(a)

(b)

(c)

FIGURE 1 NIELLO PATTERNS: (a) The effect of different spacings and impression shapes; (b) three ways of turning a corner; (c) the effects of abrasion

broadly contemporary. The question naturally arises of whether we can hope to identify, by the sizes and shapes of the impressions, the individual tools which were used to make them. Can we go further than this? It is reasonable to assume that a limited number of individuals had the skill to carry out this kind of decoration. We can see by close inspection that it was by no means easy to maintain a consistently high standard. To keep the triangles orientated along the correct axis, to maintain a constant spacing between them and across paired rows and, above all, to execute a corner with finesse (Figure 1b) were tasks that must have called for a high level of dexterity and experience. There is room with this kind of evidence for different levels of skill to be discerned, and perhaps for the hand-work of different craftworkers to be characterized. This task has not so far proved possible on the relatively small sample of comparable brooches. However, the former task – to characterize the tools used – shows more immediate promise.

There are many difficulties in pursuing this task. Not the least of these lies in the variation in angle at which the tool might have been held relative to the surface, so that the impressed shape becomes distorted. Another problem is the effect of abrasion on the surface appearance of the tapering impressions, causing the outlines to reduce in size and even in shape (Figure 1c).

Notwithstanding these difficulties, it has proved possible to distinguish the impressions according to (i) the angle of the apex of the triangle; (ii) the presence or absence of a rectangular base to the triangle; and (iii) their dimensions. Using these criteria it appears that a total of seven tools were in more or less regular use on the sixty or so brooches (pairs are here counted as one) of Kentish origin which have niello decoration of repeating design (Leigh 1980, 255–66, revised).

Notching

There are two kinds of decoration which were designed to impart textural rather than colouristic effects. One of these involved the use of a hand-held double-pronged tool which often created an 'egg-timer' shape and when repeatedly punched at close spacing gave what is best termed a 'notched' effect, mostly used along the ridges of the chip-carving, but also sometimes on flat surfaces (Figure 2). It was used not only on Kentish jewellery, but quite liberally on a very wide range of Anglo-Saxon metalwork. The difficulties of characterizing these marks are even more formidable than was the case for niello impressions: the marks are very small, only about 1 mm long; and the scope for variation in the way the tool was applied was enormous. Taking the Kentish square-headed brooches alone, it has proved possible to divide the notch patterns into five groups, based on the size and shape of the impressions (Leigh 1980, 272–6, revised). On the evidence of this study it is impossible to judge the extent to which these groups really correspond to five individual tools.

Cd.45   Bi.42

Cd.45   Sa.4–1   Ho.7   Ku2

Fi.2–1   Ca1   Ho2

Bi3   Ho.21   St.2

Do1   Bi1   He1   Ho.   Ic1

Ho1   Mi1   Ct.2   Sa.4–2   Ku1

He5   Bi.51   Cd.40

Fa1   Cd10

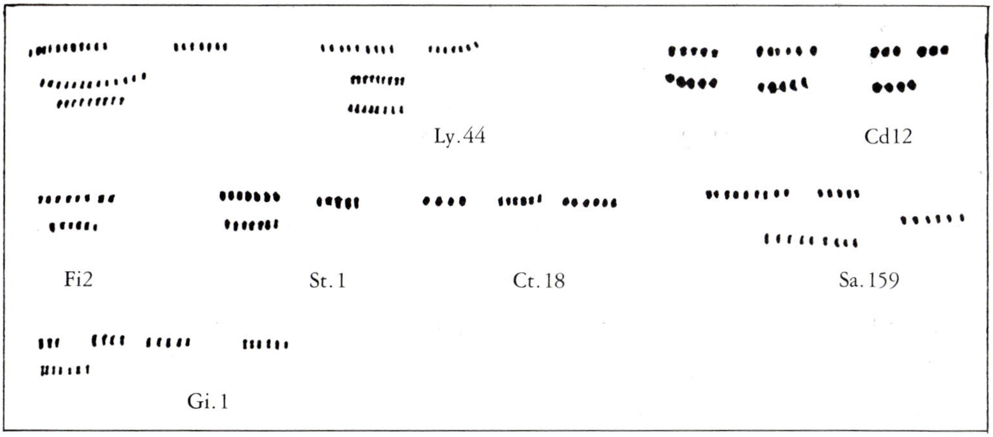

FIGURE 2   A SELECTION OF 'NOTCHING' EFFECTS produced on ridges and on flat surfaces

Stamped Patterns

The other form of textural decoration derives from the repeated use of punched shapes. These are very widespread on Anglo-Saxon jewellery and are therefore potentially the most promising for this kind of analysis. While the search for tools ought to be relatively easy in the case of the more unusual shapes such as triangles and crosses, whose form and dimensions are fairly simple to identify, the search for identity among circular punch marks is going to be far more difficult. Unless these are grossly different in diameter it is almost impossible by ordinary visual means or even by low-power microscope to differentiate one from the other with any degree of certainty.

A search among the Kentish square-headed brooches has so far revealed only one certain match between non-circular punches on different brooches (not counting deliberate pairs on which the same tool was invariably used). The shape is a triangle with rounded corners (Plate 1), a central pellet and an exactly matching defect and it is found on a brooch from the cemetery at Stowting (Figure 3: St. 1; Aberg 1926, figure 142) in Kent and on a trio of brooches from the cemetery at Chessel Down on the Isle of Wight (Figure 3: Cd12; Arnold 1982).[1]

Among the circular impressions, it has been possible to distinguish on the basis of size alone three possible groups of brooches (consisting of two, five and four brooches respectively (pairs are here counted as one) in which the members within each group share punching with what may perhaps have been the same circular-tipped tool (Leigh 1980, 267–71, revised).

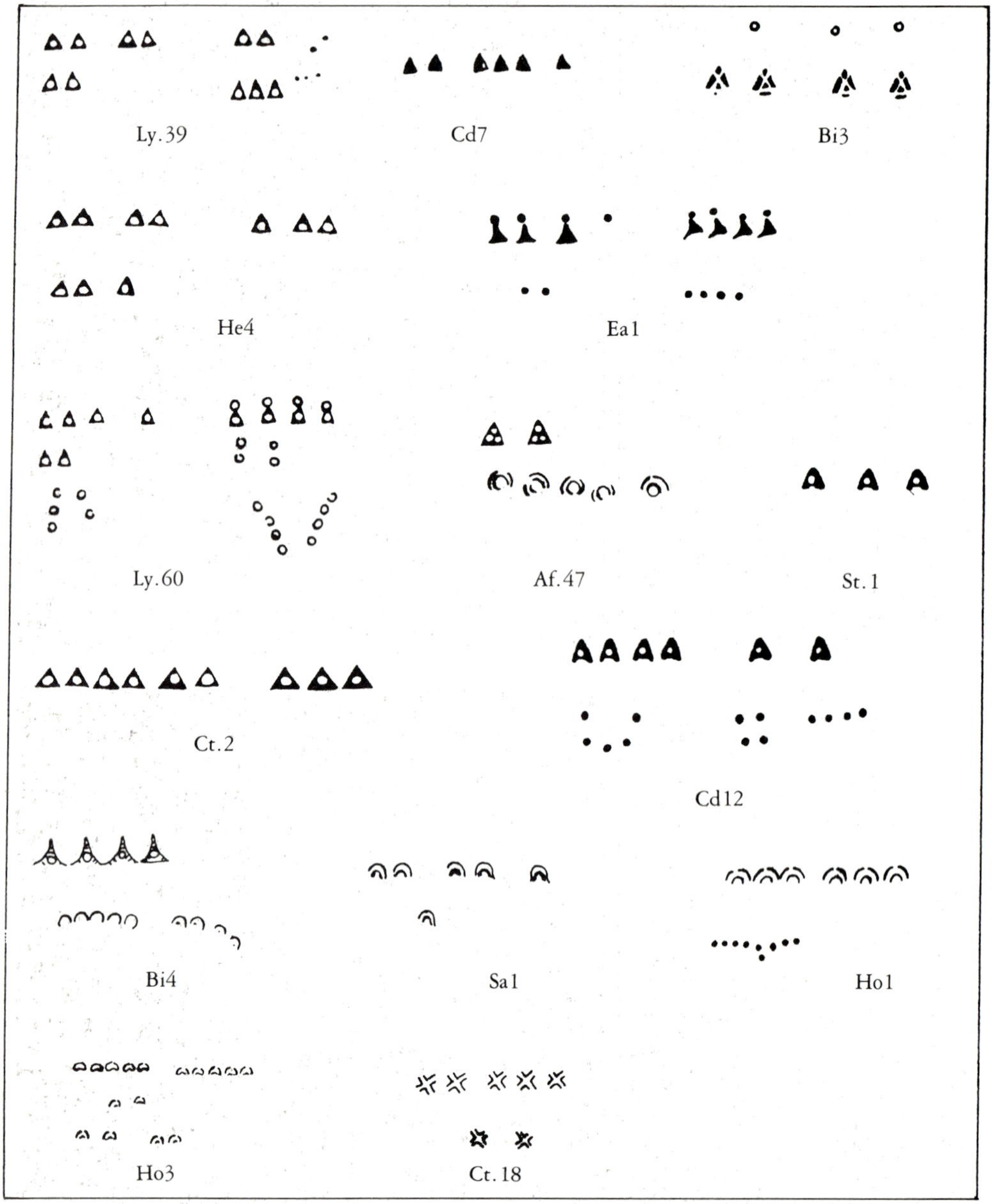

FIGURE 3   NON-CIRCULAR IMPRESSIONS on Kentish square-headed brooches

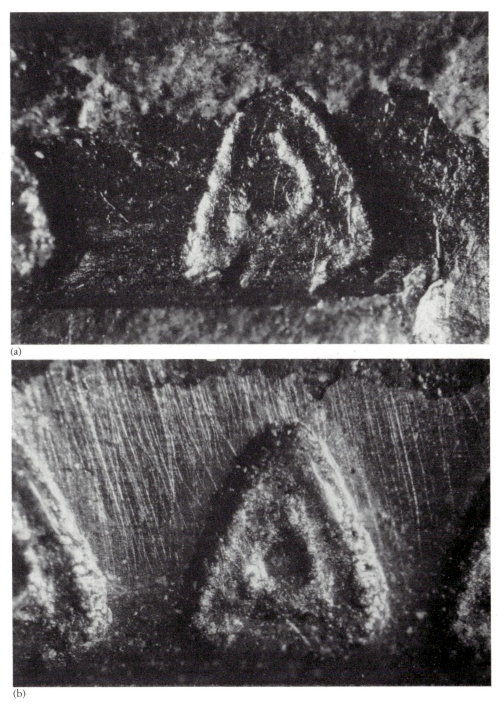

PLATE 1   STAMPED IMPRESSIONS on two Kentish square-headed brooches: (a) Stowting, Kent (b) Chessel
Down, Isle of Wight

Correlation of Tool Marks

Many brooches bear the impressions from more than one type of tool: niello and notching; or notching and punching; some have all three. There are thirty brooches (pairs are counted as one) which bear the marks of at least two types of tool. Among these, and using the tentative identifications above, there appear to be nine instances of the same two tools having been used on more than one brooch.

The significance of this conclusion at this stage is difficult to assess. It certainly adds weight to the theory that the tooled brooches were produced in a limited number of workshops, perhaps only a single one which was responsible for the whole Kentish output. But should we expect more or fewer correlations than we do; and is the triangular-tipped punch less well represented than it might be; and why is there only one repeat of a non-circular punched shape?

Answers to these questions depend on many imponderables. How many punches would have been in use at any one time? For how long would a single punch have lasted and on how many brooches might it have been used? If it was hard-wearing enough to make repeated indentations into silver or copper alloy, then surely it was tough enough to have survived in the workshop for use on many brooches. How many brooches survive compared to the numbers originally produced? Could it be that the output was vast, but that the total number which survived being melted down, to be buried, survive burial, and eventually be excavated was but a small or minute fraction of that original output? We have no idea whether all the jewellery buried represents the totality rather than a sample of the fine possessions of those buried, or whether burial of costume accessories was an exceptional luxury, reserved perhaps for only the most wealthy. If metal was in short supply, as seems likely at this period, then re-melting would have provided an obvious raw material for new jewellery in the latest style; and loss by burial might not have been a favoured option. Whatever the cause, it may well be that the low incidence of these punch marks is a measure of the smallness of our sample.

Pure speculation might provide other answers. Could it be that individual punches and their shapes were reserved for the brooches of particular families, and so were infrequently used? Could it be that there was some taboo against the re-use of punches? Although we may never be able to answer such questions definitively, we shall get a good deal closer once the whole collection of punch-decorated objects in Anglo-Saxon England has been carefully studied. One of the stumbling blocks to such a study will be circular punches, for there are many of these, all very similar. We shall have to improve our inspection techniques. Despite the virtues of photomacro- and micrographs used for the work described above, the best way of securely characterizing the original tools is to record their marks under a scanning electron microscope, either viewing the objects themselves or silicon rubber impressions of them. This technique has been used to great effect on Iron-Age metalwork (Lowery, Savage and Wilkins 1971); and also by Larsen (1987) in Denmark, who has thereby characterized the tools used on various Dark-Age products bearing rich punched decoration, including the Gundestrup cauldron.

DESIGN PRINCIPLES

The consistency of form, proportions and decoration of Northern square-headed brooches point to the existence of agreed or at least widely recognized principles of design. It would be most interesting to discover what these were and whether they were formally set down, perhaps according to some numerical rules, or were simply carried out in the mind's eyes of brooch designers. Some clue is provided by comparing the shape and general design of different brooches. In Figure 4 I have superimposed the outlines and internal frameworks of the footplates of two brooches, one from the cemetery of Howletts, near Littlebourne, Kent (Avent 1975, no. 29) and the other from Finglesham, Grave E2 (Hawkes 1958, figure 11a, pl. IV: A; Avent 1975, no. 8). The Howletts brooch is closely matched by another from Dover (Hawkes and Pollard 1981, 356; Bakka 1981, 24, Plate V.6, figure 2, F8; Evison 1987, figure 64.9).

Although there are many obvious differences between these two footplate designs, they do show a general relationship in their proportions and overall layout which one might well expect from brooches produced within a short time span and in a single workshop, as these almost certainly were. But beyond this, there is a surprising degree of concordance between them: for example, the centres of the garnet settings are extremely close; and the width of the footplate at the level of the side lobes is identical. It would seem that a single principle of design geometry has been employed for these two brooches. Further comparisons of Kentish brooches of this general type, and of headplates as well as footplates, lead to similar conclusions.[2]

In Figure 5 are shown separately and superimposed the footplate designs of three

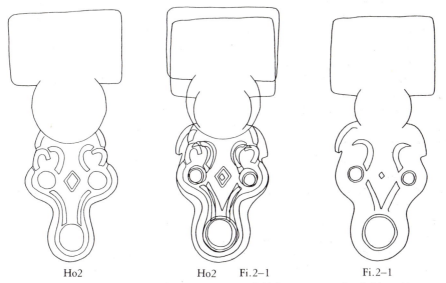

Ho2   Ho2   Fi.2–1   Fi.2–1

FIGURE 4   FOOTPLATE OUTLINES AND FRAMEWORKS overlaid for two square-headed brooches: Ho2, Howletts; Fi.2–1 Finglesham Grave E2

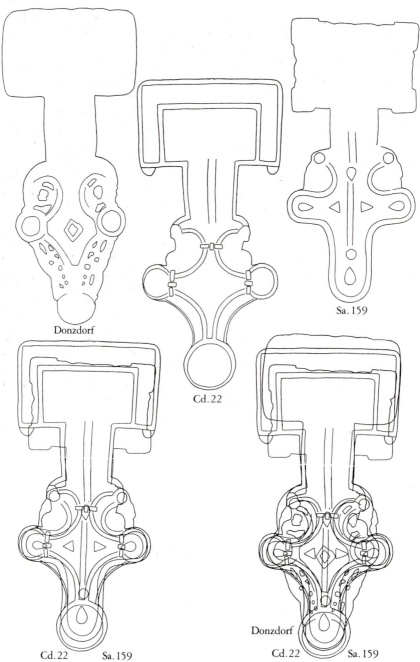

FIGURE 5   FOOTPLATE OUTLINES AND FRAMEWORKS overlaid for three square-headed brooches: Donzdorf, Württemberg, Grave 78; Cd. 22, Chessel Down, Isle of Wight, Grave 22; Sa. 159, Sarre, Kent, Grave 159

other brooches. These are one of a pair from Grave 78 in the cemetery of Donzdorf, near Wurttemberg, West Germany (Haseloff 1974, plate VI, c; 1981, Abb. 24); another from Grave 22, Chessel Down on the Isle of Wight (Arnold 1982); and another from Grave 159, Sarre, Kent (Leeds, 1949, no. 84). The Donzdorf brooch is one which Haseloff claims to have been produced in the Jutland region, and which is among the earliest brooches executed in Salin's Style 1. The large, heavily gilded Chessel Down brooch is not generally thought of as Jutlandic; nor are there other Jutlandic indicators in the Chessel Down grave assemblages. It is stylistically a later product than the Donzdorf brooch, although Hines places it among his earliest phase of the English square-headed brooches (Hines 1984, 180). The large and splendid Sarre brooch stands in relative typological isolation, best matched by one or two non-Kentish brooches (e.g. Leeds 1949, no. 85), and by the now missing brooch from Herpes in the Charente (Leeds 1949, no. 83), and is placed alongside these in Hines' second phase (Hines 1984, 180).

The visual comparison of these three otherwise somewhat disparate brooch footplates shows an unexpected degree of conformity. The overall dimensions, the proportions, the spacing of nodal points in the design – all these correspond in a tantalizing way. Yet these designs fit into a more extensive family of Kentish brooches than can be illustrated here, a family moreover that is characterized by close correspondences of headplates as well as footplates. Among them is another Jutlandic and Kentish brooch, that from Grave 41 in the cemetery of Bifrons, Kent (Leeds 1949, no. 3; Haseloff 1981, Abb. 25).

Correspondences such as these seem to go beyond mere coincidence. It is a matter of conjecture whether they also go beyond a generalized, unstated design consciousness among the jewellers of the fifth and sixth centuries AD; and whether there were distinct geometrical and numerical principles or even physical devices which determined the transfer of measurements and proportions from one design to another. Whatever the answer, these observations hint at a sophisticated level of craftsmanship and an effective medium for the transmission of design concepts.

REDISCOVERED IMAGES

Two Brooches from The Faussett Collection

The Faussett Collection in Liverpool Museum contains two Kentish square-headed brooches, one from Grave 48 in the cemetery of Gilton, Kent (Plate 2; Leeds 1949, no. 4; Haseloff 1981 no. 13, Abb. 27, Taf. 22,1), the other from Goldstone, Cop Street, Kent (formerly referred to as from Richborough) (Plate 3; Leeds 1949, no. 5; Haseloff 1981, no. 14, Abb. 28, Taf. 22,2). Both are made of silver; both

(a)   (b)

PLATE 2   SILVER SQUARE-HEADED BROOCHES from the Faussett Collection: (a) Goldstone, Cop Street,
Kent ('Richborough') (M6963) (b) Gilton, Kent, Grave 48 (M6004)

are also gilt, though not much gold now remains; and both have zigzag niello patterns
along the main ridges forming the frameworks of their pictorial fields.

These brooches have occasioned relatively little scholarly interest since their
discovery, despite or perhaps because of their bewilderingly complex surface designs.
Certainly, their strange and apparently incoherent devices seem to give hints of eyes and
limbs and other bits of animals; but what more could have been described with any
confidence? (e.g. Hawkes 1958, 47ff; and 1958a, 53ff; Bakka 1958). Until, that is, the
work of Haseloff who has stripped the designs down to their component parts and
reassembled them in superb analytical drawings, thanks to which we can now describe
these brooches with the utmost clarity (Haseloff 1981, Abb. 27, 28 and Abb. 53–71).

Looking first at the features which these brooches have *in common* (Figure 6), we see on
their *footplates* three circular lobes. Between these are the weirdest of creatures having
one or two feet each (i.e. a quadruped in profile). They appear to face towards the side
lobes and have heads the natures of which are made the more difficult to interpret by
severe abrasion, but which were almost certainly human.

Above the two side lobes are some other heads. These are somewhat easier to
understand, and help to explain the lower animals. They are human faces seen in profile,

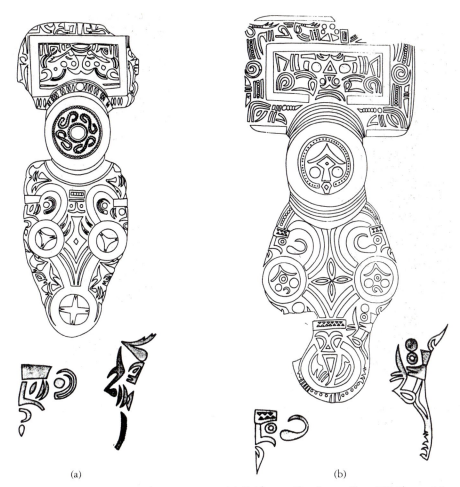

FIGURE 6   SILVER SQUARE-HEADED BROOCHES: (a) Goldstone, Cop Street, Kent ('Richborough')
(b) Gilton, Kent, Grave 48. (After Haseloff 1981)

each with a straight forehead line or band. While they can no longer be interpreted as biting animal heads (e.g. Leeds 1949, 9), there is something zoomorphic about these otherwise human profiles. Their cheeks extend into curved devices, recalling the lower jaws of genuinely zoomorphic heads found in just this position on other northern brooches (Haseloff 1981, 94–98). Furthermore, the pair of heads on the Goldstone brooch have animal bodies attached to them.

It is now perhaps easier to believe that the animals between the lobes also have profile human heads, as demonstrated by Haseloff (1981, 115–7, Abb. 68, 8.9) even if the Goldstone head lies *within* the body!

Turning to the *headplates*, we find within the main panels two symmetrical designs consisting of an apparent jumble of incoherent features. At their centres the staring eyes of a mask stand out clearly enough. To either side are contorted, backward-bent animals

FIGURE 7   SILVER SQUARE-HEADED BROOCH: Apple Down, West Sussex. (After Down and Welch 1984)

(Haseloff 1981, 118–20, Abb. 71,3.4). Furthermore, these animals also have human profile heads. It is important to note, however, that it is almost impossible to perceive both the central mask and the human aspect of these animal heads simultaneously. Only one or the other is apparent on any one view as the brooch (or drawing or photograph) is revolved.

There are, of course, many features which these brooches do *not* share. Among these are the designs of the headplate border animals which differ considerably. The Gilton brooch is blessed with four additional masks: two profiles in the footplate side lobes; one fullface on the terminal lobe – also with a headband; and one very strange face on the bow. An additional small mask lies at the top of the Goldstone footplate.

In summary these brooches display the following decorative schemes: (i) A footplate whose chief motif consists of pairs of affronted animals having animal and/or human heads converging on circular lobes which, in one case, contain human heads. (ii) A headplate whose central field shows two affronted and very contorted animals having both human and animal heads converging on a central human mask. Surrounding the headplate panels are pursuing creatures, some of them with arguably human heads.

Haseloff has shown that such schemes, or ones very like them, are common among some of the earliest square-headed brooches, those which he claims originated in Jutland – his so-called Jutlandic group.

A New Brooch from Sussex

A recent brooch find which is in many respects very similar to these two from the Liverpool Faussett Collection comes from a South Saxon cemetery at Apple Down in West Sussex. It was excavated by Alec Down and published by him and Martin Welch, to both of whom I am grateful for permission to inspect this brooch and for an original photograph (Figure 7; Down and Welch 1984).

By analogy with the Gilton and Goldstone brooches we can see on the footplate of this new brooch pairs of crouched creatures and animal-man heads (Figure 8b) menacing the human heads (Figure 8a) seen in profile within the circular lobes. The headplate main panel has a matched pair of confronted quadrupeds (Figure 8c), though this time without a central human mask. Down and Welch describe the animals in the following terms: 'Each animal has a flared nostril and open jaw, chubby cheek and pointed ear, with the jaw supported by the downward-curving front paw'. They go on to describe the rest of the animal, with its front and hind legs and paws (1984, 409–10).

While there can be little argument with this interpretation, reference to the two Faussett Collection brooches suggests that these animals might also be susceptible to an alternative interpretation. To help in understanding this it is helpful to look at a very clear representation (Figure 8e) of this kind of headplate design on a pair of brooches which are also of Haseloff's Jutlandic group. These are the brooches already referred to from the German cemetery of Donzdorf (Figure 5). Here, as on the Goldstone and Gilton examples, are a pair of contorted animals affronting a human mask. Concentrating on the heads of these animals, we see especially how the ears stick out backwards in a somewhat unusual orientation. We find a similar design scheme (Figure 8g), complete with just such animal heads, on the glamorous brooch from Dover B, referred to above, as well as on the aforementioned Howletts brooch.

Like the Goldstone and Gilton animal heads, these from Apple Down are also anthropomorphic in character, as can be seen by turning the images through ninety degrees. The Donzdorf and Dover heads confirm this beyond doubt (Figure 8f, h), even if the others are less immediately apparent. On most of these examples the following features can be clearly discerned: an open mouth; a cheek; an eye; a nose; in some cases what might be a moustache; and across the forehead a straight or curved band. Above this is a crest-like device. Suddenly the animal ear takes on a more believable role.

It is now apparent that the innocuously zoomorphic creature described by Down and Welch on the new Sussex brooch has a really convincing and impressive human head (Figure 8d). The headband is not straight, but curved, to continue the nose line; the 'flared nostril' becomes an open mouth; the 'open jaw' becomes a moustache; and there are also the cheek, the eye and finally the 'pointed ear' which has become a feather-like crest.

So we see that on this Sussex brooch, as on others both of the Jutlandic group and at least one later Kentish brooch (that from Howletts), and on both footplates and headplates, there is abundant use of ambiguous creatures, termed *Tiermenschen* or animal-men by Haseloff. I have argued elsewhere (Leigh 1984) that these creatures were meant to be seen as animals in the first place (just as Down and Welch saw the Apple

FIGURE 8   DETAILS FROM SQUARE-HEADED BROOCHES: (a)–(d) Apple Down; (e), (f) Donzdorf; (g), (h) Dover

Down creatures); and then to be seen as humans when viewed differently; and were possibly not meant to be seen as having an instantaneous dual personality.

Others have argued that in images of this period there is to be found evidence for a belief in metamorphosis – notably on the Scandinavian gold bracteates; and that such a concept might be related to early Germanic beliefs typified by the mythical trans-formations of men into animals (Hauck 1972; Davidson 1964). If this is so and if this is a phenomenon which we could reasonably expect to see reflected in the designs of square-headed brooches – personal possessions which may themselves have had some amuletic as well as functional purpose (Vierck 1967) – then perhaps these ambiguous creatures are also a manifestation of this idea. I hold no particular brief for such a theory. It may be that these are meant to be truly hybrid creatures – simultaneously both animals and men. It may equally be the case that they had no mythological or symbolic significance. Perhaps the design of these brooches – indeed all Style 1 art – was no more than 'dinner plate art'; pure decoration for decoration's sake; barely even art for art's sake. If so, then we shall have to find some other explanation for the repeated, consistent and apparently very deliberate depiction of these bizarre and totally unlifelike creatures.

Yet, if the truth does lie more in the realm of belief than mere ornament, then in order to realize the potential of early Anglo-Saxon art for revealing the subtler side of Anglo-Saxon human experience we shall have to be scrupulous in our analysis of brooch decoration. Zoomorphs can no longer be taken at face value. Beneath every sheep's clothing we must look for and expect to find a rather fierce man sporting a headband and a feather.

Acknowledgement

My thanks to Howard Mason of University of Wales College Cardiff for his assistance with the drawings.

Notes

1. The comparison of photographs in Plate 1 is less persuasive than intended. The apparent differences may be attributed to different lighting at high magnification, to differing states of abrasion and corrosion, and to variation in the depth of punching. The reader is asked to accept the author's assurance that visual comparison through the microscope and of a series of photomacrographs confirms the unique identity of the tool used on both the brooches beyond all reasonable doubt.
2. It will be apparent in this and the next comparison that the outlines of the complete brooches do not correspond. We find that either the footplate outlines can be made to overlap in this way or the headplate outlines, but rarely both together. This discrepancy arises from the manufacturing process which involved the patterns for the two parts, probably of wax, being made separately and attached to the bow at an early stage in production. This was rarely carried out with complete consistency of orientation or spacing (Leigh 1980, 161–171).

Bibliography

Aberg, N. 1926: *The Anglo-Saxons in England*, Uppsala.

Arnold, C. 1982: *Anglo-Saxon Cemeteries of the Isle of Wight*, British Museum Publications, London.

Avent, R. 1975: *Anglo-Saxon Disc and Composite Brooches*, B. A. R. 11, Oxford.

Bakka, E. 1958: *On the beginnings of Salin's Style 1 in England*, Universitet i Bergen, Arbok, Historick Antikvarisk Rekke, No. 3.

Bakka, E. 1981: Scandinavian-type gold bracteates in Kentish and continental grave finds, in *Angles, Saxons and Jutes, essays presented to J.N.L.Myres*, Evison, V.I. (Ed.), Oxford 11–35.

Chadwick (Hawkes), S. 1958: The Anglo-Saxon cemetery at Finglesham, Kent: a reconsideration, *Medieval Archaeology II*, 1–71.

Chadwick (Hawkes), S. 1958(a): Note on an early Anglo-Saxon square-headed brooch from Canterbury, *Antiquaries Journal* 38, 52–7.

Davidson, H.R.E. 1964: *Gods and Myths of Northern Europe*, London.

Down, A. and Welch, M. 1984: A Jutlandic square-headed brooch from Apple Down, West Sussex, *Antiquaries Journal* 64, 408–13.

Evison, V.I. 1987: *Dover: The Bucklan Anglo-Saxon Cemetery. Historic Buildings and Monuments Commission for England, Archaeological Report 3*, London.

Haseloff, G. 1981: *Die germanische Tierornamentik der Volkerwanderungszeit. Studien zu Salins Style 1.* (Vorgeschichtliche Forschungen, 17), Berlin. New York.

Hauck, K. 1972: Zur Ikonologie der Goldbrakteaten IV: Metamorphosen Odins nach dem Wissen von Snorri und Amulettmeistern der Volkerwanderungszeit, *Festschrift fur Siegfried Gutenbunner*, Heidelberg.

Hawkes, S.C. and Pollard, M. 1981: The gold bracteates from sixth-century Anglo-Saxon graves in Kent, in the light of a new find from Finglesham, *Fruhmittelaiterliche Studien* 15, Berlin. New York.

Hines, J. 1984: *The Scandinavian Character of Anglian England in the pre-Viking Period*, B.A.R. 124, Oxford.

Lamm, K. 1973: The manufacture of jewellery during the Migration Period at Helgo in Sweden, *Bulletin of the Historical Metallurgy Group* 7, 1 ff.

Larsen, B. 1987: SEM-identification and documentation of tool marks and surface textures on the Gundestrup cauldron, in Black, J. (comp.), *Recent Advances in the Conservation and Analysis of Artifacts*, University of London, Institute of Archaeology, Jubilee Conservation Conference, Summer Schools Press, 393–408.

Leeds, E.T. 1949: *A Corpus of Early Anglo-Saxon Great Square-Headed Brooches*, Oxford.

Leigh, D. 1980: *Square-headed brooches of sixth century Kent*, unpublished Ph.D. Thesis, University College, Cardiff.

Leigh, D. 1984: Ambiguity in Anglo-Saxon Style 1 Art, *Antiquaries Journal* 64, 34–42.

Lowery, P.R., Savage, R.D.A., and Wilkins, R.L. 1971: Scriber, Graver, Scorper, Tracer, *Proceedings of the Prehistoric Society*, XXXVII, 167–82.

Oddy, W.A., Bimson, M., and La Niece, S. 1983: The composition of niello decoration in the antique and medieval periods, *Studies in Conservation*, 28, 29–35.

Vierck, H. 1967: Ein Relieffibelpaar aus Nordendorf in Bayerisch Schwaben (zur Ikonographie germanisches Tierstil I), *Bayerische Vorgeschichtsblatter*, XXXII, 104–40.

CHAPTER SEVEN

SCRAP OR SUBSTITUTE: ROMAN MATERIAL IN ANGLO-SAXON GRAVES

Roger White

It must be borne in mind that the Romano-British population was in matters of art more advanced than the Teutonic immigrants, and if British ladies had exercised rule in the new homesteads they would certainly have introduced therein their own style in trinkets and ornaments.[1]

Although this statement of Baldwin Brown, published in 1915, is referring to art styles rather than objects, the argument that native women marrying and moving into Anglo-Saxon villages would have carried with them their own 'trinkets' as heirlooms is an old concept. Indeed this interpretation of Roman material in Anglo-Saxon graves has been so widely accepted for so long that it is only very recently that the idea has been seriously criticized and that there has been a move to reassess the quality and quantity of the evidence. It was the presence of Roman material, notably coins, in some of the Kentish cemeteries excavated by Faussett that led him into the delusion that he was excavating the graves of 'Britons Romanised'.[2] The error was partially corrected by Douglas in 1793 when he reasoned that the presence of Roman coins in Anglo-Saxon graves merely gave a *terminus post quem* but that the occurrence of Byzantine coins, or their copies, gave a truer historical date for the graves.[3] Correction of Faussett's dating was only half of the battle however; the question of what the material was doing in the grave remained unsolved.

There are still remarkably few studies of Roman objects in Anglo-Saxon grave contexts. Among the earliest was that by Leeds on the penannular brooch, which he correctly viewed as being a Roman and Celtic brooch type. He argued for substantial native influence in the production of annular and quoit brooches[4] and it is only within the last few years that this view has been challenged. At the same time he suggested that the presence of penannular brooches, and thus perhaps by inference annular and quoit brooches, indicated that the interred were of native origin. This view is, however, untenable, since artefacts cannot, necessarily, tell us the ethnic origin of the person buried. To anticipate the conclusions of this paper, it must be firmly stated that the presence of Roman material in graves tells us nothing of the ethnic identity of the deceased.

Other studies have followed the approach taken by Leeds and have tended to concentrate on particular categories of objects. Thus a pioneering article by Harden in 1956 catalogued the incidences of Roman glass in Anglo-Saxon graves[5] and in 1961, Kent proved that the occurrence of Roman coins in Anglo-Saxon graves could not be used to demonstrate the survival of a money economy into the post-Roman period.[6] No alternative explanation of their use was offered, however. In the same year, Hawkes and Dunning published their catalogue of late-Roman military metalwork from British sites, both Anglo-Saxon and Roman.[7] Their conclusion that many of the finds indicated the presence of *foederati* in British villas and towns is one that has been questioned but their overall contribution remains significant. In 1965, Evison catalogued some of the more miscellaneous Roman material from cemeteries and suggested that its presence indicated the settlement of the Romanophile Franks.[8] The subject really came to the boil in 1967 with a debate on the significance of a Roman brooch reused in a woman's grave at Londesborough, Humberside.[9] The argument centred on whether this ring brooch, which was argued to have continental affinities, could be used to identify the ethnic origin of the user. The debate was ended by Brown who pointed out that whatever her ethnic origin, she was using the brooch as an amulet and not wearing it. This was followed up by a note in which Myres suggested that the finding of scrap copper alloy in amulet bags might indicate a form of barter economy in which these small fragments might play the role of small change.[10] This is a view reached independently by Dickinson who was the first person to compile a corpus of Roman material from one area and assess its importance.[11] She formed the opinion that the material tended to reflect the sites which were around the cemetery area and were thus unlikely to reflect direct continuity between the late-Roman population and the emerging Anglo-Saxon kingdoms.

Roman pottery from Anglo-Saxon graves was examined in brief by Evison but no real conclusions were reached about such occurrences and the latest substantial work to deal with the occurrence of Roman material in graves is that of Meaney.[12] Her work is not so much a catalogue as an assessment of the unjustly neglected subject of amulets used by the Anglo-Saxons. She takes up and expands upon Brown's work with further examples and textual support including Douglas' pioneering work.[13] The writer's work on the Roman and Celtic material[14] from Anglo-Saxon cemeteries falls into two parts based upon the use to which the objects were put. Thus the largest group, objects of personal adornment, includes brooches of Roman date, penannular brooches, coins, finger rings, bracelets, late-Roman belt equipment, pins and beads. The second group, accessory objects, consists largely of vessels in metal, pottery and glass, spoons, keys, house furniture and other more miscellaneous material.

To deal with the personal objects first, the most numerous group are the brooches. There are over one hundred examples of penannular brooches alone and this group has been one of the most difficult of the categories to deal with. This is mainly due to the fact that they continue into the Post-Roman period without a break. The classification followed is that proposed by Fowler which is a chronological sequence lettered from A to I based on the form of the terminal.[15] This has not been fully accepted as there appears to be a slight break in the manufacture of these brooches in the second and early third century within the empire,[16] manifested by a change in the hoop shape found particularly in Class C and D brooches. Criticism has also been levelled at some of the subdivisions within groups which have been seen to lack significance as often the differentiation rests solely on file marks made on the terminals.[17] These problems are best demonstrated by the largest group, Class C. In this brooch form, the terminals which prevent the pin from slipping off the hoop are simply curled round on themselves in the same plane as the hoop. This brooch form is found on late-Iron-Age and early-Roman sites both in Gaul, Germany and Britain.[18] It continues in use throughout the first and probably the second century, declining in popularity. It makes its reappearance in northern Gaul in the later third century in the slightly modified form of the flat-sectioned hoop with incised, often diamond-shaped, linear decoration.[19] From this region it spread throughout the northern part of Gaul into Lower Germany and Britain. The flat-sectioned hoop had been used earlier but is a rare, continental variety; it now became the mainstay of the type. A second variant developed at roughly the same time with a small hoop which was often beaded or grooved and had a round section. The development of the beaded hoop should probably be related to the function of preventing slippage of the pin head. The spread of this brooch type into the *limes* area in the fourth century meant that the Germans must have become familiar with the type and towards the end of the fourth century it is found in graves containing late-Roman belt equipment probably in use holding a *chlamys* or military cloak.[20] Bearing in mind the familiarity which the Germans had with this brooch type, particularly in Classes Aa, C and D,[21] it is no surprise to see that the brooch is well represented in this country in precisely these classes. Most are of Class C and many appear to have been used in Germanic fashion as pairs holding together a peplos-type dress (Figure 1, 1 and 4). Others are mismatched with other classes of penannulars of similar size, as at Pewsey 102,[22] or even with other Germanic brooch types. Many have also been manufactured in iron, a material rarely used by the Romans to manufacture penannular brooches, although one example has been published from Barnsley Park, Gloucestershire.[23] Some of the copper alloy brooches such as those from Girton Group C, Cambridgeshire or Nassington, Northamptonshire also demonstrate Germanic traits such as extremely wide hoops and stamped decoration.[24] Of the smaller group of single brooches, many are of the Celtic post-Roman classes (A5, E, F, G and H) (Figure 1, 2). These may be divided into two groups. The first group (Classes A5 and F) have large hoops and flattened terminals which sometimes have simple graved ornament or may be enamelled. These are cloak pins and appear either over the midriff as at Highdown 74[25] or on the shoulder. The other type, represented by E and G, are smaller and would perhaps have been used on dresses. This is certainly the case with Class G, a brooch popular with the Germans.[26] The distribution of these Celtic brooches is markedly different from that of the other classes and clearly demonstrates the operation of trade at a frontier zone (Figure 2 and Figure 3). Such contact may also have been responsible for the adoption of the single brooch worn at the shoulder, a Romano-Celtic fashion. This lengthy consideration of the penannular brooch is necessary primarily to demonstrate the extreme diversity of the type and the problem of actually identifying which brooches are Roman and which are post-Roman. Some of the grave-finds are clearly of Roman date and have been reused, sometimes with new iron pins; for example the D5 brooch from West

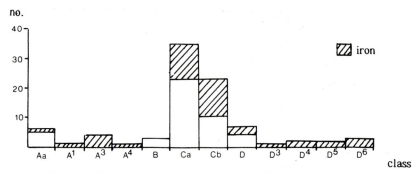

1.   Quantity of Roman & Anglo-Saxon penannular brooches by class

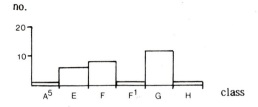

2.   Quantity of Celtic penannular brooches by class

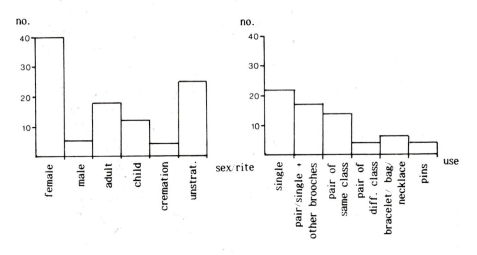

3.   Quantity of pennanular brooches by
     sex or rite

4.   Use of penannular brooches in graves

FIGURE 1   HISTOGRAMS showing quantity and use of penannular brooches in Anglo-Saxon graves

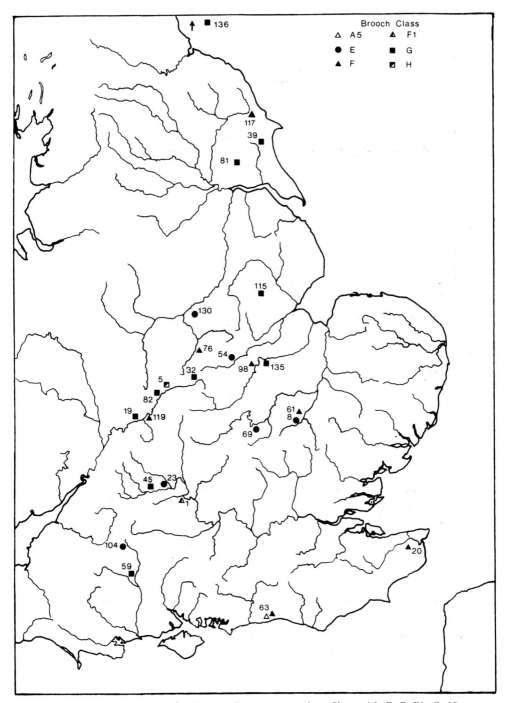

FIGURE 2   DISTRIBUTION of Celtic post-Roman penannulars (Classes A5, E, F, F1, G, H)

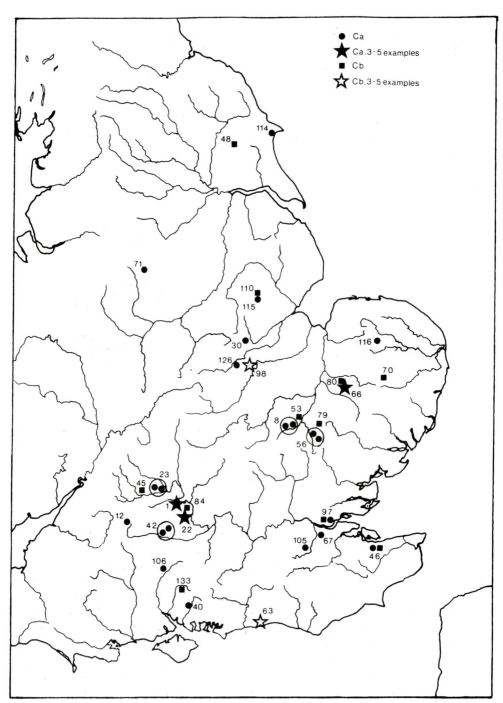

FIGURE 3   DISTRIBUTION of Class C brooches

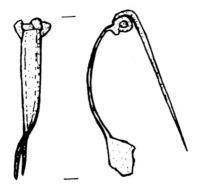

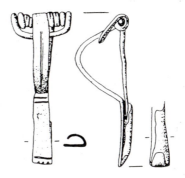

1. Little Wilbraham 11, CMAA
    48.1340

2. Westerham A, after Böhme
    1974, Taf. 44,9

3. Gilton 67, LM M.6063

4. Chessell Down 45, after Arnold
    1982, Fig. 13,45xiii

FIGURE 4   GERMANIC AND ANGLO-SAXON BROOCH TYPES and contemporary imitations using Roman
brooches

Overton 4, Wiltshire.[27] Others may be Roman or Anglo-Saxon; the pair from Wakerley
10 have been interpreted in both ways.[28]

The final class for consideration is the large terminal H brooch. The five examples
from Anglo-Saxon cemeteries listed by Fowler have all been misidentified and the writer
can find no true H brooches in Anglo-Saxon cemeteries.[29] This would appear to mean
that a dating in the middle to late sixth century for the start of the true H brooch would
be in order. The only H-type brooch that the writer has been able to identify is a small,
unrepresentative example from Baginton, Warwickshire, originally classified as a G
brooch.[30] In summary, the penannular brooch must be seen as a small but consistent
element of Germanic dress accessories in the fifth to seventh centuries. Their familiarity
with the type means that there is no need to argue, as Leeds does, that the production of
these brooches must be linked to surviving elements of the native population.

Of the other brooch categories, the most important are the simple Nauheim and
Colchester type bow brooches and the late-Roman disc-brooch with central setting. To

take the earlier category first, fifteen of these brooches are known from Anglo-Saxon cemeteries.[31] Some are in a fragmentary condition and could never have been used; Dunstable Five Knolls 54, Bedfordshire is a case in point. Others are, however, in a usable condition and their reuse 500 years after their manufacture is something of a mystery. That such brooches were used has been proven at Portway Down, Hampshire where graves 22 and 67 both used Nauheim brooches.[32] Thus the substantial group from Linton Heath B, Cambridgeshire and two examples from Little Wilbraham, Cambridgeshire,[33] can be seen in their true context. Although the question of whether they were in use has been answered, the question of why they were reused has not. It may be suggested, however, that these early-Roman brooches with their flattened and simply decorated hoops with coiled springs on either side of the head closely resemble the fourth-century *Armbrustfibel* which the settlers were familiar with from their homeland (Figures 4, 1 and 2). Germanic examples of these brooches are rare in this country and it is possible that the early settlers used Nauheim brooches as imitations or substitutes for brooches that they were unable to obtain otherwise. The brooch types are not exactly alike but perhaps this would have been unimportant at a time when brooch production was at such a local level. The alternative hypothesis that these brooches were reused simply for the practical reason that they were often still functional when found may also have more than a grain of truth in it but, as will be shown below, the theory of imitation is not limited to Nauheim brooches alone.

The case for the reuse or continuing use for the late-Roman gilded disc-brooch has been argued previously by Dickinson who used it as the basis for her argument that the type was the precursor of the Saxon disc-brooch.[34] The thesis was difficult to maintain in 1979 since there were none of these Roman disc-brooches that could be dated to the middle to late fourth century, a fact that Mackreth pointed out in writing up the brooch from Spong Hill 26.[35] This has now changed with the publication of a complete brooch from Nettleton, Wiltshire in a context dated to about AD 360.[36] Further brooches may be cited from New Grange in Ireland where two of these brooches were found in an horizon dated by *solidii* of the house of Valentinian.[37] This does not, however, resolve the problem of when the Anglo-Saxon disc-brooch began to be manufactured as Welch argues that their appearance should be dated to the last quarter of the fifth century and not the third as Dickinson maintains.[38] There are in all sixteen of these late-Roman gilded disc-brooches from Anglo-Saxon cemeteries but only six of these have recorded associations.[39] Only one site can boast two examples, East Shefford, Berkshire but both are unassociated. Two other examples serve to illustrate some of the pitfalls in interpretation that may occur in dealing with Roman material in general. At Collingbourne Ducis 11, Wiltshire, one of these brooches was found, its gilded and stamped decoration in good condition but lacking its central setting, at the shoulder of a prone male burial.[40] The only associated object was an inlaid iron buckle which is dated to the later fifth or early sixth century. The brooch had an iron pin suggesting that it had lost its original pin but was still functional. In addition, it was being worn in Roman fashion at the shoulder of the interred. There was no weapon or knife in the grave, an unusual fact given the presence of inlaid metalwork. The brooch from this grave has all the hallmarks of an heirloom or of use in a Roman fashion suggesting the assimilation of the local Celtic-speaking population.

In contrast, the second grave, at Gilton 87, Kent, had an example of this brooch type at the throat of a female inhumation.[41] Given that the brooch was three hundred years old when buried, it is in good condition although it has no central setting. The body had been placed in a coffin and the only other accompanying artefacts were a small necklace from which the brooch may have been suspended, some iron chain links with miniature tools suspended from the waist and the remains of a box at the feet. There were no objects in the box when it was excavated but this does not rule out organic contents. The chatelaine did not survive lifting. The grave may be dated to the early seventh century on analogy with similar graves in the cemetery. The position of the brooch is correct for the female costume of the later sixth century onwards which by the early seventh century in Kent consisted of a large brooch at the centre of the chest and sometimes small paired brooches or pins at the shoulders.[42] The contents of Gilton 87 are worth examining in more detail. The use of a coffin, the wearing of a chatelaine and the ownership of a box suggest a wealthy burial but there are anomalies. The box was empty of the usual paraphernalia of the high-status Anglo-Saxon woman of this period; notably cowrie shells, rock-crystal beads etc. The chatelaine, although present, was small and of poor quality as Faussett was able to lift more substantial examples with ease. Her necklace was also small and would have represented little wealth. The picture given of this burial is of a woman of middling rank in society unable to afford the luxuries of life but able to afford substitute equipment to give the social standing necessary in society. It is in this context that the disc brooch should be viewed: as a contemporary imitation of an Anglo-Saxon keystone or composite disc brooch. Gilton 87 is not an isolated case either. In Gilton 67, a small enamelled ring brooch of second century date was found also at the neck of a woman.[43] This example is very battered and must have been suspended from a necklace. The only other association was a knife. The clue to the reuse of this brooch lies in the 'keystone' areas of dark red enamel on the ring: surely these may be seen as imitating the small keystone garnet disc brooches of the time (Figures 4, 3 and 4). The enamel is very close in colour and shape to the garnets of the period and would have been seen as an adequate imitation of the real thing. Finally, a second enamelled brooch from Gilton 70 is used in the same position and may also have been used in imitation of contemporary brooches.[44]

The last category of brooches to discuss are those of the Quoit Brooch Style. Ager's discussion of the style itself has reopened the question of who was making these brooches and the writer feels that it must now be accepted that these are creations of Germanic workmen.[45] This is not, however, to deny that their debt to late-Roman art and metalworking techniques is considerable and this is reflected by the range of brooches decorated in the style. Ager's discussion was limited to the Quoit brooches themselves, the best known of the group, but there are two other brooch forms decorated in the style; disc and penannular brooches[46] (Figure 5). The former are clearly inspired in form and decoration by the late-Roman gilded and stamped brooches already discussed above but the latter are a new development which the writer believes demonstrate the essential Germanic nature of the pieces. Their novelty lies not, of course, in their form but in their use. A true penannular may be defined as a brooch which functions by passing the terminal of the brooch (of whatever form) under the pin which has already been pushed through the cloth. The hoop is then rotated to lock it: the pin will not slip through the gap because the terminal prevents it from doing so. When the three Quoit Brooch Style penannulars are examined, it is clear that they could not have functioned in this way.

1. Alfriston 43, after Welch
    1983, Fig. 19,a

2. Horton Kirby II 22, after
    Evison 1965, Fig. 28,i

3. Lyminge II 10, after
    Ager 1985, Fig. 14,e

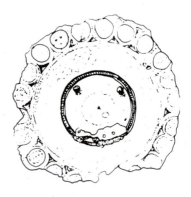

4. Faversham, after Hawkes
    1961, Fig. 1

5. Higham, after Hawkes
    1961, Pl. XVI,a

FIGURE 5   QUOIT BROOCH STYLE penannular brooches (1–3), Quoit brooch style disc brooches (4–5)

The only brooch with a freely moving pin (Alfriston 43) has the pin located not on the wide and extensively decorated hoop but on a subsidiary wire above it. The brooch from Lyminge II, 10 has the pin head pushed through a hole which has been bored through the hoop opposite the opening. The arrangement of the decoration reflects the fact that the pin was unable to move freely. Clearly, this brooch was worked not by turning the hoop to lock it but by lifting the pin over the terminal. Finally, the brooch from Horton Kirby II, 22 may have operated in the same way. The Quoit Brooch Style penannulars appear to demonstrate that they were created by people who did not wish to use the penannular form in the normal way but adapted it to suit their decorative style.

Now that the style may be dated with greater clarity and the likely source of manufacture has been identified, it only remains to discuss the reason for their manufacture. This needs to be assessed principally because of the existence of buckles and other military belt fittings in the Quoit Brooch Style (below). Ager has argued that the Quoit brooch itself was largely intended for use by women,[47] a fact that certainly has a grain of truth in it when the existence of the pendants from Bifrons is taken into consideration. But this may not be the case with those brooches already discussed: the large quoit brooches, the disc-brooches and the 'penannular' brooches. These are certainly the earliest of the style and are closely linked, as already suggested, with metalwork largely imitative in form and decorative style of late-Roman military metalwork. The occurrence of both brooches and military metalwork in the late or immediately post-Roman period automatically raises the suspicion that both brooches and buckles were used together as badges of office or even as part payment for the services of military officials. The forms of the brooches would appear to be modelled on late-Roman brooches of which the penannular would have been very familiar to the settlers and the same is probably true of the disc-brooch. When originally worn, there is no reason not to consider them as badges of office worn by *foederati* on terms that are now unclear. That the equipment appears with women as well need not weaken the case as late-Roman buckles are also found with Germanic women as well (e.g. Mucking II 987 and 989; see below).

Turning next to the late-Roman belt equipment, it is clear that the former classification of Hawkes and Dunning must be abandoned in favour of that now developed on the continent by Bullinger and Böhme, among others.[48] This is not a particularly radical alteration but should eliminate the criticisms levelled at the original classification in recent works.[49] The buckles may be divided into three or two piece sets (Figure 6). The former are the earlier and may be subdivided into four major groups with variants. Group A1 are equivalent to Hawkes and Dunning's group IIA buckles. These have hoops composed of opposed dolphins holding a pellet between their jaws. The substantial crest is another feature of this group. They appear to be the earliest group which appear in Britain as they are found in graves at Lankhills, Hampshire.[50] Some chronological development is hinted at by the fact that the earliest of these buckles

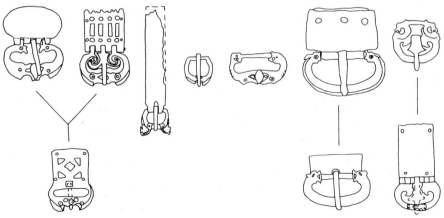

FIGURE 6   BUCKLE GROUPS

have solid buckle plates whereas a later British development have openwork plates and may be dated to *c.* AD 360 which is approximately ten years after the introduction of the former variety.[51] These are followed by group A2 of which there are three identifiable variants. A2a is the British buckle formerly classified as IB. It is characterized by the conversion of the crest into outward facing horses' heads but the dolphins are also represented. This group appears to be linked particularly to women.[52] Group A2b and A2c, formerly group IA, are similar in that they are debased versions of the normal dolphin buckle. The difference lies in the fact that they lack the involuted tails of A1 buckles and thus the body of the dolphin merges directly with the hinge bar in the case of A2b or has a secondary animal head interposed between the body and the hinge bar in the case of A2c. These latter buckles with secondary animal heads of the same form as A3 and B2 buckles are clearly contemporary with them and may thus be dated to the period after AD 390.[53] Further subdivision is possible but probably merely reflects the fact that these buckles were widely produced throughout the south of England in different workshops. The third group, A3, formerly IIIA, have large oval hoops which are terminated by the hinge bar with lion or leopard heads. The plate is usually rectangular. None of these have been found in Anglo-Saxon graves. The final three piece buckle set is group A4, formerly group IIC, represented by the well-known examples from Bifrons and Highdown.[54] In this group, the involuted tail of group A1 is reintroduced with the addition of animal terminals. The tongue is also involuted to mirror the shape of the buckle. The hoop is otherwise without zoomorphic forms. The buckle plates associated with this group remain to be identified but there is the possibility that they did not have any. The two piece buckles mirror the development of group A. Group B1, formerly group IIB, is a rare form in which the hoop and openwork buckle plate of A1 buckles are cast in one. Only two examples are known.[55] B2 buckles, formerly IIIB, are exactly similar in form to A3 buckles with the exception that the buckle plate is cast integrally. Finally B3 buckles are a group in which the hoop of A4 buckles are cast with a large rectangular buckle plate. This may be either openwork or solid with inlaid wire decoration. This group were formally published by Evison as Quoit Brooch Style buckles[56] but unlike all other Quoit Brooch Style metalwork a fragmentary example is known from a Roman context at Richborough, Kent[57] suggesting a Roman date and an early fifth-century date of manufacture. Strap ends and other late-Roman fittings are classified following terms used by Clarke.[58]

When the date of deposition of these buckles in Anglo-Saxon graves is examined, it becomes clear that the bulk of the dateable contexts belong in the late fifth or early sixth century (twenty-two out of thirty-one examples). Of these thirty-one graves, sixteen are female inhumations with a further four unsexed graves. Identifiable male graves with buckles only include Woodingdean 5, East Sussex, a late sixth- or seventh-century grave and Alfriston 14, East Sussex, a late fifth-century grave.[59] Other male graves with complete sets of belt fittings dating to the early fifth century were found at Dorchester I, Milton-next-Sittingbourne, Mucking II (979) and Kempston (14).[60] Three female graves of the same date were all wearing group A2a buckles (Dorchester I, 2; Mucking 987 and 989).[61] The other thirteen graves are mostly of the last quarter of the fifth or the beginning of the sixth century which would rule out the possibility that they had acquired them directly from late-Roman sources. Two possibilities may be suggested to fit this fact. One is that these are, exceptionally, heirloom objects. The other is that they

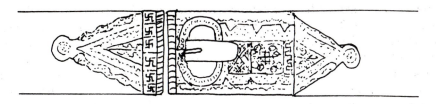

1. Broad Belt Set

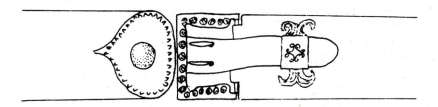

2. Narrow Belt Set, type A

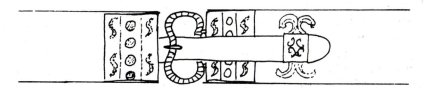

3. Narrow Belt Set, type B

FIGURE 7   QUOIT BROOCH STYLE BELT SETS

are using these buckles to imitate the contemporary taste for inlaid iron buckles. In favour of the former hypothesis is the fact that A2a buckles in particular consistently appear in female graves in both Roman and Anglo-Saxon contexts and that they continue to be worn at the waist as intended, even if repaired or broken. Few buckles are known from bag collections but particularly favoured in this context are fragments of group A1 buckle plates (e.g. Droxford, Sarre 94 etc.).[62]

It is necessary next to re-examine the Quoit brooch-style belt sets. That these are modelled on Roman buckle sets becomes particularly clear once the variants of belt designs are reconstructed (Figure 7). The first, represented by Mucking II 117, is from a broad belt but is clearly not of Roman manufacture in that it is cast in one piece unlike similar Roman pieces.[63] The other two forms are from narrow belts and consist of a heart-shaped counter plate and a rectangular hoop, probably with a double tongue originally (e.g. Highdown 34) or a second form with rectangular or square plates and a kidney-shaped hoop with inlay (e.g. Alfriston 17).[64] The form of the hoop on this latter belt set clearly provides the inspiration for the inlaid iron belt sets of the later fifth century. Both the narrow sets could have utilized the Highdown belt slide and the various forms of strap ends. The existence of narrow belt sets may point to their use by women as well as men.

The next category, coins, have been examined by Kent, as already noted. He concluded that it was impossible to demonstrate that the coinage in Anglo-Saxon graves had been used as the basis for a money economy. Till now there has, however, been no attempt to quantify the material. In all nearly two hundred and fifty graves with coins are known representing over four hundred and fifty coins. These have been identified where possible and the results drawn up by issue period following the methodology of Reece[65] (Figure 8). The writer has also taken the opportunity of discussing the results with Dr Reece in order to search for any anomalies in the histograms drawn up. The first point that arises from the histogram of issue periods is that the only period not represented is the last (XVI): the House of Theodosius. Here, if proof were still needed, is the evidence of a complete break with the late-Roman economy. The only other serious anomaly is the large number of issue period XIIIa coins which corresponds to the issue of the *follis*. The total of twenty-three *folles* from Anglo-Saxon graves is certainly higher than one would normally expect. Conversely, the total of irregular coins of third and fourth century date, except for a few examples of good quality, is also low when compared with settlement sites. Dr Reece has suggested in discussion that the lack of issue period XVI and irregular coins should probably be related to their small diameter, generally under 15 mm, which appears to have militated against their selection. This is probably a function of the use of coins as pierced ornaments in Anglo-Saxon graves: those under 15 mm would not be worth piercing while those of the *follis* size would be very noticeable when pierced. Of the coins in issue periods I–X, the bulk of the

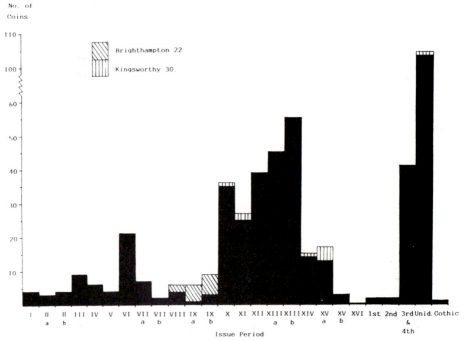

FIGURE 8   HISTOGRAMS to show incidence of Roman Coins in graves by Issue Period (after Reece, 1972).
Total: 469 graves

examples catalogued are *sestertii* or *dupondii* rather than *denarii*, of which only one or two examples may be cited. The reason for this imbalance will be discussed below. For the third century, the low silver *antoninianii* predominate and in the fourth century the AE3 size coins (roughly 16–21 mm) predominate. When the histogram is compared with Roman settlement sites such as Gadebridge Park villa,[66] it is clear that the overall pattern is similar, given the anomalies noted above suggesting that there has been a random selection of coins from Roman sites with favour being given to the heavy coinage in the early periods and the lighter third- and fourth-century issues.

When the information on who was actually selecting these coins is plotted, a very interesting histogram emerges (Figure 9). This demonstrates that the bulk of the coinage found is in female Anglo-Saxon graves deposited singly or, more infrequently, in two or threes. These single coins were often pierced and were usually associated with strings of beads or were worn in the neck or chest area. Larger groups are, however, known. Principal among these are two groups of ten coins, one from Brighthampton 22, Oxfordshire and a second from Kingsworthy 30, Hampshire.[67] All of these coins were pierced. At Brighthampton they were found strung on a necklace and at Kingsworthy they were found in a bag collection with beads suggesting the same arrangement. The distribution of the Brighthampton coins by issue period strongly suggests that they are part or all of a hoard of early third-century *antoninianii* and *denarii*. The Kingsworthy

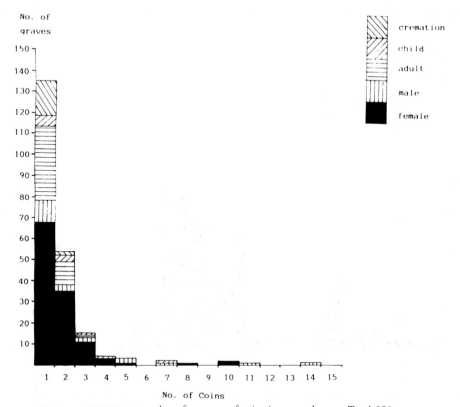

FIGURE 9   HISTOGRAMS to show frequency of coins in graves by sex. Total 321 graves

group also clusters, less convincingly, around the period of the House of Valentinian and the late third century. The single group of fourteen coins on the histogram brings us onto the other use of coins, that of weights. This group is from a male grave at Dover II.[68] Five are of *sestertii* or *aes* of first and second century date and most have been modified by having their surfaces filed or trimmed. Other modifications include the insertion of a plug of lead into a *sestertius* of Faustina to increase its weight. The rest of the coins from this group are of issue period XI where identifiable. Many are quite fresh again suggesting the finding of a hoard. Other coins, such as those from Ozingell, Kent, show the addition of punch marks to act as weight denominations.[69] Whilst the use of coins as weights is reasonably clear, their use as pendant jewellery is less so. Clearly, selection for use as pendants militated against heavy coins such as the *sestertius* and *dupondius* whilst the lighter third- and fourth-century coins would have been favoured. Coins in precious metals are noticeable by their absence which suggests that when found, they were immediately used as bullion rather than as ornaments. This would suggest that the use of coinage was in some way amuletic and was not related to social status. This conclusion has already found favour with Meaney and seems to be borne out by their use by the most vulnerable elements of the population, women and children.[70] If the two groups are compared, however, it is noticeable that the latter are under-represented and it may therefore be argued that the coins performed some prophylactic function related to childbirth. On the question of dating graves with coins in them, most appear to be linked to the later fifth to middle sixth century, although coins are known in graves from the very earliest to the very latest period. There is, however, a demonstrable change in the use of coinage after the change in dress style in the later sixth and seventh century when coins are increasingly relegated to bag collections rather than being worn. Finally, it is of interest to note that only one genuine example of coins being placed in the mouth has been found in an Anglo-Saxon cemetery and that only a few graves have coins placed by or in the hand.[71] Thus, both these Romano-British customs can be seen to have rapidly died out and no continuity can be argued.

The final category of objects in this section are objects used for personal adornment i.e. finger rings (including intaglios), bracelets, pins and beads. All of these objects are found with reasonable frequency in Anglo-Saxon graves, this being especially true for finger rings and intaglios of which the writer has catalogued thirty-one. The quasi-magical quality of intaglios and monogrammed rings such as those from Harnham Hill 40 and 53 need not be dwelt upon.[72] Pins occur only infrequently and are often of such simple construction that they may have been made in either the Roman or the Anglo-Saxon period. Some, such as the late- or post-Roman pin from Cassington and the late-Roman pin from Gilton are easily categorized however.[73] The same difficulty in assigning date applies also to a certain extent with bracelets; twenty-nine examples have been catalogued. The occurrence of beads has been excluded here largely because they deserve a study in themselves and also because it is so difficult to distinguish between late-Roman and early-Anglo-Saxon beads, although recent work has greatly elucidated the dating of many types.[74]

The second section is devoted to the much smaller category of accessory objects, consisting mainly of vessels. Pottery is the most common, with forty-nine examples of varying forms and fabrics. Many of these graves may be late Roman in date and are only included because poor excavation has lead to confusion as to their date and context: those found at Girton, Cambridgeshire are a good example. There are, however, numerous associations which are genuine. In some of the Kentish cemeteries, the looting of Roman cemeteries provided some seventh-century graves with samian dishes; Smith asserts that at Ozingell as many as a dozen were found.[75] About fourteen of the vessels are colour-coated beakers or bowls which being late Roman in date may well have been acquired by settling peoples. At Highdown 82, West Sussex, a complete indented beaker of fourth-century date was an isolated find in a grave.[76] Cut-down beakers have also been found in grave 16 at Chessell Down and at Kingsworthy 98.[77] The cutting down of these vessels and their worn appearance strongly suggests their use as heirlooms. A second substantial group is jugs and flagons. Their popularity rests largely on their ability to be reused for cremations. Indeed, five Roman jars were found at Caistor-by-Norwich alone.[78] These are of second or third century date and their presence on the site may be explained by the finding of a kiln in the area of the cemetery which was producing the same wares. There is one other vessel of Roman date that is worth mentioning and that is a small Roman bottle-vase from Westbere, Kent[79] (Figure 10). As the excavator noted at the time, it bears a very close resemblance to the prestigious imported Frankish bottle-vases encountered in sixth- and seventh-century graves in Kent. Is it possible that this vase could be seen as an imitation of a contemporary artefact? The significance of the final group of pottery vessels, post- (or sub) Roman wares is unclear. They are very few in number and there is no strong reason to equate them with the assimilated Roman population as has often been done before.

With metal vessels, there is very little to discuss as there are only five examples of definite Roman date. The vessels represented include a *bassin uni* from Faversham, Irchester-type bowls from Dover II 137 and Higham, a skillet base from Cliffe-at-Hoo and a late-Roman pan.[80] This last vessel, from grave 26 at Long Wittenham I, Oxfordshire is perhaps the most illuminating.[81] It was buried in a male grave and was worn and patched when discovered. Dickinson compares it with Egger's type 117 which is found in Free Germany. The dish may, therefore, have been an heirloom imported into Britain by a settler who died at the end of the fifth or the beginning of the sixth century. The other vessels are two palm cups of possible Roman date from Horton Kirby and Howletts 16.[82] Two other imported vessels may be considered. These are the Gallo-Roman vessels from Long Wittenham I 93 and the reused vessel now known as the Strood horn mount[83] (Figure 11). Both vessels may date from the end of the fourth to the mid-fifth century.

The question of hanging bowls in Anglo-Saxon graves is one that has been much discussed in the past. The writer has been able to list fifty-seven examples from cemeteries, the bulk of which were deposited in the early to mid-seventh century. Two groups may be noted. The larger group is that where the bowl appears to have been buried in one piece although generally worn and patched and a second group where only the decorative escutcheon is found, generally as a pendant in a female grave, for example Camerton 32, Somerset.[84] These graves tend to be of mid- to late-seventh century date. Many of the bowls are found in male graves but there is a small proportion from female graves as well e.g. Kingston Down 205.[85]

Finally, glass vessels comprise the only group that has been comprehensively discussed previously. Harden's basic division of the Roman material into type-fossils and

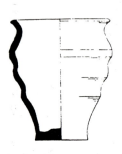

1. Ruskington, after
    Thompson 1956, Fig.
    2,1

2. Oudenburg 104, after
    Böhme 1974, Taf, 96,9

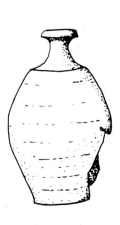

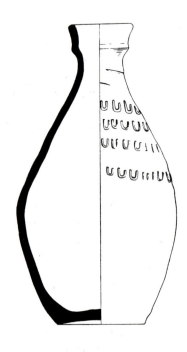

3. Westbere, after Jessup
    1946, Pl. IV,4

4. Sarre 12, after Evison
    1979, Fig. 9,c

FIGURE 10   CONTINENTAL POTTERY VESSELS and contemporary imitations using Iron Age and early
Roman vessels

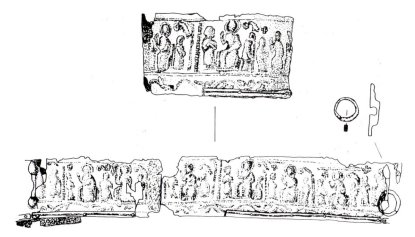

FIGURE 11   GALLO-ROMAN VESSEL FRAGMENT (Strood, LM M.6399) reused as an Anglo-Saxon horn mount

prototypes is still valid. Vessels of the former category, such as indented bowls of Isings form 117 (four examples), amphorae (Mitcham 199), bowls with folded rim and foot and Isings forms 96 and 115 were mainly buried before the middle of the fifth century where contexts are known. The second, prototype, category includes cone-beakers such as those from Chessell Down 1, Highdown 32 and Alfriston 60[86] as well as unassociated vessels from East Shefford, Faversham, Westbere and Chessell Down.[87] A second group is represented by the unique claw-beaker from Mucking II 843, Essex.[88] These vessels are sometimes deposited as late as the mid-sixth century when they would have been well over one hundred years old. Their survival is almost certainly due to their resemblance once again to contemporary vessels. They would not have looked out of place on a dinner table of the period whereas the type-fossils would have done. It is also likely that, as with the metal dish from Long Wittenham I 26, these vessels were carried over by the settlers themselves as they were all made in the Rhenish glass factories.

The next group of accessory objects are spoons and keys. Only seventeen examples of the former are known but two of these (Chartham Down 26 and Desborough) are probably seventh century in date.[89] Of the other spoons, all except that from Icklingham, Suffolk, have had their handles removed,[90] the break often being smoothed with wear. Few of the spoons are from recorded contexts but one that is fortunately provides a clue as to the use of the rest. At Little Wilbraham 3, Lethbridge found a Roman spoon bowl corroded on to a conventional girdle hanger at the waist of a mid- to late-sixth-century female inhumation[91] (Figure 12). Next to the spoon was an oak apple mounted in copper alloy slings; the parallel is, of course, provided by the well-known gilt strainer spoons and crystal balls found in richly attired female graves. Meaney, in her book on Anglo-Saxon amulets provides the written sources for the uses of oak apples in medicine of the later Anglo-Saxon period.[92] The use of Roman spoons in this way is again another way of imitating a contemporary fashion for exotic objects. The same source also tells us that keys were symbolic of the functions of the housekeeper and this is borne out by the fact that all the Roman examples are found with women (except that

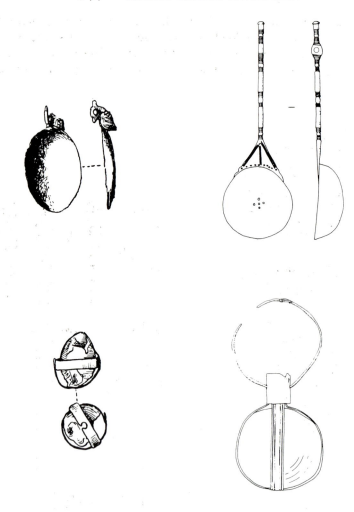

1. Little Wibraham 3, after
   Lethbridge & Cater
   1928, Fig. 4,2 & 3

2. Chessell Down 45, after
   Arnold 1982, Fig.
   11,45ii & iii

FIGURE 12   ANGLO-SAXON STRAINER SPOON and crystal ball in slings and contemporary imitation using Roman spoon and suspended oak gall

from Stowting 4). Their use may perhaps be seen again as alternatives to expensive contemporary objects or, when found in bags as at Barrington B 82, Cambridgeshire,[93] because they are smaller and thus more portable.

A third major category of objects is represented by horse harness fittings and terrets. These are surprisingly common, totalling twenty-one. Some have been reused as buckles, as at Long Wittenham I 134 but many are found in bag collections along with other rings whose function appears to be amuletic. Some, however, were reused in a more ingenious fashion as the 'Donside' terret from Linton Heath B9 shows[94] (Figure 13). Here, the projecting internal knob has been used to suspend a home-made key or girdle hanger to wear at the waist. Other small categories of objects such as bone inlaid caskets, mirrors, openwork knives, bells and seal boxes occur rarely and none appear to be significant.

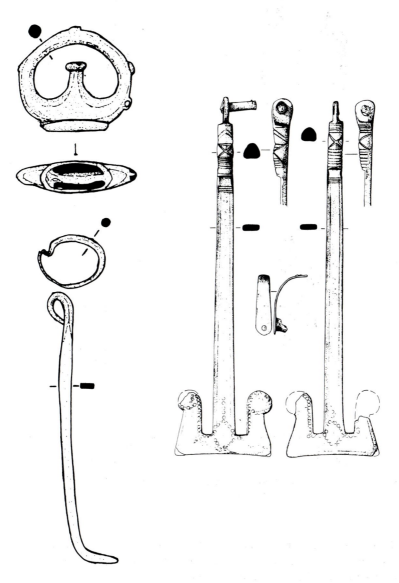

1. Linton Heath B 9.
    CMAA 48. 1523 &
    1524c

2. Spong Hill 28, after
    Hills et al. 1984, Fig.
    91,1 & 4

FIGURE 13   ANGLO-SAXON GIRDLE HANGER and contemporary imitation using terret and key

In conclusion, several points can be drawn from the evidence presented here. Perhaps the most important is that this material cannot be used to demonstrate the survival of the Romano-British population into Anglo-Saxon England. The material is not selected randomly but conforms to a pattern of usage which is related to, and mirrors the use of, contemporary Anglo-Saxon artefacts. Some of the material, particularly vessels, may be seen as objects carefully retained after the collapse of the Romano-British economy at the end of the fourth century as there were no replacements. These tend to be buried before the middle of the sixth century at the latest. Some of this material is also selected and used because of its fortuitous resemblance to contemporary vessels. Whether this usage was due to the unavailability of certain objects or, more probably, due to the fact that those using Roman objects could not afford to get contemporary objects is unclear. Roman material is selected, in an apparently *ad hoc* fashion, from known Roman sites. This can be demonstrated by the fact that the closer a cemetery is to a Roman settlement site or cemetery, the more objects are found. Thus, at Gilton, Kent, a cemetery founded on top of a Roman cemetery, there are sixteen graves with Roman objects. At Stowting, Kent, a probable hoard of second-century house furniture is dispersed through several graves. At Brighthampton 22, a hoard of *antoninianii* were reused for jewellery. This would tend to suggest that there is little truth in the theory of an economy based on barter in scrap-metal. Sites were easy to find and when material was needed, it was looked for. The theory of the use of Roman objects as imitations of contemporary objects also appears to be borne out by the little Anglo-Saxon settlement evidence that has been published. At West Stow, Suffolk, all the groups catalogued here are represented with the exception of keys and vessels although there seems to be a much higher concentration of coins from this site than is reflected in the cemeteries.[95]

The final point to consider is that the material examined in this study is largely derived from inhumation cemeteries. Cremations very rarely use Roman material and even coins appear only sixteen times. Whether this imbalance in the use of Roman objects is real or merely a reflection of the burial rite is impossible to say but the latter seems likely.

Those looking for the surviving Romano-British population who were, undoubtedly, assimilated into Anglo-Saxon society will have to look, therefore, in other directions. One possible line of enquiry is an assessment of Romano-British customs such as the wearing of a single brooch at the shoulder or the survival of Romano-British burial customs. The use of the coin in the mouth has been shown to have quietly disappeared in Britain, unlike Merovingian Gaul, but the rite of decapitation is known in at least twenty-two cemeteries.[96] The crucial problem is still one of how it is possible to detect a population that has adopted Anglo-Saxon dress styles and customs by marriage and conquest. The answer is probably that it is impossible to do so convincingly. If this is so, then it is pertinent to ask how much does it matter that the British population is untraceable. The assimilation is known to have occurred as place-name studies and documents demonstrate; that they are undetectable archaeologically is not surprising as even in areas where they are known to have survived, they remain difficult to find. There has been too much confusion caused already by the chasing of tribal identities in what must have been an already thoroughly mixed population, a fact that Lethbridge pointed out some time ago.[97] The interest in the problem of the use of Roman objects in Anglo-Saxon graves lies not in the question of survival but in the demonstration of the ingenuity of a newly-formed society in reusing elements of an old way of life in new fashions.[98]

Acknowledgements

I would like to thank the many people who have helped me in my work on the thesis on which this article is based. In particular, the Keepers of the Anglo-Saxon collections at the British Museum, Ashmolean, Liverpool Museum, Cambridge Museum of Archaeology and Anthropology who are, respectively, L. Webster, D. Brown, E. Southworth and M. Cra'ster. In addition, I would like to thank S.C. Hawkes for allowing me to study material from her excavations, G. Grainger for information on Ozingell, D. Miles for access to the unpublished site of Berinsfield and K. Annable for information on Pewsey. C. Scull provided details on objects from Watchfield and G. Kinsley information on finds from Willoughby on the Wolds. I am particularly grateful for these contributions although I would stress that the interpretation of their data is my own. I would also like to thank all those who agreed to the reuse of illustrations from their own work. All such sources are acknowledged on the illustrations.

Notes

1. Brown 1915, 51.
2. Faussett 1856, 192–3.
3. Douglas 1793, 96–7.
4. Leeds 1936, 3; 1945, 44–9.
5. Harden 1956, 134–7.
6. Kent 1961, 18–22.
7. Hawkes and Dunning 1961, 9–10, 40–1.
8. Evison 1965, 27–8.
9. Dickinson 1982, 54 n.94.
10. Brown 1977; Myres 1978.
11. Dickinson 1976, 237–43, especially 240.
12. Meaney 1981.
13. Douglas 1793.
14. Celtic is used throughout to denote areas outside the control of the pagan Anglo-Saxon kingdoms, however hazy that distinction might be. It also covers pre-Roman Iron Age and Roman Iron Age objects.
15. Fowler 1960 and 1964.
16. Fowler 1964, 114–6; 1983, 19.
17. Mackreth 1982a m/f 2, B07.
18. Simpson 1979, 329–30; Tuitjer 1986, 121–2, type 2.
19. Fowler 1983, 19.
20. e.g. Rhenen 818; Böhme 1974, 268 *Taf.* 59, 1–11.
21. Tuitjer 1986.
22. Information K. Annable, class D and E brooches.
23. Mackreth 1982b, 144–5 no. 162 Figure 37.
24. Girton: Hollingworth and O'Reilly 1925 18 Plate 3; Nassington: Leeds and Atkinson 1944, 112 Plate 23 b, c.
25. Welch 1983, 65–7.
26. For a discussion of this class, see Dickinson 1982, passim.
27. Eagles 1986, 113, 115 Figure 13; 14 no. 120–2.
28. Cook 1978, 232–3; Mackreth 1982a m/f 2, B06.
29. For a full catalogue, see White 1988, 20–21.
30. Fowler 1964, 141; Dickinson 1982, 50 n. 80.
31. A full listing is given in White 1988, 33–35.

32. Dunstable 54: Dunning and Wheeler 1931, 202 Figure 5; Portway Down: Cook 1985, 95.

33. Linton Heath B, grave 2, 28, 43 and 100 (Neville 1854, 96, 102, 105 and 113); Little Wilbraham 11 (Neville 1852, 14).

34. Dickinson 1979, 40–1; 48–53.

35. Mackreth 1984, 36–7.

36. Wedlake 1982, 148 Figure 23, 5.

37. O'Kelly 1982, 74–5 Plate 27.

38. Welch 1983, 56–7.

39. White 1988, 26–30.

40. Gingell 1978, 78–9.

41. Faussett 1856, 28–9.

42. Vierck 1978, 248–251.

43. Faussett 1856, 23–4.

44. Faussett 1856, 24.

45. Ager 1985, 6–16.

46. Disc brooches from Faversham and Higham, Kent (Hawkes 1961, 33– 5 Figure 21 6 and 7); Penannular brooches from Alfriston 43, E. Sussex (Welch 1983, 64–5), Horton Kirby II, 22, Kent (Evison 1965, 116) and Lyminge II, 10, Kent (Hawkes 1961, 39).

47. Ager 1985, 3.

48. Bullinger 1969, passim; Böhme 1974, 79–89.

49. e.g. Clarke 1979, 286–8; Evison 1981, 129. For the classification, see White 1988, 46–48.

50. Clarke 1979, 273–6.

51. ibid., 276.

52. Hawkes 1974, 393.

53. Clarke 1979, 276–7.

54. Hawkes and Dunning 1961, 57–9.

55. Clarke 1979, 270. The Anglo-Saxon example is from Sleaford, Lincs. (Hawkes and Dunning 1961, Figure 19, a).

56. Evison 1968.

57. Cunliffe 1968, Plate XXXV, 104.

58. Clarke 1979, 278–284.

59. Welch 1983, 507 and 351.

60. Kirk and Leeds 1953, 65–7; Hawkes and Dunning 1961, 4–5; Evison 1981, 139; Kennett 1983, 88–90.

61. Kirk and Leeds 1953, 67–9; Evison 1981, 138–9.

62. Evison 1968, Figure 4, i; Hawkes and Dunning 1961, Figure 18, 1.

63. B. Ager, pers. comm.

64. Welch 1983, 469 and 352.

65. Reece 1972.

66. Neal 1974, Figure 52.

67. Akerman 1860, 86; S.C. Hawkes, pers. comm.

68. Grave group published in Evison 1967, 85–6. This article was written before the publication of the Dover Buckland cemetery in 1987.

69. Smith 1853, Plate IV.

70. Meaney 1981, 220.

71. The burial with a coin in the mouth is Broadstairs, Bradstow School, Kent, grave 71. The coin was a Merovingian tremissis which suggests that the burial was heavily influenced by Frankish customs; see White 1988 157–158. I am indebted to L. Webster for this information. For coins in the hand, the best example is Sleaford 85, Lincs. (Thomas 1887, 393).

72. Akerman 1853, 263–4.

73. Leeds and Riley 1942 66–7; Van Es 1967, 126 Figure 3.

74. Guido 1978 66–7.

75. Smith 1853, 5.

76. Welch 1983, Plate VI.

77. Arnold 1982, 22. S.C. Hawkes, pers. comm.

78. Cremations N6, N72, P43, P48, Y4. (Myres and Green 1973, 149, 163, 177–8, 198).
79. Jessup 1946, 19 Plate 4, 2.
80. Kennett 1971, 137 no. 9 Figure 14; Dover and Higham vessels White 1988, 119–120; Cliffe-at-Hoo (Smith 1880, 562).
81. Dickinson 1976, 364.
82. BM MLA; Evison 1978, Figure 2, j.
83. Akerman 1860, Plate XVII. The Strood Horn Mount is in Liverpool Museum (M.6399).
84. Horne 1934, 48–9, Plate VI.
85. Faussett 1856, 77–9.
86. Arnold 1982, 19; Welch 1983, 462 and 366.
87. Harden 1956, 158 and 170.
88. Evison 1982, 45–6.
89. Jackson 1892, 117–8. For a full catalogue, see White 1988, 137–141.
90. Ashmolean M.; White 1988, Figure 80.6.
91. Lethbridge and Carter 1928, 102.
92. Meaney 1981, 61.
93. Foster 1883, Plate V, 5.
94. Neville 1854, 96–8.
95. For a full discussion, see White 1988, 159–160, Figure 98. There are 289 coins from West Stow (Curnow 1985, 76–81).
96. White 1988, Appendix 2, 233–234.
97. Lethbridge 1956, 113–4.
98. The author would here like to correct a mistake in White, 1988. On p. 161 and 164, reference is made to brooches found in graves at Pagans Hill, Somerset. L. Watts, who reported these finds to the author, has asked him to correct the site name to Henley Wood. No burials were found at Pagans Hill. The author apologises to her for the confusion between the sites; the fault is entirely his own.

Bibliography

Ager, B. 1985: "The smaller variants of the Anglo-Saxon Quoit brooch" in *Anglo-Saxon Studies in Archaeology & History 4*, Hawkes, S.C., Brown, D. and Campbell, J. (eds.), 1985, 1–58.

Ahrens, K. (ed.) 1978: *Sachsen und Anglesachsen*. Exhibition Catalogue, Hamburg.

Akerman, J.Y. 1853: "An account of Excavations in an Anglo-Saxon Burial Ground at Harnham Hill, near Salisbury." *Archaeologia 35*, 259–278.

Akerman, J.Y. 1860: "Second Report of Researches in a cemetery of the Anglo-Saxon period at Brighthampton, Oxon." *Archaeologia 38*, 84–97.

Arnold, C.J. 1982: *The Anglo-Saxon cemeteries of the Isle of Wight.* London.

Böhme, H.W. 1974: *Germanische Grabfunde des 4 bis 5 Jahrhunderts.* Munchner Beitrage Vor-und Fruhgeschichte 19, Munchen.

Brown, B. 1915: *The Arts in Early England, Vols III & IV: Saxon Art and Industry in the pagan period.* London.

Brown, P.D.C. 1977: "The significance of the Londesborough Ring Brooch." *Antiquaries Journal 57*, 95–97.

Bullinger, H. 1969: *Spatantike Gurtelbeschlage. Typen, Herstellung, Trageweise und Datierung.* Diss. Arch. gand. XII Bruges.

Clarke, G. 1979: *The Roman cemetery at Lankhills.* Winchester Studies. 3. II: Pre-Roman and Roman Winchester. Oxford.

Cook, A.M. 1978: "Catalogue of Anglo-Saxon material and discussion." In Jackson, D.A. and Ambrose, T.M., 1978, 228–234.

Cook, A.M. 1985: "The Anglo-Saxon Cemetery." In Cook, A.M. and Dacre, M.W., 1985, 22–113.

Cook, A.M. and Dacre, M.W. 1985: *Excavations at Portway, Andover, 1973–1975.* Oxford University Committee for Archaeology Monograph. 4 Oxford.

Crummy, N. 1983: *The Roman small finds from excavations in Colchester 1971–9*. Colchester Archaeological Report 2. Colchester.

Cunliffe, B.M. 1968: *Fifth Report on the Excavations of the Roman Fort at Richborough, Kent*. Report of the Research Committee of the Society of Antiquaries London XXIII. Oxford.

Curnow, P.E. 1985: "The Roman Coins." In West, S., 1985, 76–81.

Dickinson, T.M. 1976: *The Anglo-Saxon burial sites of the Upper Thames Region, and their bearing on the History of Wessex c. A.D. 400–700*. Unpublished D.Phil thesis, University of Oxford.

Dickinson, T.M. 1979: "On the origin and chronology of the Early Anglo-Saxon disc brooch." in *Anglo-Saxon Studies in Archaeology and History 1*, Hawkes, S.C., Brown, D. and Campbell, J. (eds.), 1979, 39–80.

Dickinson, T.M. 1982: "Fowler's Type G Penannular brooches Reconsidered." *Medieval Archaeology 26*, 41–68.

Dolley, R.H.M. (ed.) 1961 *Anglo-Saxon coins. Studies presented to F.M. Stenton*. Oxford.

Douglas, Revd J. 1793: *Nenia Britannia: or A sepulchral history of Great Britain from the earliest period to its general conversion to Christianity*. London.

Dunning, G.C. and Wheeler, R.E.M. 1931: "A barrow at Dunstable, Beds." *Archaeological Journal 88*, 193–218.

Eagles, B.N. 1986: "Pagan Anglo-Saxon burials at West Overton." *Wiltshire Archaeological Monograph 80*, 103–120.

van Es, W.A. 1967: "Late Roman Pins from Xanten/Dodewaard and Asselt." *Berichten Rijksdienst voor het Oudheidkundig Bodemonderzoek 17*, 121–128.

Evison, V.I. 1965: *The Fifth Century Invasions south of the Thames*. London.

Evison, V.I. 1967: "The Dover Ring Sword and other sword rings and beads." *Archaeologia 101*, 63–118.

Evison, V.I. 1968: "Quoit Brooch Style buckles." *Antiquaries Journal 48*, 231–246.

Evison, V.I. 1979: *Wheel-thrown pottery in Anglo-Saxon graves*. Royal Archaeological Institute Monograph, London.

Evison, V.I.(ed.) 1981: *Angles, Saxons and Jutes. Essays presented to J.N.L. Myres*. Oxford.

Evison, V.I. 1981: "Distribution maps and England in the first two phases." in Evison, V.I. (ed.), 1981, 126–167.

Evison, V.I. 1982: "Anglo-Saxon glass claw beakers." *Archaeologia 107*, 43–76.

Faussett, B. 1856: *Inventorium sepulchrale. An account of some antiquities dug up at Gilton, Kingston, Sibertswold, Barfriston, Beakesbourne, Chartham and Crundale in the county of Kent*. Smith, C.R. (ed.) London.

Foster, W.K. 1883: "Account of the excavation of an Anglo-Saxon cemetery at Barrington, Cambridgeshire." *Cambridge Antiquarian Society 5*, 5–32.

Fowler, E. 1960: "The origins and development of the Penannular brooch in Europe." *Proceedings of the Prehistoric Society 26*, 149–177.

Fowler, E. 1964: "Celtic metalwork of the Fifth and Sixth centuries A.D.: A reappraisal." *Archaeological Journal 120*, 98–160.

Fowler, E. 1983: note in Crummy, N., 1983, 18–19.

Gingell, C.J. 1978: "The excavation of an Early Anglo-Saxon cemetery at Collingbourne Ducis." *Wiltshire Archaeological Monograph 70–71 (1975–6)*, 61–98.

Guido, M. 1978: "The beads." In Gingell, C.J., 1978, 66–7.

Harden, D.B.(ed.) 1956: *Dark Age Britain. Studies presented to E.T. Leeds*. Oxford.

Harden, D.B. 1956: "Glass Vessels in Britain and Ireland A.D. 400–1000" in Harden, D.B.(ed.), 1956, 132–167.

Hawkes, S.C. 1961: "The Jutish Style A. A study of Germanic Animal Art in Southern England in the fifth century A.D." *Archaeologia 98*, 29–74.

Hawkes, S.C. 1974: "Some recent finds of Late Roman buckles." *Britannia 5*, 386–393.

Hawkes, S.C., Brown, D. and Campbell, J. 1979: *Anglo-Saxon Studies in History and Archaeology 1*. B.A.R. 72.

Hawkes, S.C., *eadem* 1985: *Anglo-Saxon Studies in History and Archaeology 4*. Oxford.

Hawkes, S.C., and Dunning, G.C. 1961: "Soldiers and Settlers in Britain in the fourth to fifth century: with a catalogue of animal-ornamented buckles and related belt fittings." *Medieval Archaeology 5*, 1–70.

Hills, C., Penn, K. and Rickett, R. 1984: *The Anglo-Saxon cemetery at Spong Hill, North Elmham. Part 3 Catalogue of inhumations.* East Anglian Archaeology 21.

Hollingworth, E.J. and O'Reilly, M.M. 1925: *The Anglo-Saxon cemetery at Girton College, Cambridge.* Cambridge.

Horne, Revd P. 1934: "Anglo-Saxon cemetery at Camerton, Somerset pt. II." *Proceedings of the Somerset Archaeology and Natural History Society* 79 (1933) 39–63.

Jackson, C. J. 1892: "The spoon and its history; its form, material, and development, more particularly in England." *Archaeologia* 53, 107–146.

Jackson, D.A. and Ambrose, T.M. 1978: "Excavations at Wakerley, Northants., 1972–75." *Britannia* 9, 115–242.

Jessup, R.F. 1946: "An Anglo-Saxon cemetery at Westbere, Kent." *Antiquaries Journal* 26, 11–21.

Kennett, D.H. 1971: "Late Roman bronze vessel hoards in Britain." *J.R.G.Z.M.* 16 (1969), 123–146.

Kennett, D.H. 1983: "The earliest male grave at Kempston." *Bedfordshire Archaeological Journal* 16, 88–91.

Kent, J.P.C. 1961: "From Roman Britain to Saxon England." in Dolley, R.H.M. (ed.), 1961, 1–22.

Kirk, J.R. and Leeds, E.T. 1953: "Three early Saxon graves from Dorchester, Oxon." *Oxoniensia* 18, 63–76.

Leeds, E.T. 1936: *Early Anglo-Saxon Archaeology.* Oxford.

Leeds, E.T. 1945: "The Distribution of the Angles and Saxons Archaeologically Considered." *Archaeologia* 91, 1–106.

Leeds, E.T. and Atkinson, R.J.C. 1944: "An Anglo-Saxon cemetery at Nassington, Northants." *Antiquaries Journal* 24, 100–124.

Leeds, E.T. and Riley, M. 1942: "Two early Saxon cemeteries at Cassington, Oxon." *Oxoniensia* 7, 62–70.

Lethbridge, T.C. 1956: "The Anglo-Saxon Settlement in Eastern England: a reassessment." in Harden, D.B. (ed.), 1956, 112–122.

Lethbridge, T.C. and Carter, H.G. 1928: "Excavations in the Anglo-Saxon cemetery at Little Wilbraham." *Cambridge Antiquarian Society* 29, 95–104.

Mackreth, D.F. 1982a: "The Brooches." in McWhirr, A., Viner, L. and Wells, C., 1982, m/f A13–B07.

Mackreth, D.F. 1982b: "The Brooches" in Webster, G. and Smith, L., 1982, 140–145.

Mackreth, D.F. 1984: "The Romano-British brooch 26/6." in Hill, C., Penn, K. and Rickett, R., 1984, 36–37.

McWhirr, A., Viner, L. and Wells, C. 1982: *Cirencester Excavations II. Romano-British cemeteries at Cirencester.* Gloucester.

Meaney, A. 1981: *Anglo-Saxon Amulets and Curing Stones.* B.A.R. 96 Oxford.

Myres, J.N.L. 1978: "Amulets or Small Change." *Antiquaries Journal* 58, 352.

Myres, J.N.L. and Green, B. 1973: *The Anglo-Saxon cemeteries of Caistor by Norwich and Markshall, Norfolk.* Report Research Committee of the Society of Antiquaries, London. XXX. Oxford.

Neal, D.S. 1974: *The Excavation of the Roman Villa in Gadebridge Park, Hemel Hempstead 1963–8.* Report Research Committee of the Society of Antiquaries London. XXXI. Oxford.

Neville, R.C. 1852: *Saxon Obsequies illustrated by ornaments and weapons discovered . . . in a cemetery near Little Wilbraham, Cambridgeshire.* London.

Neville, R.C. 1854: "Anglo-Saxon cemetery excavated January 1853." *Archaeological Journal* 11, 95–115.

O'Kelly, M.J. 1982: *Newgrange: Archaeology, Art and Legend.* London.

Reece, R. 1972: "A short survey of the Roman Imperial Coins found on Fourteen Sites in Britain." *Britannia* 2, 269–276.

Simpson, G. 1979: "Some British and Iberian Penannular brooches and other early types in the Rhineland and the *Decumates Agri.*" *Antiquaries Journal* 59, 319–342.

Smith, C.R. 1853: *Collectanea Antiqua vol. 2.* London.

Smith, C.R. 1880: "A Saxon Cemetery at Cliffe." *Archaeologia Cantiana* 13, 562.

Thomas, G.N. 1887: "On excavations in an Anglo-Saxon cemetery at Sleaford in Lincolnshire." *Archaeologia* 50, 383–406.

Thompson, F.H. 1956: "Anglo-Saxon sites in Leicestershire: unpublished material and recent discoveries." *Antiquaries Journal* 36, 181–199.

Tuitjer, H.G. 1986: "Iron Age Penannular brooches from Northern Germany." *Antiquaries Journal* 66, 121–124.

Vierck, H. 1978: "Die Anglische Frauentracht." in Ahrens, K. (ed.) 245–253.

Webster, G. and Smith, L. 1982: "The excavation of a Romano-British Rural Establishment at Barnsley Park, Gloucestershire, 1961–70. Part II c. AD 360–400." *Transactions of the Bristol and Gloucester Archaeological Society* 100, 65–189.

Wedlake, B.J. 1982: *The Excavations of the shrine of Apollo at Nettleton, Wiltshire.* Report Research Committee of the Society Antiquaries London XL. Oxford.

Welch, M.G. 1983: *Early Anglo-Saxon Sussex.* B.A.R. 112 Oxford.

West, S.E. 1985: *West Stow, the Anglo-Saxon village.* East Anglian Archaeology 24. Hadleigh, Suffolk.

White, R.H. 1988: *Roman and Celtic objects from Anglo-Saxon graves: a catalogue and an interpretation of their use.* B.A.R. 191 Oxford.

CHAPTER EIGHT

THE ALTERNATIVE QUOIT BROOCH: AN UPDATE

Barry Ager

I n the present author's recent catalogue, details were given of forty-four examples of the smaller type of quoit brooch (Ager 1985); of new discoveries four more were mentioned in postscript. Publication of the quoit brooch from Charlton Plantation, Wiltshire, burial 12 (Davies 1984, figure 15) now shows that it was as well to speak of a catalogue and not of a corpus. It is unfortunate that this brooch is from a salvaged grave, but we must be grateful for it nevertheless.

The use of the term 'quoit brooch' has varied in the past, so an attempt has been made in the catalogue to define it, in agreement with general usage, as an annular brooch with a broad band and some form of 'notch-and-stops' fastening – as on the well-known brooch from Sarre, Kent (Hawkes 1961, plate 14; Ager 1985, figure 14a, title transposed to b) – the feature which distinguishes the quoit brooch from the mass of Anglo-Saxon annular brooches. In order to fasten the brooch, the pin is pushed through the fabric of the clothing, then passed up through the notch and placed to the outside of one of the stops, where it is held in place by the drag of the fabric. In this respect, quoit brooches are similar to penannular brooches.

The finely decorated quoit brooches from Sarre and Howletts are well documented and need no repetition (Leeds 1936, plates 2a, c and 3a; Hawkes 1961, plates 14 and 15a–b; Evison 1965, plates 10c, 11b, 12c). The aim of the catalogue, therefore, was to bring together the smaller and less elaborately decorated variants, occasionally mentioned in footnotes, but not previously given much coverage, although they make up some nine-tenths of the total of the class as a whole.

The smaller brooches have been divided into four main types, D1–D4, and given the prefix 'D' in order to relate them to the typological classification suggested by Leeds in his celebrated 1945 monograph (Leeds 1945, 46–49). Type D1 has riveted stops, on D2 they are folded up, on D3 cast (either in one piece with the band or soldered on), and on D4 they are rolled back; the numbers are the author's own addition.

The brooch from Charlton Plantation is an example of type D1, of which seventeen others are known. The ornament is simple and includes a ring of punched half-masks on the inner border, which connect the brooch with objects decorated in what is now generally known as the Quoit Brooch Style. Very similar punches can be seen on the inner border of the buckle-plate from Mucking, Essex, grave 117 (Evison 1968, plate 53 top left) and opposite the pin-slot of the penannular brooch from Alfriston, East Sussex, grave 43 (Hawkes 1961, plate 17e), both of the fifth century. This punch design does not appear on objects decorated in Salin's Style I and can therefore probably be taken as an indicator of a fifth-century date for the Charlton brooch. The decoration of many of the D1 brooches connects them more or less closely with the Quoit Brooch Style (Ager op. cit., 9–10). The decoration of the later types D2–D4 has no demonstrable connection with the Quoit Brooch Style.

It is interesting to note a non-matching pair of type D2 from Abingdon, now in Oxfordshire, grave B85 (Ager op. cit., figure 23c–d). Where grave contexts have been recorded, half the total of the smaller quoit brooches were worn in identical pairs and almost another fifteen per cent in non-matching pairs. On the other hand, the larger examples of the Sarre and Howletts types B and C were all worn singly. Comparison can be drawn here with square-headed brooches where the large or 'great' form was worn singly and the smaller versions in pairs, while Leeds's 'great' form can be seen as superseding the larger types of quoit brooch (at the same time as their ornamental Style I supplanted the Quoit Brooch Style). The wearing of brooches in identical pairs tends to be regarded as the Anglo-Saxon norm; in fact there was considerable variation in practice. To take button brooches as another example, almost a third were worn in identical pairs, but the rest in some other combination (Avent and Evison 1982, table 2). Similarly type D quoit brooches could be paired with another brooch type altogether, e.g. the D1 brooch with an equal-arm brooch from Mucking grave 637 (Ager op. cit., figure 26g–h). The manner in which quoit brooches were worn therefore conforms with Anglo-Saxon practice, not with the Frankish or sub-Roman as is sometimes suggested.

The distribution patterns of the various types are noted in the author's catalogue. In addition to the French connection, illustrated by the B and D1 brooches from Bénouville, Normandy and Herpes, Charente, there is a small but increasing corpus of metalwork connected with the Quoit Brooch Style found in France – not in the Frankish heartland, but in areas settled to some degree by Anglo-Saxons, as shown both by place-names (Morris 1973, map on p. 289) and by archaeological evidence, as at Vron and Frénouville, the latter of which appears to bear out Gregory of Tours' mention of Saxons settled around Bayeux (History of the Franks, 10,9). Apart from the quoit brooches mentioned, this corpus includes a buckle from Amiens and a D-sectioned tubular belt-fitting from Réville (Evison 1981, 133–4) as well as another tubular fitting (but undecorated) from Herpes (Brit. Mus. reg. MLA 1905, 5–20, 783). The type E broad-band annular brooch from Hoogebeintum, Holland must be Frisian (Karras 1985, 167–8), though is based on the Anglo-Saxon type.

The quoit brooch from Bénouville (Plate 1) is rather corroded, but the remains of slots around the inner edge relate it to the Sarre and fragmentary Howletts brooches of type B. The decoration, however, is incised, not chip-carved. The grave associations suggest that it is from a male burial, but it is perhaps an heirloom piece.[1]

Since the 'notch-and-stops' fastening of the quoit brooches appears on a number of

PLATE 1 'BRONZE' QUOIT BROOCH from Bénouville, Normandy (Scale approx. 5:4)

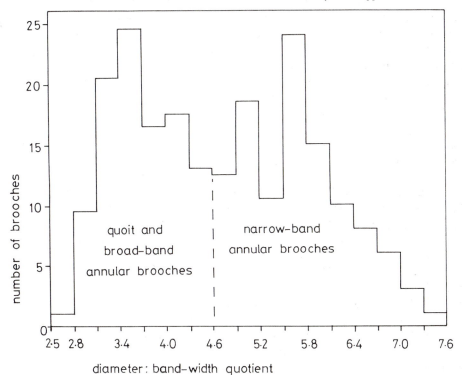

FIGURE 1   HISTOGRAM of diameter: band-width quotients of Anglo-Saxon quoit and annular brooches

annular brooches too, an attempt has been made to distinguish them according to the relative width of their bands; otherwise the term 'quoit brooch' has no real meaning as it is nothing more than a special form of the latter. The diameter of quoit and annular brooches was divided by the band width to give a numerical quotient and it was suggested that a division between the two could be drawn at about 4.5. A more recent check on a much larger number of annular brooches has been carried out (119 against 92 quoit and broad-band annulars combined) and the results tabulated in histogram form (Figure 1). This reveals a two or possibly three-humped distribution with no concrete division between broad and narrow forms, though a trough still in the region of 4.5 shows that this figure provides a working basis for a definition.

The notch-and-stops fastening has been derived from a type of ring-brooch known in *Germania libera* from the late third century onwards, an example of which has been found at Londesborough grave 7, Yorkshire. Tania Dickinson has suggested that it might have been made in Britain (1982, 56), but its unfinished state does not prove the case, while its ring-and-dot decoration and dotted terminals can both be found on Continental examples (Roes 1965, plate 15a–b), so that we need not link it with insular penannular brooches of Fowler's type G. A possibly late- or sub-Roman example from the Thames at Kempsford is also noted by Dickinson (ibid., 54–7), but as it is a river-find from outside the distribution area of the early forms of quoit brooch, its relevance to the discussion of the origins of the latter is uncertain.

Leeds sought to derive the quoit, and indeed all forms of annular brooch from the penannular class, which he regarded as purely native. But this results from his fundamental misunderstanding of the construction of the Sarre brooch, which he described as a combination of the flat annular form with a cast penannular ring that was 'attached by its finials and two subsidiary struts at various points of the inner circumference of the main ring' (Leeds 1945, 46). From this description it is clear that either he had never looked at the back of the brooch, or, if he did, he failed to see how it was made. The penannular collar is in fact purely decorative and non-functional; it is not attached to the 'struts' but to the inner edge of the band left by the three slots cut in it, and can be entirely dispensed with, as on the Bénouville brooch. Even if there were influence from penannular brooches, it can now be demonstrated that those of Fowler's type C from Anglo-Saxon graves are derived from Germanic forms, so there is no need to invoke native influence. The broad annular form (and the narrow too) is best compared with north German and Scandinavian types. Building on his mistake, Leeds sought to make a special type of the more elaborately decorated and larger quoit brooches and identify them as pre-dating Anglo-Saxon settlements. While he rightly criticized the hypothesis of a 'golden age of Arthur' put forward by Sir Thomas Kendrick, who had claimed to detect a native British style in the manufacture of Kentish disc brooches, Leeds himself adopted exactly the same illogical method of slicing off a group of objects from assured Anglo-Saxon contexts and then treating them as unusual in an illusory isolation of his own making. Yet, from that day to this, neither a quoit brooch (large or small, elaborate or not so remarkable), nor any object decorated in the Quoit Brooch Style, has been found in either a late- or sub-Roman or central Frankish context — although, as we have seen, both are found outside England in areas known to have been settled by the Anglo-Saxons, on a limited scale, in France.

Leeds's further suggestion, that the plain annular brooch was 'evidence of the need of women-folk, seized like the Sabine women, from among the natives of the invaded areas' is quite fantastic. But the parallel between the founding of the Roman Empire and what might be seen as the very beginnings of the recent British one is revealing in an article written just a year before the outbreak of war against modern-day, would-be emperors. Although Leeds himself recognized the many affinities of the Quoit Brooch Style to Germanic styles, it would hardly have been politic to lay too much stress on this in the late 1930s and his interpretation of fifth-century events may well have been coloured by those of the twentieth.

Leaving aside the ethnic question of who wore these objects (which cannot by themselves tell us anything definite about the origin of their wearer; cf. Roger White's paper in this volume), it is possible to argue that the form of the quoit and annular brooches is demonstrably Germanic in origin. A similar cultural background has been claimed for the Quoit Brooch Style, as an Anglo-Saxon imitation of late-Roman designs.

For example, the copper alloy belt-plate from Faversham, Kent (Plate 2),[2] which can now be identified as being decorated in the geometric version of the Quoit Brooch Style described by Professor Evison (1965, 62–66), derives its form and elements of decoration from those of the late provincial-Roman belt-plates, cf. the plate with the saltire ornament from St Julien, France, grave 9 (Böhner 1980, 132, no. 183b). The

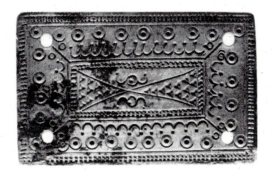

PLATE 2, A–B DOUBLE-SIDED 'BRONZE' BELT-PLATE from King's Field, Faversham, Kent. Side (b) was decorated first (Scale 3:2)

punches include the diagonal rows of minute base to apex triangles and pellet-in-triangles noted by Evison, the triple-dotted plant-like motif and 'winged' ring-and-dot of the Mucking 117 buckle and the triple-dotted arcs of quoit brooches of type D1 from Abingdon and Highdown. But, although these and others on the plate can be derived from late-Roman Continental metalwork, they are not always identical. The 'plant' appears on a strapend from Tongern, Belgium (Böhme 1974, Taf. 106, 11), except that the Roman craftsman has used double semicircles instead of single ones, while 'winged' ring-and-dots belong only to the quoit brooch school.

A preliminary tabulation of Continental and Anglo-Saxon metalwork punch designs is not intended to be all inclusive or particularly systematic (Ager 1985, figure 15), but serves to show how many are of late-Roman origin and that a number besides are Germanic innovations. Some, as we have just seen, are particularly associated with the Quoit Brooch Style; others appear only later, together with Style I. Some, therefore, seem to have a value as chronological indicators. The subject would repay further investigation, always bearing in mind the obstacles to identifying punches caused by variations in depth and angle that have been discussed by David Leigh (this volume). The differing lengths of the arcs on the front of the Faversham plate – all likely to have been produced with the same punch – further illustrate the problem.

The Mucking 117 belt-suite too is clearly based on late-Roman military belt equipment, but details of its ornament and construction show that it is distinct (Evison 1968, 231–4). There is no strong evidence to support suggestions that it formed part of equipment issued by native British authorities to Germanic mercenaries or *foederati*. It is from an Anglo-Saxon grave and it is accordingly proposed here that it is an Anglo-Saxon imitation of a provincial-Roman Continental form. Whether the owner was an official federate or not, we cannot be certain, although it still does not seem improbable.

There is clear evidence that Germanic craftsmen did produce copies of Roman belt equipment in other regions, e.g. the imitations of amphora strapends produced in the Elbe area (Böhme 1974, Karte 18). The map also shows that Roman belt fittings were widely available for copying, and no doubt they were thought fashionable, as items of militaria often still are today, without meaning that the wearer held an official rank. From another area, Böhme suggests that his Ehrenburg-Jamoigne type of buckle (ibid., Karte 14) represents an Alamannic imitation.

In connection with the Quoit Brooch Style, an inscribed copper alloy disc engraved with legionaries, animals and birds now in the Bibliothèque Nationale in Paris (Myres 1986, figure 11) has been given prominence on more than one occasion.[3] However, it is quite wrong to say that it is probably from France, as has been stated recently. All that we know for certain is that at the end of the seventeenth century it was in Italy in the collection of the Cardinal of Carpegna; it was first published in Rome and not in France (Buonarroti 1698, 17–19, plate 38). The animals have very little affinity with those of the Quoit Brooch Style – some even have four legs! They are also running free and not in the set poses employed by the style. Furthermore, Roman scholars are inclined to place the disc in the third century, which is far too early to have any bearing on the style.

Closer to home, comparison is made in the latest Sutton Hoo volume (Bruce-Mitford 1983, 278, figure 213a) between the moulded bird figures of the Sarre quoit brooch and the model creature riveted to the centre of an enamelled Roman disc brooch of unknown provenance, but possibly from Britain. However, the creature's dorsal fin, snub nose and leaping posture, which all become evident in a side-on view, confirm that it is in fact a dolphin, as described by Brailsford (1964, 20, figure 12, 38) and Thomas (1966, 134–7, Abb. 5, 2). Similar brooches from the Continent are dated from the late second to the early third century, but an example from Hammoor burial 15, from an urn of Plettke's form C of the fourth or fifth century, shows that the Anglo-Saxons could have been familiar with the idea of riveting model creatures to jewellery before ever they migrated to England. Like the legionary disc, the dolphin brooch must be rejected as evidence for a native British origin for the Quoit Brooch Style.

It has often been said that the confronted pairs of parcel-gilt animals of the Sarre brooch have no obvious connection with the later Style I – as if those of the Nydam or Equal-Arm Brooch Styles are any closer. It is not an argument of any great weight against a Germanic origin. In fact, as Sonia Hawkes has shown in her 'Jutish Style A', it could be argued that the Quoit Brooch Style has closer links in some respects with Style I than do other northern Germanic styles. Haseloff remarks that the absence of sea-creatures distinguishes the Continental Style I from its predecessors, but in England they do occur in Style I, as well as in the antecedent Quoit Brooch Style. The pair of interlaced Style II animals on the gold sword pommel from Crundale, Kent (Speake 1980, plate 14b) shows an advanced stage in the long period of development of the Sarre motif.

The connections between the Quoit Brooch Style and approximately contemporary fifth-century Scandinavian metalwork are often remarkably close, as between the pieces from Sarre, Howletts and Bifrons and the brooches from Sejlflod, Denmark and Hol, Norway, although allowance must be made for the possibility of parallel development from a common source. But a hitherto unnoticed link can be seen in the dotted lozenge pattern of the strapend from Chessell Down, Isle of Wight, grave 3 (Hawkes 1961, figure 2). Unconvincing attempts have been made to connect the pattern with the much more finely cross-hatched, undotted and non-inlaid lozenges of late-Romano-British buckleplates. A much closer comparison can, however, be drawn with the pattern on the neck of the bird at the top-left of the mid-fifth-century scabbard-chape from Nydam (Salin 1904, Abb. 491). As if to clinch this point, the scale-like pattern on the neck of the opposite bird on this chape can be seen on the unpublished fragment of a Quoit Brooch Style bracelet from East Shefford, Berkshire (Ager forthcoming).

Apart from the development of their form, that can be traced from the fifth into the early seventh century, the number of quoit brooches alone demonstrates that they are just as much to be considered as Anglo-Saxon as equal-arm or supporting-arm brooches. On the other hand, Quoit Brooch Style belt equipment is mainly restricted to the fifth century and does not therefore, at first sight, appear to be typically Saxon. But fashions and styles changed, sometimes quite dramatically, in the Early Saxon period – square-headed brooches and Style I are typical of the sixth century, but are unknown in the early to mid-fifth and later seventh; pin-suites and pendent crosses are in vogue in the seventh, but non-existent in the fifth. What is typical for one division of the period is, then, often unknown for another. The metalwork of the quoit brooch school can be justifiably regarded as typically Anglo-Saxon for the middle quarters of the fifth century.

In the past, scholars of the so-called Dark Ages appear to have been embarrassed by the lack of material evidence (particularly in the fifth and sixth centuries) for the survival of the native British population and, rather than come to terms with it, in some cases seem to have attempted to explain it away. Leeds never sought to explain how the Quoit Brooch Style, which he himself recognized was Continental in origin, came actually to be produced in this country rather than merely imported. Nor did he cite any evidence from a non-Saxon context in order to provide the essential missing link in his argument. Theories of Jutish and Frankish origins have considerably advanced the debate, but have not been fully accepted. The present author has therefore taken up Bakka's alternative suggestion that the style represents an Anglo-Saxon imitation of provincial-Roman style, a view which adequately accounts both for the importation of the elements of the style and for the apparent amalgamation of Gallic and northern Germanic features. It also fills the stylistic blank that otherwise exists between the first arrivals of the Anglo-Saxons, certainly in the first half of the fifth century, and the introduction of Style I, probably not long after *c.* 475, since neither the Nydam nor the Equal-Arm Brooch Styles seem to have taken root here. The closeness of the Quoit Brooch Style to the late Roman may well have made it quite acceptable to native taste and, if so, it is possible to see the lack of early material evidence for sub-Roman presence in Saxon-settled areas as a sign of cultural assimilation, which makes them almost undetectable in the archaeological record much before the seventh century.[4]

Notes

1. The author is extremely grateful to Dr M. Welch for his generous permission to use the plate of this brooch.
2. Brit. Mus. reg. no. MLA1156'70. It measures 43 x 27 x 1 mm and is very slightly bowed lengthwise. Only the front has been previously published (e.g. Smith 1923, figure 37), but not so as to show the pellets of the pellet-in-triangle punches between the arms of the central saltire.
3. The writer is most grateful to Mr M. Hassall for further information (*in lit.*) on this disc, including a reference to the Corpus Inscriptionum Latinarum vol. XV, no. 7164 and to the main publication by Cagnat (1895).
4. Although modern ethnographic parallels should be treated with caution, they do show that far-reaching cultural change can be a rapid process, if only outwardly. Twentieth-century Japan provides an obvious example.

The important article by Professor Böhme (1986) came too late for consideration at the conference but, in the author's view, the basic conclusions expressed above still stand. No attempt has been made to incorporate discoveries of Quoit Brooch Style objects reported after 1986.

Bibliography

Ager, B.M. 1985: "The smaller variants of the Anglo-Saxon quoit brooch", *Anglo-Saxon Studies in Archaeology and History*, 4, 1–58. Oxford.

Avent, R. and Evison, V.I. 1982: "Anglo-Saxon button brooches", *Archaeologia*, 107, 77–124.

Böhme, H.W. 1974: *Germanische Grabfunde des 4. bis 5. Jahrhunderts zwischen unterer Elbe und Loire.* Munich.

Böhme, H.W. 1986: "Das Ende der Römerherrschaft in Britannien und die angelsächsische Besiedlung Englands im 5. Jahrhundert", *Jahrbuch des Römisch-Germanischen Zentralmuseums Mainz*, 33, 469–574.

Böhner, K. et al. 1980: *Gallien in der Spätantike.* Römisch-Germanisches Zentralmuseum, Mainz.

Brailsford, J.W. (2nd ed.) 1964: *Guide to the Antiquities of Roman Britain.* British Museum.

Bruce-Mitford, R. 1983: *The Sutton Hoo Ship-Burial.* Vol. 3. British Museum.

Buonarroti, F. 1698: *Osservazioni istoriche sopra alcuni medaglioni antichi*. Rome.

Cagnat, R. 1895: "Note sur un disque en bronze du cabinet de France", *Revue Archéologique*, 3rd ser., 26, 213–220. Paris.

Davies, S.M. 1984: "The excavation of an Anglo-Saxon cemetery (and some prehistoric pits) at Charlton Plantation, near Downton", *Wiltshire Archaeological and Natural History Magazine*, 79, 109–154.

Dickinson, T.M. 1982: "Fowler's type G penannular brooches reconsidered", *Medieval Archaeology*, 26, 41–68.

Evison, V.I. 1965: *The Fifth-Century Invasions South of the Thames*. London.

Evison, V.I. 1968: "Quoit Brooch Style buckles", *Antiquaries Journal*, 48, 231–249.

Evison, V.I. 1981: "Distribution maps and England in the first two phases" in Evison, V.I. (Ed.), *Angles, Saxons and Jutes. Essays presented to J.N.L. Myres*, 126–167. Oxford.

Hawkes, S.C. 1961: "The Jutish Style A. A study of Germanic animal art in southern England in the fifth century A.D.", *Archaeologia*, 98, 29–74.

Karras, R.M. 1985: "Seventh-century jewellery from Frisia: a re-examination", *Anglo-Saxon Studies in Archaeology and History*, 4, 159–177. Oxford.

Leeds, E.T. 1936: *Early Anglo-Saxon Art and Archaeology*. Oxford.

Leeds, E.T. 1945: "The distribution of the Angles and Saxons archaeologically considered", *Archaeologia*, 91, 1–106.

Myres, J.N.L. 1986: *The English Settlements*. Oxford.

Roes, A. 1965: "Continental quoit-brooches", *Antiquaries Journal*, 45, 18–21.

Salin, B. 1904: *Die altgermanische Thierornamentik*. Stockholm.

Smith, R.A. 1923: *A Guide to the Anglo-Saxon and Foreign Teutonic Antiquities*. British Museum.

Speake, G. 1980: *Anglo-Saxon Animal Art and its Germanic Background*. Oxford.

Thomas, S. 1966: "Die provinzialrömischen Scheibenfibeln der römischen Kaiserzeit im freien Germanien", *Berliner Jahrbuch für Vor- und Frühgeschichte*, 6, 119–178.

CHAPTER NINE

THE ANGLO-SAXON CEMETERIES OF THE ISLE OF WIGHT: AN APPRAISAL OF NINETEENTH-CENTURY EXCAVATION DATA

Christoper Arnold

I n 1982 the British Museum published the first list of graves and their contents, as far as they were known, from the early Anglo-Saxon cemeteries of the Isle of Wight (Arnold 1982). The reasons for assembling the material were to make the evidence available to all students and to provide a full and secure database for research into subject areas which had not previously received systematic attention. The lists of graves were based on the surviving notes of the excavators, some of which had lain unseen by archaeologists for nearly one hundred and thirty years in the Isle of Wight Record Office. It had been assumed that such records did not exist and as a result a number of artefacts had been studied in isolation of their associations and contexts. Summaries of such studies were given with grave-lists so as to draw the entire body of knowledge and opinion concerning these nineteenth-century discoveries together.

Many of the archaeological studies relating to the early Anglo-Saxon period that have been published over the last thirty to forty years are either detailed examinations of regions or studies of particular artefact types. The regional studies serve to bring to wider attention specifically local sequences and changing patterns, but the potential links and differences between areas tend to be played down. Studies of specific artefact types serve to highlight the range of types which are shared over the greatest distance, but far less attention has been given to studying their contexts, to see possible subtle differences between sites and regions. The question of traditions running in parallel and the varying degrees to which clear regional groups can be discerned has hardly been tackled at a mature level.

There is no need here to reiterate the details of the Isle of Wight cemeteries, but it is appropriate to draw together a number of studies made before and after their publication. It is first necessary to highlight the shortcomings of the data and then to indicate what can be achieved with such evidence. Any research carried out on data recovered so long ago is bedevilled by a lack of information about the original extent of the cemeteries, their often small size (as excavated) which makes statistical analysis spurious, and the almost total lack of detail, or certainty as to its accuracy, about the graves and their occupants. Despite the quality of the data significant patterning can be found by the application of contemporary research techniques and traditional interpretations are at times found to be weak.

On the Isle of Wight there are, as yet, no known early Anglo-Saxon settlements. As a result any discussion of the cemeteries in relation to settlement patterns must be cautious and can easily be misled by the introduction of additional types of evidence, such as place-names (Arnold 1975). Nevertheless a number of observations can be offered about the distribution of the cemeteries which may, in turn, be constructive in understanding the overall settlement pattern and use of the island's landscape. Studies of the location of cemeteries and settlements in England during the sixth and seventh centuries have indicated a common pattern which may guide us when considering cemeteries in isolation (Welch 1985; Arnold 1988, 17ff). Excavated settlements are frequently located on adjacent ground to the cemeteries, in areas of light fertile soils at low altitudes close to water.

On the Isle of Wight we may divide the evidence into two parts. Firstly there are the cemeteries of Bowcombe, Rancombe, Arreton and Chillerton which are located immediately above steep-sided coombs, now often dry valleys (to this list might be added Carisbrooke Castle, where the excavation of early Anglo-Saxon graves by C. Young has been reported to the author by M. Welch). These comprise small isolated areas of sheltered, light, fertile soils which are located on the edges of the principal block of downland which forms the east-west spine of the island. We may note that in these cemeteries some or all of the burials are placed in prehistoric burial mounds. It may emphasise how some of the post-Roman occupants of the island may also have been following the bronze age strategy of farming the coombs and burying their dead on the downland above. It may however only be the ritual landscape that was being replicated, making use of existing burial structures for the sake of the economy, veneration or appeal to mythical or real ancestors.

Secondly there are cemeteries such as Chessell Down and Shalfleet which lie immediately adjacent to, or on, the larger tracts of equally fertile alluvium which border the downland. No cemeteries are known on or near the heavier clay soils which lie beyond the alluvium, nor are they found on the extremely propitious soils located on sections of the island's coastline.

There are, in addition, differences in the nature of the cemeteries associated with the two land-use models. The cemeteries adjacent to the coombs are considerably smaller in size than, for instance, Chessell Down. The size and longevity of the cemeteries, and perhaps their settlements, may be reflecting the carrying capacity of the adjacent blocks of arable land. A number of problems arise with such conclusions, particularly in relation to the reuse of prehistoric barrows. We might ask to what extent the known pattern of early Anglo-Saxon cemeteries reflects the research interests of nineteenth-century antiquaries in their pursuit of prehistoric barrows. The majority of the post-Roman cemeteries were discovered by accident while excavating prehistoric barrows. For an analysis of the settlement pattern based on cemeteries to be valid we have to ignore those cemeteries where the accidental discovery of one or a few Anglo-Saxon burials did not lead to more extensive investigations, thereby increasing the validity of the sample. If we adhere to that rule it can be said that the reuse of prehistoric burial mounds only occurs at heights greater than 350 ft and that the larger cemeteries occur at the lowest altitudes; the former observation is governed by the distribution of the prehistoric barrows, the latter is not, unless we argue that they deliberately avoided landscapes containing barrows.

It is possible to filter out the effects of the reuse of the prehistoric burial pattern and observe significant patterns in the relationship between location and mortuary ritual in the early Anglo-Saxon cemeteries. Nearly all of the possible permutations (Figure 1) of cremation, inhumation, under visible barrows as primary or secondary deposits, or in flat-grave cemeteries are to be found, although there are seemingly significant negative correlations. As we have seen flat-grave cemeteries are not found at the higher altitudes, nor are barrow burials of any type found at low altitudes. In some of the cemeteries primary Anglo-Saxon burials under barrows occur alongside secondary deposits in prehistoric mounds.

Here again there are many problems as the absence of visible burial mounds at any location may only be a reflection of the succeeding land-use pattern. Subsequent ploughing can easily have caused the destruction of smaller barrows especially on the more consistently cultivated low-lying arable land. The available evidence does suggest

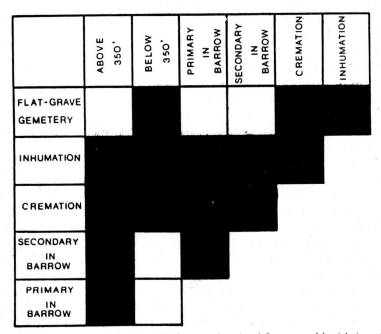

FIGURE 1   MATRIX showing the relationship between locational features and burial rites of early Anglo-Saxon cemeteries on the Isle of Wight

that more elaborate forms of burial, cremation and barrows, are found at higher altitudes in the smaller cemeteries (Figure 2). The dating of these downland cemeteries in which barrows are used is consistently late fifth and early sixth century. Such elaborate forms of burial occur again towards the end of the pagan period, at first as part or wholly barrow cemeteries, and later with rich barrow burials, although no examples of the latter are known on the Isle of Wight. It has been argued that elaborate and visible forms of burial occur at times of stress in society, although the nature of the stress during the periods of barrow building is unlikely to be the same. Stress may have been caused during the earliest phase by the effects of migration and initial settlement, by the turbulent political and economic state of affairs in the latter, when individuals were asserting their power roles. On the other hand, Shephard (1979) has suggested that isolated barrows of the early seventh century onwards, symbolized the stability of the social system through the emergence of paramount rank, and that the earlier barrow cemeteries reflect a system regulated by a higher degree of organization than the flat-grave cemeteries. Shephard did not, however, consider the earliest phase of barrow use represented on the Isle of Wight at, for instance, Bowcombe Down.

Just as any discussion of settlement/cemetery location can become a barren pursuit when there are many gaps in the data, the absence of whole categories of data from the cemeteries themselves both limits and controls the approaches that are made to the cemeteries. The grave-lists that were made available in 1982 perpetuate the domination of the grave-goods, as there is little or no reliable data regarding the graves themselves or of the physical anthropology of the occupants. This unfortunately encourages a materialistic approach to the study of cemeteries and robs us of the opportunities of

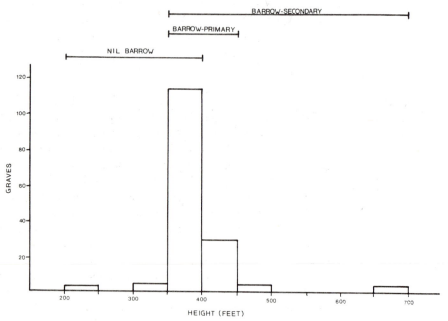

FIGURE 2   FREQUENCY DIAGRAM OF GRAVES within specified height ranges in relation to the use of barrow burial

using other categories of data, for instance the structure of the graves or the health/diet of the occupant as means of seeking ranking in the cemeteries independently of the grave-goods. Similarly the available data would be of little use to the types of research which are geared to seeking significant correlations in all possible factors.

The potential reliability of such grave lists and grave-goods inevitably draws the student to the grave-goods and far greater attention has been paid to those graves with a greater volume of artefacts. Many of these grave-groups, or more often individual objects from them, have been discussed at great length. But there are many other graves which, either because of the unusual nature of the grave-goods, or because of the near total absence of them, are hardly touched by traditional methods of research. They are however included in synthetic approaches to grave-goods in the search for order, ranking and types of research which seek a wide variety of potentially significant correlations. For example, drawing at random from the available details we may think of Chessell Down grave 78, with its bone spindle whorl, small fragment of Samian pottery, small piece of Roman glass, and perforated pebbles; this grave contains no elaborate Anglo-Saxon metalwork and might be considered unusual because of the Roman material. We cannot assume that such Roman material is residual although it is much harder to demonstrate deliberate deposition. Similarly Bowcombe Down grave 21, with its arrowhead, half a horseshoe, shreds of coarse pottery, a clasp, iron ring and a bead.

The concentration on graves with a multiplicity of objects, especially highly diagnostic examples, has resulted in the symbolic content of grave assemblages and the numerous other factors which go together to form the material component of complex ritual being seriously underplayed. With cemeteries such as those on the Isle of Wight, this is arguably inevitable if the data which might assist in extending our understanding of the significance of a wider range of graves had been recorded. But with cemeteries where the level of recording is high, one would surely expect as much research being applied to aspects of ritual and symbolism as the study of the objects. However, the desire to say the last word about early Anglo-Saxon ritual should not now become the new excuse for the failure to publish cemeteries; the primary objective should be to publish the data alone, and without unnecessary delay.

Very little progress can be made in analysing mortuary ritual with the Isle of Wight cemeteries. At Chessell Down, where the level of recording was perhaps highest, Hillier claimed that the normal body position was extended and lying on the back, but variations from the norm receive special notice. Hillier mentions five graves as being unusual, two where the bodies were lying on their sides with no grave-goods (graves 26 and 50), grave 8 in a stone cist with no grave-goods, one (grave 9) also unaccompanied with the legs flexed, and grave 48 with charcoal at the head and feet with again no artefacts. Is it common for unusual burial positions to be unaccompanied? The excavator mentions in passing that some graves were covered with small heaps of stones. Elsewhere on the island we find stones on a body at Shalfleet (grave 2); at Bembridge Down two inhumations side by side but with opposing orientations; at Bowcombe Down graves 1 and 21 had stone either under the body or surrounding it but with grave-goods, the head was absent from the unaccompanied grave 5 and grave 18 contained a flexed skeleton with grave-goods. These few graves whose body position is given, along with the more numerous observations about the varying positions of the hands, are hardly the material for detailed research, but taken in conjunction with a larger sample may well begin to throw up patterns which may be significant in terms of life and death ritual and belief.

A variety of methods of analysis have been used to examine the range and variety of grave-goods in Anglo-Saxon cemeteries such as Chessell Down and others in southern England. These have included a monothetic divisive technique and methods based on quantity and quality (Arnold 1980). There are also subtleties in the assemblages of grave-goods which such analyses do not detect. It is well known that within female graves there is more likely to be a multiplicity of types of object which is in part due to the frequency of occurrence of dress items. But very few male graves have more than one of any type, even those with large numbers of grave-goods. At Chessell Down there are five graves where there is such a multiplicity (59, 76, 99, 105, 106) one having more than one knife, the others a number of spears; what may link them together is that all but one is accompanied by a sword but no unusual, exotic or large quantities of objects.

Even with such poor data it is possible to extract a type of artefact from its context, where that is known, and apply techniques of analysis which may have considerably greater precision than an art-historical appreciation of form and decoration, and which can produce useful if challenging results. Such techniques manipulate and extend the database and may open a variety of doors. The pottery from the island may be taken as one example (Arnold 1981a).

Only two of the pottery types, isolated in terms of form and decoration, are known from more than one cemetery, the linear decorated wares and the undecorated types which nevertheless share a similar form; that form, however, is common to a large proportion of undecorated pottery. Each of the remaining vessels are unique to the cemetery in which they were found and, at times, to the island.

Much of this pottery is consistently dated to the late fifth and early sixth centuries. This might give us grounds to question the dating because of what it implies. The early dating of much of this pottery and the types themselves are paralleled in Kent and where it may represent an initial phase, followed by a near absence of pottery in cemeteries. Taken literally it makes the remainder of the period aceramic (Arnold 1981b). If it were assumed that pottery was continually in existence in society and that the chronology was correct it may point to an important change in the use of pottery in the burial rite. This may be correct as the majority of the vessels on the Isle of Wight are associated with primary cremations below barrows, and no types are found with both cremation burial and inhumation. The few pieces of pottery which are dated on typological grounds to the sixth century were associated with inhumation graves.

All of the thirty-eight vessels from the island, which have survived or had been found when the study was made (a sad total of thirteen), have received microscopic petrological examination and textural analysis, making the Isle of Wight one of the few counties, albeit a small one, where all of the pottery of a particular period has been studied in this way. Seriation of the results and other known factors reveals a potential relationship between form, decoration, mortuary ritual and fabric. Those supposedly earliest vessels from the island have undistinguished local fabrics and, whether plain or decorated, are associated with cremation and have typological links with Kent. They constitute the largest group of pottery on the island. The more distinct fabrics belong to vessels which are all given later dates, are associated with inhumation burials, are more highly decorated and/or have more unusual forms. To some extent, although one might be hesitant in advancing general observations on data of this quality, it may be observed that the more elaborate forms of cemetery with either primary or secondary burials in barrows, using cremation or inhumation, at higher altitudes, have the supposedly earlier and simpler types of pottery, whereas the less elaborate, larger flat-grave cemeteries also contain the more elaborate forms. This may suggest that the symbolism of the form of the burial and the grave-goods are in some way alternatives.

A number of potential explanatory models have been proposed to explain these observed patterns, but their validity depends on whether they are constrained by Myres' evolutionary scheme or not (Myres 1969). The pattern may simply be a reflection of what types of pottery are appropriate for particular forms of burial and chronology may or may not be a relevant factor. Other explanations have been based on economic factors relating to migration, the developing socio-economic structure of the communities and stress (Arnold 1981a).

The pottery, like other artefacts on the Isle of Wight, displays a strong link with Kent. There is little similarity between the Isle of Wight assemblage and the ceramic material from either Hampshire or Sussex; some general similarities occur, but they are no stronger than can be found with any part of south-east England, and the differences far outweigh the similarities. The strongest axis of similarity is with Kent, except for two of the more exotic items one of which is an import from the Continent, the other having only one 'parallel' in Derbyshire.

The natural temptation is to associate the supposedly earlier forms of pottery with Jutish settlement from Kent. However, if the earliest material with at least a Kentish connection was taken together to represent the historical migration and viewed in conjunction with all the available archaeological evidence, we find a bizarre mixture. Such material need not be taken literally to represent the graves of actual Jutish/Kentish settlers, but may merely indicate the direction from which some settlers came resulting in their influence manifesting itself in ceramic material. It is only fair to point out that we do not actually know how or whether a Jute would symbolize membership of that identity group, if indeed it was considered to be one at the time the event was supposed to have occurred.

If the evidence was taken to represent such settlers it should be realized that there are very few graves which can now be shown to display such a link, that they are thinly spread across the island and the individuals are buried in a variety of ways. If Chessell Down grave 22 containing the great square-headed brooch is included in the list, we are faced with one inhumation with a brooch, tweezers, knife and buckle; one vessel from either an unaccompanied inhumation (107), or one with a knife (42) or a grave of unstated burial rite (95); from Chillerton Down a possible cremation urn; from Bowcombe (grave 3) an unaccompanied cremation; and from Bembridge Down a vessel with an otherwise unaccompanied inhumation. In addition there is one unprovenanced vessel. On whatever basis you were to assess them, these material correlations are hardly a coherent group.

We should not forget that there has really not been any research carried out on cemeteries of this period to analyse the extent to which the form of burial is determined by ethnic affinity, religion or other factors; there is general agreement that rank plays a role in the quantities and nature of the grave-goods, and that the designs and decoration on some artefacts can be traced to particular geographical regions, but that is as far as work has proceeded, which in itself weakens any attempt to attribute ethnic labels to graves.

If some pattern emerges from the petrological and stylistic study of ceramic material, similar results may be obtained from decorated metalwork, especially brooches, and detailed studies have been made of technical and stylistic aspects. In broad terms the Isle of Wight brooches fall into two main groups: the larger, more elaborate and therefore distinctive brooches have strong links with Kent; smaller, less distinctive examples have links with most areas of southern Britain. Some of the material is dated within narrow chronological brackets, particularly that with Kentish associations, the rest is placed into such wide brackets as to be virtually useless for detailed analytical purposes. The actual number of brooches from the Isle of Wight for which a Kentish origin has been proposed is about fifteen pieces out of a total of forty surviving brooches from the island; rarely do the other artefacts associated with them have such strong Kentish connections. Of the dated pieces a couple are attributed to the first decades of the sixth century, about four to the second quarter and about six to the third quarter of the century. The dating brackets rarely carry any precise indication of whether they refer to manufacture and/or deposition; they are necessarily wide. It is therefore very difficult to establish whether they represent a steady trickle of material over about seventy-five years (about one brooch every five years) or a smaller number of bulk imports. The associations of over half of these brooches are not known making it difficult to state with certainty the number of individuals with whom they were buried. But if we combine the number of brooches ascribed to known graves with the number of pairs and singletons it suggests one death by a person with such material every ten and a half years, a maximum of seven females. While this may only be a fraction of the total it hardly implies very strong contact, or a shared material culture, and may represent nothing more than the movement of people or objects between families maintaining a traditional link between Kent and the island. Assuming that this was a two-way movement, it is unfortunate, and perhaps instructive, that there does not appear to be any distinctive form of metalwork whose manufacture can be attributed to the Isle of Wight and which can be traced in Kent.

There is the possibility of relatively weaker links with other areas such as Hampshire and Sussex. Of the recently excavated cemeteries on the opposite mainland there is Charlton Plantation (Davies 1984) in the Avon valley near Downton (the data published quickly within four years of the excavation) where there are a few links. Burial 37 contained a small bronze pendant very similar to that from Chessell Down grave 3. Burials 1 and 6 provided two more examples of vessels with repoussé arcade and dot decoration along with some further unprovenanced pieces, perhaps the most that has yet come from any one cemetery. The type has been shown to be very common in central southern England, including the Isle of Wight (Arnold 1982, 58–9) and reinforces the pattern which may be taken to indicate manufacture in the area; there are two examples in Kent. There are a few other items from Charlton Plantation which can be matched on the Isle of Wight but their significance here is lessened as they are also found more generally in southern England. There is no Kentish material in the traditional sense. Compton Appledown, near Marden, Sussex is reported as having produced a similar story, including in this case some Kentish material mixed with grave-goods more usual to the area, but this material has only recently been excavated.

It should be noted that the Isle of Wight graves which contain sixth-century Kentish material, albeit limited to the female side, comprise about 13 per cent of the total graves at Chessell Down. The significance of that figure can only be measured by some consideration of the proportion of female graves in a Kentish cemetery with such diagnostic artefacts. This is made difficult when the number of large cemetery samples excavated this century which are freely available for study from Kent can easily be counted on the fingers of one hand. Ridiculous as it may seem one has to go back to the nineteenth-century excavations to obtain suitable, if inadequate, published accounts, and in this respect early Anglo-Saxon archaeology has regressed since the last century. Of the graves from Lyminge which have been published so far, 5 per cent contain brooches which might be defined as 'Kentish', at Sarre 4 per cent, and it is only at Bifrons, with 12 per cent that we come at all close to the Chessell Down figure.

Another way in which the material culture of cemeteries and regions can be characterized to highlight cultural affinities is by examining the proportions of object types, a method used by Welch (1983, 163–75). A comparison between Sarre, Bifrons and Chessell Down (Figure 3) reveals a quite different pattern at each cemetery, although the value of such comparisons might be greatly reduced if the actual chronology of the cemeteries, the rate of burial through their lifespan, and the varying means by which the objects were acquired, were better understood. But taking the distributions at face value would lead to the conclusion that quite different processes were at work, perhaps as complex as the varying means of acquiring the objects and/or the desire to indicate membership of separate identity groups.

It may also be noted in passing that males are rarely buried with artefacts decorated in such a fashion that enables us to attribute an origin; we at least do not recognize the signs. While we must allow the possibility that group identity, if that is what it represents, may be symbolized in other, less durable, ways, it remains true on present evidence that it is women alone who display such identity in durable artefacts in a form which we can observe. This may be important for any discussion of the role of women and men within early Anglo-Saxon society. It would, however, present us with the basis for strongly contrasting interpretations.

The last few years have seen the publication of studies of objects, some of which come from the Isle of Wight. Leigh's detailed technical study of the Kentish great square-headed brooches (1980) has led to many important conclusions about the methods of manufacture employed, although questions regarding the organization in broad terms of that industrial activity are not necessarily much clearer. The principal conclusion is that all such Kentish brooches were made in one workshop and can be divided between three generations of craftsmen. There are examples of the products of each generation on the Isle of Wight. The trio of brooches from Chessell Down grave 45, for example, is particularly revealing as one differs sufficiently from the others to imply that they were not all made at the same time; from the extent of wear on the brooches Leigh argues that the pair is later. We may ask whether two stages of manufacture have to be envisaged to create the trio before they were transferred to the island and eventually buried, or did one brooch return to Kent to be copied? These are interesting, if unanswerable, questions because of the social and chronological implications that they carry.

There can now be little doubt as a result of the research carried out on the technical aspects of the Kentish brooches that the Isle of Wight examples are derived from the same source and even, at times, the same craftsmen as the Kentish square-headed silver

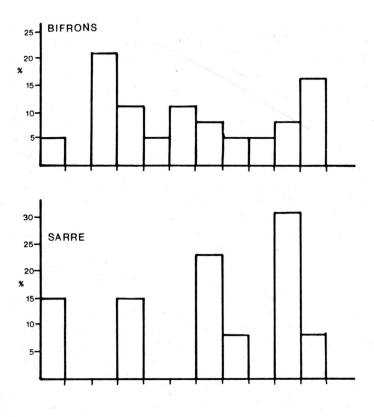

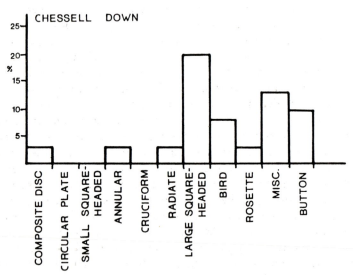

FIGURE 3   FREQUENCY DIAGRAMS OF BROOCH TYPES in southern English cemeteries

brooches. The Kentish link also extends in the case of Chessell Down grave 45, at least, to the total assemblage and the manner of deposition of the artefacts; this type of grave is not limited to Kent and the Isle of Wight but also occurs in other areas of England as far north as Leicestershire and we may be witnessing a number of different processes whereby these configurations appear. First, an important implication is that the items were in use in every-day life in a similar manner to which they are found as grave-goods, for how else would such a social norm be transmitted over such a wide geographical area; it points to the extent of social interaction at least between elite members of society. Secondly, there are more detailed considerations as to the actual mechanisms involved. On the one hand the movement of a woman with her symbolically charged artefacts, or the procurement of complete sets of items, by whatever means, for use in another area may cause such replication. On the other hand it may be a case of emulation, that is providing the items in a local genre for a local person, or producing the goods locally to satisfy a person who has moved into the area. Some of these permutations may imply a change of social identity, others may not.

It has been shown that a high degree of similarity between cemeteries is also found in such matters as the distribution of general types of objects between graves, and of the frequencies of such types, despite there being considerable differences in specific terms. This may suggest to us that there were many processes at work at both a local and regional scale which combine to create differences and similarities at various levels and intensities. In more specific terms we have to consider the possibility of isolating such factors as the movement of people, the social exchange of goods, both items and people, for such purposes as cementing alliances, new and long standing, which may occur once or repeatedly, or emulation of facets of another region's culture; the operation of processes relating to economic, social and political development which, with interaction between regions, can result in very similar formations. The desire to maintain an individualistic group identity may continue to underlie other similarities and differences.

The nature of the economic success of the Isle of Wight might best be understood in terms of a prestige-goods economy. Objects may bestow prestige both by their excellence of craftsmanship and as a result of their availability being restricted. We might note how runic inscriptions convey some form of power both by their apparent codification of meaning and by their restricted availability; it is relevant to note how a high proportion of the identified early English examples are in Kent and the Isle of Wight, where they are restricted to rare and exotic items. Prestige items may be necessary parts of certain transactions, for instance as a dowry, with the inbuilt result that it is also possible to control such transactions; this may be the appropriate framework with which to view much of the sixth-century Kentish material on the island, which is also notable for having an exclusive character. Another means of maintaining such exclusivity is by controlling the supply of exotics; the directional nature of amber distribution in southern England, which may be seen in this light, has been discussed elsewhere (Arnold 1980). The extent to which such prestige items are inherited is important as it may provide a means of accumulating wealth and power, whereas burial may take place when their immediate function comes to an end. There are reasons for seeing a number of artefacts as being old when buried; but therein lies the important point that when they enter the archaeological record they are being disposed of, whether or not they have passed through more than one generation.

By drawing together the pieces of research that have been carried out with a view to isolating a variety of possible processes, certain overall conclusions and prejudices concerning the Isle of Wight cemeteries may be stated. The earliest Anglo-Saxon activity is represented by cremation burials at a minimum of three separate locations, which could be taken to represent the settlement of small groups in individual farmsteads during a time of stress. Some of these locations continue in use through the sixth century, others are terminated relatively quickly. The graves are at first often unusual, elaborate and impoverished, often with material which is difficult to date any more precisely than the fourth to sixth century AD. There is a demonstrable link, especially in ceramic material, but also with a limited amount of metalwork, with Kent at this time, but by no means all of the early graves evince that identity in the form of decoration on artefacts. Indeed throughout the sixth century there is no distinctive identity which manifests itself in grave-goods beyond the continuing Kentish link. Two of the cemeteries, Bowcombe Down and Chessell Down, contain graves with artefacts dated to the early sixth century which may be taken to indicate individuals, males of high rank, and which appear amongst the earliest inhumation graves on the island.

Through the sixth century Chessell Down continues to be used as a cemetery while the others appear to gradually go out of use altogether; the evidence of Chessell Down suggests a growing community, the overall size of the cemetery being five times greater than its nearest rival on the island. There were increasingly varied small-scale external contacts demonstrated especially by ceramics, weaponry and brooches, and the island had the power to attract exotic items in quantities sufficiently large to imply that the movement of such goods was directional and controlled. As the community entered the second half of the sixth century it had developed a clear hierarchy dominated by no more than three families, perhaps segments of the same family with women at least emulating Kentish modes of dress and artefact. More probably they were individuals who had actually come from Kent with trappings reflecting their senior rank, and by means of controlled marriage they had entered into the high ranking families of the Isle of Wight. It is more than likely that the size of this element is being overstated as the result of assuming that the sixth-century Kentish material represents the movement of a number of people, whereas it may all have arrived as the result of a single transaction, but only a proportion being the property of a person who was part of that transaction.

Adjacent cemeteries appear to share some of the characteristics of the community buried on Chessell Down; Shalcombe and Shalfleet join Bowcombe Down in being the only ones to produce swords. Shalfleet is only known from a couple of chance discoveries in the edge of a small marl pit, but may well represent another large flat-grave cemetery which has never been explored. The society buried at the western end of the island was as wealthy and as socially and politically developed as any others in southern England. The size of the cemetery on Chessell Down may be the result of its being a centralized depository for a number of dispersed communities, although the implication would be that there was a common bond to encourage the sharing of a single cemetery. If it belonged to a single community its size, about twenty-five to thirty people alive at any one time, may be a reflection of, and a reason for, its success in the economics of political life; we should not forget that human beings are an important resource and an essential element to permit growth.

This state of affairs is brought to a sudden end with the cessation of burial after *c. 575*. There is at least nothing dateable to the seventh century from the island. This may represent the disappearance or the dispersal of the population or a change in burial rite. Irrespective of the actual fortunes of the population, the disappearance of the élite class can be viewed in terms of the shifting of power in southern England; the alliances that had been formed by such communities as Kent and the Isle of Wight were broken when a number of the southern English population conglomerates were forcefully incorporated into larger political units. Society was generally on a track of political and economic growth which may be observed through primary and secondary data. The late sixth and early seventh century was a period of considerable stress, and the shifting of power has already been examined from a number of viewpoints, most recently in terms of the chronolgy and distribution of rich graves in southern England which were viewed as central to political units for reasons of security and veneration (Arnold 1987). Their presence and absence in certain areas at particular times produces both an interesting and challenging pattern. Power shifted from the Isle of Wight possibly to reappear with the creation of the maritime centre of industry and commerce on the River Itchen on the opposite mainland, controlled by the larger polities which the seventh century had seen develop.

That little can be achieved from the examination of nineteenth-century excavations. How much more could be achieved if all the cemetery samples from southern England, both large and small, which have been excavated since the second world war were available for research.

Bibliography

Arnold, C.J. 1975: *The Anglo-Saxon settlement of the Isle of Wight.* Unpublished B.A. Thesis, University of Southampton.

Arnold, C.J. 1980: "Wealth and Social Structure: a matter of life and death" in *Anglo-Saxon Cemeteries 1979*, Rahtz, P., Dickinson, T. and Watts, L. (Eds.), B.A.R. 82, Oxford pp. 81–142.

Arnold, C.J. 1981a: "Colonisation and Settlement: the Early Anglo-Saxon pottery of the Isle of Wight". *Proceedings of the Isle of Wight Natural History and Archaeology Society* 7, 419–435.

Arnold, C.J. 1981b: "Early Anglo-Saxon pottery: production and distribution" in *Production and Distribution: a Ceramic Viewpoint*, Howard, H. and Morris, E.L. (Eds.), B.A.R. 120, Oxford pp. 243–55.

Arnold, C.J. 1982: *The Anglo-Saxon cemeteries of the Isle of Wight*, London.

Arnold, C.J. 1987: "Territories and Leadership: frameworks for the study of emergent polities in early Anglo-Saxon southern England" in *Power and Politics in Early Medieval Britain and Ireland*, Driscoll, S. and Nieke, M. (Eds.), Edinburgh, pp. 111–127.

Arnold, C.J. 1988: *An Archaeology of the Early Anglo-Saxon Kingdoms*, London.

Davies, S.M. 1984: "The excavation of an Anglo-Saxon cemetery (and some prehistoric pits) at Charlton Plantation, near Downton". *Wiltshire Archaeological and Natural History Magazine* 79, 109–54.

Leigh, D. 1980: *The Square-headed Brooches of Sixth Century Kent*, unpublished Ph.D. Thesis, University College, Cardiff.

Myres, J.N.L. 1969: *Anglo-Saxon Pottery and the Settlement of England*, Oxford.

Shephard, J.F. 1979: "The social identity of the individual in isolated barrows and barrow cemeteries in Anglo-Saxon England" in *Space, Hierarchy and Society*, Burnham, B.C. and Kingsbury, J. (Eds), B.A.R. International Series 59, Oxford, pp 47–80.

Welch, M.G. 1983: *Early Anglo-Saxon Sussex*, B.A.R. 112, Oxford.

Welch, M.G. 1985: "Rural Settlement Patterns in the Early and Middle Anglo-Saxon Periods". *Landscape History* 7, 13–25.

CHAPTER TEN

MODELS OF BURIAL, SETTLEMENT AND WORSHIP: THE FINAL PHASE REVIEWED

Andy Boddington

INTRODUCTION: EXAMINING THE MODEL

> A man may bury his brother with dead
> And strew his grave with the golden things
> He would have him take, treasures of all kinds,
> But gold hoarded when he here lived
> Cannot allay the anger of God
> Toward a soul sin-freighted

Captured here, in the Anglo-Saxon poem *Seafarer*, are the sentiments of a Christian recalling the heathen practice of burial with grave-goods and preaching its futility (Alexander 1983). These words reflect the contrast between the burial practice in later Anglo-Saxon England when burial was unadorned and confined to churchyards, and that current a couple of centuries earlier. At that earlier time the dead were interred in pagan burial grounds equipped with the weapons, tools and jewellery of every-day life. This transformation of burial arrangements is one of the most dramatic archaeological statements of the Anglo-Saxon period.

For the archaeologist the transformation is preserved as two major-event horizons. The first is the end of pagan burial – the decline or closure of existing burial grounds along with the end of burial with grave-goods. The second is the inception of churchyards. In terms of the history of the Anglo-Saxon period the two sets of events are inevitably intertwined, but in terms of the archaeology of the period they are remarkably separate. While activity in the pagan grounds is minimal by the beginning of the eighth century, it is not until the tenth century that there is any quantity of archaeological evidence for churchyards. Evidence for churchyard burial prior to that date is by and large confined to the minsters. As yet there is no plausible evidence for a pagan burial ground that subsequently acquired a church (but see Morris 1983, pages 60–61, for a list of pagan finds from churchyards). Equally it has not yet been possible to extensively excavate pagan, 'transition' and Christian cemeteries within the same Anglo-Saxon estate or parish. In terms of landscape archaeology the English Christian churchyards are part of a web of town, village, manor and open fields. On the other hand, the pagan burial grounds belong to a sharply different landscape, one that is still imperfectly known. In some areas at least, it seems to have taken the form of dispersed hamlets without urban or village nuclei. The archaeological evidence for the end of pagan burial and the creation of Christian churchyards is thus polarized. This dichotomous structure has encouraged separate examination of the pagan and Christian evidence.

This paper focuses only on the first part of that evidence, the end of pagan burial. In particular it examines a model that has become known as the 'Final Phase'. This model originated in East Anglia in the 1930s when T.C. Lethbridge pursued the idea that some burials with grave-goods were Christian rather than pagan. During the subsequent forty years his initial suggestions have been developed into a detailed model. Surprisingly, this model has never been subject to rigorous review.

This paper traces the origins and development of the Final Phase model. It concentrates on the data from those cemetery excavations which were most influential in the definition of the characteristics of the Final Phase. It might be thought useful to compare in detail all those cemeteries considered to be Final Phase (for a list see Morris 1983, 55–6) with those of the sixth century. This proves impractical chiefly because the assignment of Final Phase status has been uneven and, as a result, there is no consensus on a 'corpus' of Final Phase cemeteries. A review of the artefact-based chronology of the period also seems inappropriate. Typology cannot produce the precision required to map in detail the decline and abandonment of burial grounds. In any event it is somewhat lame in a period when the frequency of artefact occurrence is declining. In preference this paper concentrates on comparing the physical attributes of cemeteries; that is, features such as artefact frequency, artefact type, grave orientation and the relationship of the burial grounds to the contemporary landscape.

Certain technical conventions are followed. On the matter of alignment, the position of the head of the skeleton is always quoted first; thus W–E indicates that the head lay to the west. For clarity and precision the various numeric values quoted are given in brackets according to the following format – (number of observations/number of possible observations/percentage observations). For example, at Burwell about one half of the burials were accompanied by artefacts (62/129/48). The figures indicate that of the one hundred and twenty-nine burials for which records are available, sixty-two (or 48 per cent) were accompanied by artefacts.

Acknowledgements

Much of the research necessary for this paper was conducted at the Department of Archaeology, University of Durham. Professor Rosemary Cramp has provided support, encouragement and constructive debate throughout that research and the drafting of this text. My interest in burial alignment goes back further and much of the statistical analysis was conducted at the School of Archaeological Sciences, University of Bradford, under the watchful eyes of Arnold Aspinall, John Haigh and Rick Jones. The text of the paper, diagrams and the detailed statistics were processed using the resources of the Academic Computing Service of the Open University. Graham Cadman and Sue Gill kindly commented on drafts of this paper.

STEPS FROM PAGANISM TO CHRISTIANITY:
THE DEVELOPMENT OF A MODEL

When E.T. Leeds produced his *Anglo-Saxon Art and Archaeology* in 1936 he headed its concluding chapter 'The Final Phase'. In this chapter he reviewed the character of seventh-century assemblages in Kent and elsewhere. He did not, though, see such a phase as representing a separate group of cemeteries. His intent, in dedicating an entire chapter to the subject, was to fully refute the view that: 'When Christianity was adopted in any given district the pagan burial-places fell into disuse, and the practice of depositing personal possessions, whether arms, jewellery, or other equipment with the deceased quickly came to an end' (1936, 96). His primary concern was that the historical timetable for the introduction of Christianity should not compress the period available for the development of artefact styles. 'Pagan practices', he stressed, 'died slowly'. The chain of discoveries that led to the Final Phase model had, however, begun a few years earlier. In 1925 T.C. Lethbridge conducted the first of five seasons of excavation at Burwell, Cambridgeshire. Burwell was just one of several cemeteries in that area excavated by Lethbridge during the late 1920s and early 1930s. Initially he saw the seventh-century burials at Burwell as poor but pagan (1926, 79), but as excavations progressed he was struck by the atypical character of the burial ground. By the end of his second season it was apparent that Burwell was 'not a cemetery of the usual local Anglian type' (1927, 122). At the close of excavations in 1929 the cemetery was still viewed as representing a late and 'obstinate pagan community' (1929, 109) but, with the publication of the final report in 1931, Lethbridge had made up his mind that the site was Christian:

> It may be thought that the explanation was staring one in the face, but it was not till I had nearly completed the excavations in the cemetery at Holywell Row that I came to the conclusion that Burwell was undoubtedly a Christian and not a pagan cemetery (1931, 48).

He summarized his reasoning in both the 1931 report and, more thoroughly, at the end of his 1936 report on Shudy Camps, a cemetery which he also considered to be Christian (1936, 27–29):

1. Most of the bodies were unaccompanied by grave-goods.

2. No object of typical pagan form had been found with the possible exception of two annular brooches re-used on chatelaines and a few Roman coins treated as curiosities. Here Lethbridge was impressed in particular by the absence of weapons and brooches.
3. The cemetery appeared to date from a time when the ordinary pagan cemeteries close.

Lethbridge also considered the former presence of a church near the site to be relevant. He concluded: 'To my mind it is the highest degree probable that this new cemetery, formed in the VII century, is a Christian one laid out away from the "burial mounds of the heathen" as the Church commanded' (1931, 48). The Final Phase model was not developed further until after the Second World War when Vera Evison reported on the cemetery at Holborough, Kent. Evison added to the Lethbridge list the suggestion that some artefacts, notably crosses, had Christian connotations and that graves were consistently oriented W–E (1956). In support also of Leed's earlier analysis she concurred that 'fashion at that time did not tend to develop on local lines, but that a certain homogeneity pervaded the style of trinkets and other furniture deposited in the graves' (1956, 108). A few years later Hyslop argued that this homogeneity was a direct result of the strengthening of communications across Britain with the introduction of Christianity (Hyslop 1963, 193). The argument that some artefact forms were Christian was later used by Audrey Ozanne in her analysis of the Derbyshire barrows (1962–3). It was also in 1963 that Miranda Hyslop drew together the emerging criteria and presented a list of attributes which defined the Final Phase. Her eleven points may be summarized:

1. Cremations are absent.
2. Orientation is markedly consistent and the graves are in regular groups or rows.
3. Barrow graves occur.
4. A high proportion of graves are without artefacts, or only with a knife.
5. Features of clothing and ornamentation change. Brooches are rare, as are elaborate necklaces, pendants are common, buckles small and thread boxes occur in female graves.
6. Weapons are rare. Where they occur the scramasax is more common and the shield boss takes on a tall sugar loaf form.

Hyslop, more than the earlier writers, emphasized the separate identity of this group of cemeteries. In particular, she suggested that many of them had adjacent pagan ancestors:

> None of the late group of cemeteries contains any grave which can be dated before the 7th century, and in some places . . . a neighbouring cemetery has been found to go out of use at some point in the 7th century, precisely when the second cemetery was begun (1963, 191).

With the publication of Hyslop's paper all but one of the characteristics of the Final Phase were defined. Of all the criteria, it was the notion of the Final Phase cemeteries being a replacement, under Christian influence, of neighbouring pagan burial grounds that has become important to many reconstructions of the middle Anglo-Saxon ecclesiastical and secular landscape. Audrey Meaney and Sonia Hawkes, in particular, use the Final Phase model to explore the relationship between Winnall I and Winnall II, cemeteries which lie 1 km north-east of Winchester (Meaney and Hawkes 1970).

Hawkes' conclusions to this report form one of the most comprehensive discussions of the Final Phase. Amid a broad ranging discussion she emphasized the role of the church in the ending of burial with grave-goods:

> This was one of the old customs which died hard . . . it was a custom the church was at first prepared to wink at. In our late cemeteries offerings of food and drink had become infrequent . . . only the fastenings and ornaments worn on the garments in which the dead were buried, and indispensable adjuncts of everyday wear such as knives . . . By the 1st half of the 8th century the custom seems virtually to have been stamped out . . . even dress-fasteners were now frowned on . . . the archaeological poverty of a cemetery like Winnall II is a demonstration of the Church's success in combating one of the outward shows of heathenism (1970, 53).

Hawkes also discussed burial alignment in the Winnall report and has elsewhere attributed 'solar' alignments to burials of the Christian period (1976). The solar model explains the diverse orientations of W–E burials in terms of orientation to the sunrise on the day of burial. It is considered in detail below. Martin Biddle has emphasized the apparent correlation between the demise of Winnall II and commencement of burial in Winchester Old Minster churchyard early in the eighth century (1976, 69).

The final component of the Final Phase model was added by Margaret Faull in 1976. She considered the relationship between a large, almost exclusively cremation, cemetery (Sancton I, Yorkshire) and a smaller inhumation cemetery (Sancton II) close by the medieval parish church. Faull comments: 'Hyslop has drawn attention to the phenomenon of the establishment in southern England in the later pagan period of a second cemetery closer to its settlement than the earlier burial ground'. In fact Hyslop did not suggest that the second cemetery was closer to the settlement, this is a new addition to the model. The model presented by Faull envisages Sancton I as a central cemetery for several of the Wold-edge settlements, these are replaced by individual cemeteries adjacent to the village and finally by the Christian churchyard:

> First the cremation cemetery located on the outer edge of the cultivated land and possibly being used by all the surrounding communities; then the establishment of the smaller, predominately inhumation cemetery close to the village at the same time that inhumation cemeteries were appearing outside other settlements in the area, although perhaps with Sancton I continuing to serve as a central crematorium; and finally the Christian burial ground developing as an extension of its immediate pagan predecessor (1976, 233).

The full Final Phase model was now complete, it can be summarized as a set of eight points:

1. A new set of cemeteries are established under Christian influence.
2. These are close to the settlement, whereas their pagan predecessors tended to be further afield, often on boundaries.
3. The burials are entirely inhumation.
4. Orientation is consistent and west–east.
5. Some graves are in, or under, barrows.
6. The proportion of graves without artefacts, or only with a knife, is high.
7. Artefacts relate predominately to utilitarian clothing or are small personal tokens. Weapons are rare.
8. Some objects, notably cross forms, have Christian significance.

More than thirty cemeteries with some or all of these criteria present have now been identified as Final Phase (Morris 1983, 55–56).

More generally the model may be synthesized into three major components. Firstly, *suppression*: burial with grave-goods was gradually squeezed out. Secondly, *separation*: the Final Phase burial grounds are a discrete group of cemeteries. Thirdly, *succession*: the cemeteries replace a nearby predecessor. For these three components of the model the causation, the motivating force for change, is Christianity. Beyond this core of cause and effect there are various peripheral attributes. These are seen as an integral part of the pattern of change but are peripheral in that they are not generally thought to result directly from the adoption of Christianity. The first is orientation, i.e. that W–E burial becomes the norm. Peripherally attached to this is the solar hypothesis. Then there is the gravitation toward settlement. Finally there is the change in costume and equipment, reflected both in new clothing and in artefact styles and types.

ARTEFACTS IN DECLINE: THE LETHBRIDGE CEMETERIES

I t was during the excavation of three cemeteries, in Cambridgeshire and Suffolk, that Lethbridge developed the first stages of the Final Phase model. Burwell, a cemetery with one hundred and thirty inhumations, lies on a low area of chalk just above fenland, 7 km to the south of the River Cam and 15 km north-east of Cambridge. The Holywell Row cemetery was more extensively disturbed, although one hundred and fifteen inhumations were recovered nevertheless. It lies some 16 km further to the north-east of Burwell, on a tributary of the Little Ouse. Once again it is sited just above the fen, here on sand as well as chalk. The cemetery at Shudy Camps lies on higher ground rather further south, 21 km south-east of Cambridge near to the head of the River Granta. In all one hundred and forty-eight inhumations were recorded. For all these cemeteries Lethbridge provides a detailed catalogue of grave-goods, burial position and a general site plan; the analysis below is based on his reports (1931, 1936).

Holywell Row is typical of the sixth-century cemeteries of East Anglia. The burials are predominately oriented W–E (85/88/97), with two E–W and one S–N. They lie supine, or gently flexed, and a high proportion (85 per cent) of the burials are accompanied by grave-goods (86/101/85). No cremations were located by Lethbridge. As is normal in pagan Anglo-Saxon cemeteries, some types of artefact could be seen to be deposited exclusively with males or females, while a further group of other artefacts were deposited with both sexes.

In order to examine which artefacts occurred with which sex, the data was computer processed using the technique of multi-dimensional scaling (Shennan 1988, 281). In the method used here, account is taken of the number of graves in which each type of object occurs with each other type of object, and of the number of times that that type is present and the other is not. Skeletal sexing data is not taken into account. Grave-good types can be said to be 'similar' when they occur together most frequently and most 'dissimilar' when they do not occur together. It is thus possible to compute a measure of similarity between any two given object types (specifically the proximity measure used was DICE; SPSSX 1986). Subsequently it is possible to convert (scale) these multi-dimensional measures of similarity into a two dimensional map. The resultant map for Holywell Row is presented as Figure 1. The distances between objects on this map represent closely the association of object types in the Holywell Row graves. This is not the place to discuss the mathematics nor the full benefits of this technique. It will suffice to state that multi-dimensional scaling avoids the danger of assuming that artefact groupings are either dichotomous or hierarchical, a danger inherent in other techniques such as cluster analysis.

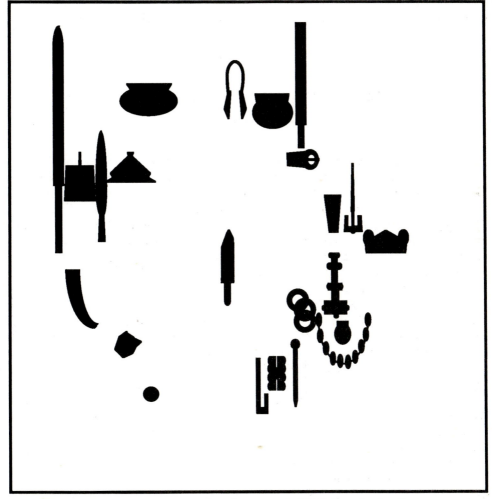

FIGURE 1   HOLYWELL ROW, SUFFOLK: grouping of grave-goods. Multi-dimensional scaling separates those objects typically found in male graves (sword, bucket, spear, shield) from those found in female graves (strapend, girdlehanger, pouchmount, brooch, various rings, pendant, beads, pin, wristclasp, key). The metal bowl and drinking horn are also apparently associated with male burials

From this diagram it can be seen that the objects fall into three groups. Swords, shields, etc. lie to the top left, clearly the group of objects associated with male burials. Beads, brooches, etc. cluster at the bottom right, clearly the female-associated group of objects. Between lie a scattered set of types which either occur with both sexes or cannot, from this data alone, be assigned to a single sex due to the small number of occurrences. Examination of the burial catalogue demonstrates that the most frequently occurring objects, knives and buckles (knives – 38/62/61, buckles – 21/62/34) occur with both sexes. It is not so clear whether the other objects, such as pots, are sex specific or whether they occur with both sexes. To summarize the artefact pattern at Holywell Row. Men are typically kitted with knives, buckles, spears and shields, less often with buckets and swords. In contrast the artefacts buried with women, while including knives, are typically associated with clothing and ornamentation. These included beads, brooches, buckles, various types of ring, girdlehangers, wrist clasps, strap ends, pendants, pins and pouch-mounts/fire-steels.

With the character of the Holywell Row assemblage sketched, it is possible to compare it with Burwell. It is immediately apparent that fewer graves have grave-goods at Burwell; just half compared to 85 per cent at Holywell Row (62/129/48). The number of object types per grave is also reduced, an average of two types per grave compared to three at Holywell Row (123/62/198 to 272/86/316). Equally remarkable is the lack of visibility of male burials in the cemetery. The sex classification of grave-goods derived from Holywell Row can be used to examine the material from Burwell (Figure 2). It is striking that, with the exception of a single scramasax, objects which are exclusively associated with male burials at Holywell Row are not present at Burwell. Three-quarters of the burials with grave-goods at Burwell had just a knife and/or buckle (46/62/74). The data from Holywell indicates that these objects occur with both sexes. Of the Burwell 'knife and buckle' group, eleven burials occur with distinctly female associated objects. In contrast twenty-eight burials with either a knife or buckle, or both, have no other associated object. This represents nearly half the total number of burials with grave-goods (28/62/45). It seems probable that at least some of these are male burials. In contrast to this undistinguished provision for the male burials, there is an equivalent range of female-associated objects at both Holywell Row and Burwell. Although at Burwell brooches, wrist clasps and strap ends are absent and rings, beads and pendants are less common, pins are more frequent and whorls, combs, beads, shears and work/thread-boxes appear. There are, therefore, three distinctive groups which summarize burials at Burwell. The female burials are evidenced by the association of distinctive items of clothing and ornament. A second group of burials are represented by 'belts' only (i.e. knives and buckles); these are presumably both male and female burials. Finally there are the burials without grave-goods.

We now turn to the seventh century cemetery at Shudy Camps. From its plan it is immediately apparent that there are two areas of burials, a predominately SW–NE aligned group to the west and a W–E aligned group to the east (Figure 3). Some 83 per cent of the burials in the west area are oriented SW–NE (including four reversed burials) while 98 per cent of the burials in the east area are W–E (73/87/83; 52/53/98). Some further data relating to these trends is given in tables 1 and 2. It is immediately evident that the proportion of burials with grave-goods in the west area, 63 per cent, is nearly twice that of the east area, 37 per cent. The presumption drawn from this evidence is

Holywell Row   Burwell

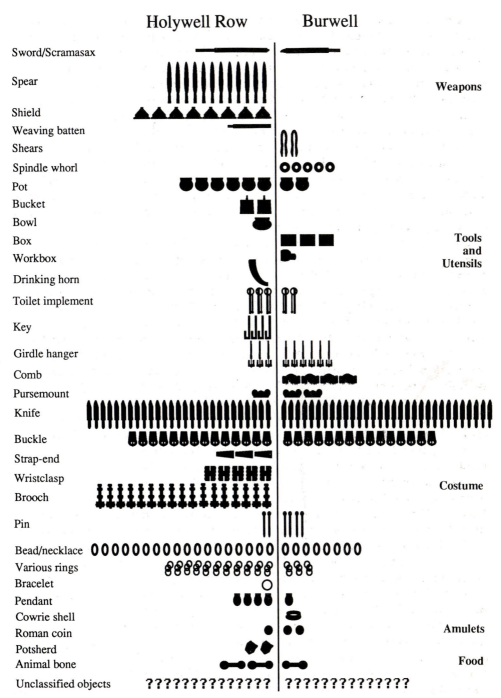

	Holywell Row / Burwell	
Sword/Scramasax		Weapons
Spear		
Shield		
Weaving batten		
Shears		
Spindle whorl		
Pot		
Bucket		
Bowl		
Box		Tools
Workbox		and
Drinking horn		Utensils
Toilet implement		
Key		
Girdle hanger		
Comb		
Pursemount		
Knife		
Buckle		
Strap-end		
Wristclasp		
Brooch		Costume
Pin		
Bead/necklace		
Various rings		
Bracelet		
Pendant		
Cowrie shell		
Roman coin		Amulets
Potsherd		
Animal bone		Food
Unclassified objects		

FIGURE 2   COMPARISON OF ARTEFACT FREQUENCIES at Holywell Row and Burwell. Each icon indicates that the object occurs in *c*. two per cent of the graves with grave-goods at that site

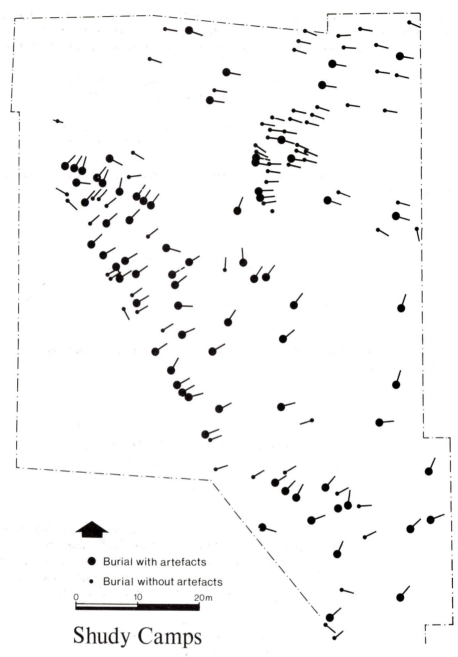

Burial with artefacts

Burial without artefacts

0   10   20m

Shudy Camps

FIGURE 3

that the east area of the graveyard was the successor to the west area. The range of artefacts overall is similar to Burwell, though three spears are present in the west area. Of those graves with artefacts, twenty-eight have just a knife and/or buckle (28/75/37).

Area	Burials	Head SE–SW	Head SW–NW	Head NW–SE	Artefacts Present	Artefacts Absent
West	93	69	15	4	60 (65)	33 (35)
East	54	0	52	1	15 (28)	39 (72)

Table 1. Shudy Camps, Cambridgeshire: occurrence of artefacts and orientation by area. Figures in brackets are percentages.

Artefacts	Head SE–SW	Head SW–NW	Head NW–SE
Present	51 (74)	23 (34)	1
Absent	18 (26)	44 (66)	4

Table 2. Shudy Camps, Cambridgeshire: occurrence of artefacts by orientation. Figures in brackets are percentages.

THE SUPPRESSION OF CONSPICUOUS DISPLAY: A QUESTION OF RESPONSIBILITY

Throughout this paper the term 'grave-goods' has been used rather loosely to signify any artefact deposited with the corpse. This single term embraces a variety of objects with a diverse set of functions. It is pertinent at this point in this exploration of the Final Phase to consider this diversity. One method of classification is by function, as the following list, with examples, illustrates:

1. Grave-furniture – coffins, biers, covers and markers.
2. Weapons – swords, spears and shields. Also seaxes and arrowheads.
3. Utensils – Domestic: knives, weaving battens, shears, hones, pots.
   – Personal: toilet implements, keys, combs, girdlehangers.
4. Costume – Dress fastenings: brooches, pins, buckles.
   – Jewellery and ornament: beads, rings, bracelets.
5. Amulets – cowrie shells, fossils, Roman coins.
6. Food 'offerings' – animal bone.

For our Final Phase cemeteries we may emphasize two characteristics. Firstly that the proportion of unadorned burials has increased. Secondly that it is the weapons that have, almost, disappeared. Most of the other classes of grave-goods are still in evidence.

What are the options for this decline of conspicuous display? They may be summarized under five headings:

1. Suppression by the church.
2. Religious belief.
3. Patterns of inheritance.
4. Conservation of resources.
5. Expression of status.

A number of scholars, including Leeds, Lethbridge and Hawkes, have been convinced that the church suppressed the use of artefacts:

> This change in long-settled funerary habits constitutes a real break in tradition. At this period it can only mean one thing: that it was the church which was responsible for the transference of burial away from the burial-grounds of the heathen fathers and forefathers. (Hawkes in Meaney and Hawkes 1970, 54.)

This viewpoint has not been universally supported. Donald Bullough has noted that 'it has long been recognized that the archaeological evidence for Merovingian and early Anglo-Saxon burial fits ill with the narrative accounts of the conversion' (1983, 185). Indeed, not a single canon or law forbids, or even frowns upon, burial with grave-goods. The earliest references in the laws to graves are essentially incidental (Bullough 1983). There are no direct references in seventh- and eighth-century documents to graveyards as distinct from churches. This point was recognized as long ago as 1903 by Baldwin Brown – 'for example the ninth and following canons of the council of Clovesho give a list of the duties of the secular priest, but omit all references to their functions with respect to the churchyard' (Baldwin Brown 1903, 261). To quote Bullough again, 'the early church showed itself surprisingly indifferent to where Christians were laid to rest' (1983, 186). So universal is the end of burial with grave-goods and so consistent is the trend, that if the church forbade it then it is of some considerable surprise that this escaped the attention of contemporary and later writers. If the church was so intent on elimination of burial with artefacts, then one might also expect to see a fairly sudden end to the practice. That this was not the case is clearly shown by the evidence from Shudy Camps where as burial progressed the proportion of the burials with artefacts gradually declined. Also the very rich graves of the seventh century, for example at Sutton Hoo and Taplow, do not suggest active ecclesiastical suppression. Neither does the richly equipped burial, and later translation, of St Cuthbert. There is a further weakness in the ecclesiastical suppression argument. It seems unlikely that the deposition of grave-goods resulted from pagan religious beliefs alone. Indeed, most archaeologists accept at least some degree of expression of social status (e.g. Hawkes in Hawkes and Wells 1983) while some see this as being the predominant factor (e.g. Arnold 1980). Given that the motives for burial with grave-goods were wide ranging, it seems improbable that the end of the practice was due to a single factor.

Burial with grave-goods represents both emphatic display of social status and conspicuous consumption of resources. Both illustrate the general practice of not passing personal tokens, tools and clothing on to the next generation. The question of inheritance and its relation to Anglo-Saxon burial practice is central to John Shephard's analysis of seventh century barrow burial (1979). Shephard argues that Germanic laws of the early ninth century record changes in inheritance patterns and that the objects that were previously buried are now inherited. These Germanic laws refer both to *Herregewate* (armour and weapons) for men and *Gerade* (jewellery and personal objects) for women. As we have seen in the Lethbridge cemeteries, while male armour is not present in the seventh-century graves, women's jewellery is virtually undiminished. Moreover, Shephard's historical references are exclusively to continental laws and we must question whether they are applicable to England. They also ignore Young's arguments that this legal explanation for the presence of artefacts in pagan graves is likely to have emerged in Christian times to account for a custom whose origins were unknown (1977, 55). There is no similar historical evidence for middle Anglo-Saxon England, neither is it clear how changes in the pattern of inheritance can be distinguished archaeologically from other influences on burial practice. Nevertheless Shephard's hypothesis serves to remind us that there are alternative causal factors for the decline of burial with grave-goods.

Given that early Anglo-Saxon burial practice disposed of considerable resources, particularly metals, it is plain that another factor operating from the early seventh century might be increased conservation of such resources. Economic pressures might result from the expansion of exchange/trading systems, as might be evidenced by the establishment of trading sites such as Ipswich (Hodges and Whitehouse 1983). It might be speculated that the end of burial with grave-goods coincided with this growth of more accessible mechanisms for exchange and a market for the recycling of materials. The appearance of the first notable evidence for the Anglo-Saxon metalwork industry in England is only slightly later in date. It was noted above that it is the weapons that virtually disappear in the Final Phase. In the alternative context of recycling of materials, it might be argued that it is the bulk iron objects that disappear! Conservation and recycling of resources is a mechanism for grave-good decline that has yet to be adequately explored.

Lethbridge observed the lack of brooches in the Burwell graves. This matter can be resolved by reference to Gale Owen-Crocker's analysis of Anglo-Saxon costume. Many of the changes in artefact provision in female graves can be explained by changes in costume during the seventh century, in particular the move away from the peplos style of costume (Owen-Croker 1986). The Christian symbolism of cross-shaped jewellery remains a matter of some debate. Barry Ager has argued, with reference to the Wigber Low (Derbyshire) cemetery, that there is nothing explicitly Christian about this form of jewellery and that 'the cross-symbol bears no specifically Christian connotations when it is used on the metalwork of the northern world' (Ager 1983, 102).

It is worthwhile to note that the Final Phase model is concerned only with the burial of the 'common man' and fails to deal with the more 'aristocratic' burials of the seventh century. At one end of the spectrum, there are burials with few grave-goods or with none. At the other, are the astoundingly rich burials such as Sutton Hoo and Taplow (Bruce-Mitford 1975). For this latter group of burials there is no question of 'artefacts in decline'.

By way of conclusion for this section, it can be stressed that it is unlikely that there was a single factor responsible for the decline and disappearance of the custom of burial with grave-goods. More probably several factors were involved, those which predominate may have been social and economic in character, religion may only have played a marginal role.

CEMETERIES IN PAIRS: PATTERNS OF SEPARATION AND SUCCESSION

The two cemeteries at Chamberlains Barn lie on sand, a few hundred metres apart on opposite sides a minor stream flowing into the River Ouzel north of Leighton Buzzard, Bedfordshire. Both were excavated by Frederick Gurney at much the same time as Lethbridge was active in Cambridgeshire (Chamberlains Barn I in 1931; II in 1936) but their significance in relation to the Final Phase was not recognized until Miranda Hyslop published them in full in 1963. Further north, at a distance of 500 m, lay a third cemetery, Dead Man's Slode. This was discovered in 1880 and little is known of it, though it appeared to be a cremation cemetery. Here within the spread of a mile are three cemeteries, potentially successive in date, with the third in sequence (Chamberlains Barn II) belonging to the Final Phase group.

Only a crude sketch of the position of the graves of Chamberlains Barn I survives (Hyslop 1963, figure 2). The graves appear almost randomly aligned, but given the circumstances of recording it may well be that the cemetery was one of mixed S–N and W–E orientation. Some three-quarters of the graves had grave-goods (14/19/74), the range of types is not dissimilar to those at Holywell. In contrast the graves at Chamberlains Barn II are predominately SW–NE (64/67/93, including four reversed burials) and according to the plan are aligned in rows (Hyslop 1963, figure 3). Only about half the skeletons are interred with grave-goods (37/69/54). The range of object types is not dissimilar to Burwell.

Less is known about the earliest cemetery at Winnall, Hampshire. The Winnall sites lie on chalk above the River Itchen to the north-east of Winchester. The first was discovered during the construction of a railway line in 1884 and now the only surviving finds are three iron shield bosses (Meaney and Hawkes 1970). The second cemetery was excavated by Audrey Meaney in 1957–8. No shields were present in this cemetery, the predominant artefacts were knives and buckles. Overall rather more than half of the graves had grave-goods (26/45/58). Once again the pattern seemed to fit the developing model.

It was the pairing of an early and Final Phase cemeteries at Leighton Buzzard and at Winnall that led Hyslop, Meaney and Hawkes to emphasize that the Final Phase cemeteries replaced nearby pagan burial grounds. Faull suggested the same pattern for Sancton (Faull 1976). Since these excavations, however, only two further 'pairs' have been detailed in publications. On the limestone slopes above the Welland valley, a seventh century cemetery of just eight burials has been discovered at Wakerley (Northamptonshire). This, it is argued, replaced a sixth-century cemetery of eighty-eight burials just 250 m to the south-west (Cook 1978). In Kent, south of the

Wantsum, the cemeteries of Eastry I and II are perceived as having been succeeded by Eastry III, which lies about 1 km to the south (Hawkes 1979).

Of these five 'pairs', only at Wakerley have both cemeteries been completely excavated. Elsewhere, the extensively excavated cemeteries of Buckland, Dover (Kent) and Finglesham (near Eastry) appear to go on into the seventh century without a break (Evison 1987, Hawkes 1976). Similarly, perhaps, at Bidford-on-Avon, Warwickshire (Humphreys *et al.* 1924 and 1925). Short of completion of a full review of all the cemeteries of Anglo-Saxon England there is little coherent data on which to decide whether the Final Phase cemeteries represent a distinct, separate phase. Certainly, the evidence of Dover and Finglesham demonstrates that the phase is not universally separate. Equally the cemeteries at Burwell, Holywell Row and Shudy Camps (analysed above) show considerable overlap of characteristics, suggesting not a synchronous creation of new cemeteries but an asynchronous pattern of abandonment and establishment.

When the wider perspective of Anglo-Saxon cemeteries and of settlement development is considered, it would seen unlikely that there is anything remarkable about the appearance of some new graveyards in the seventh century. There are, after all, numerous cemeteries which date only to the fifth century, or to both the fifth and sixth, or to only the sixth. At Chamberlain's Barn, for example, there is a potentially fifth-century cemetery to the north (Dead Man's Slode) which has sadly been ignored during the course of the Final Phase debate. In this area there is perhaps a succession of three cemeteries rather than two. The Anglo-Saxon landscape was not static but was host to a continually evolving settlement structure. With the general progression from dispersed to nucleated settlement and the introduction of open fields, it would be a surprise if the cemeteries were not periodically relocated to new sites as part of that restructuring of the landscape. The occurrence of some new cemeteries in the seventh century does not necessarily indicate a new 'phase' of burial provision.

ALIGNMENT WITH THE GODS: THE SOLAR HYPOTHESIS

T he alignment of graves is a peripheral component of the Final Phase model. While one of Hyslop's 1963 criteria (above), it has long been recognized that most pagan burials are of W–E orientation. The situation was summed up by Hawkes: 'It used to be fashionable to treat the orientation of graves as indicative of the religion of their occupants, but nowadays this is generally admitted to be an unprofitable line of approach' (Meaney and Hawkes 1970, 53). Elsewhere, though, Hawkes seems not to have totally abandoned the orientation argument: 'At Finglesham, for example, though they continued to use the heathen burial place, the seventh century people changed to west-east orientation, using sunrise bearings, and were probably at least nominally Christian' (Hawkes 1982, 48). Finglesham, a cemetery of the sixth and seventh centuries, is situated on the east coast of Kent, about 1 km inland. It was excavated in 1928–9 by W.P.D. Stebbing and by Sonia Chadwick [Hawkes] between 1959 and 1967 (Stebbing 1929, Chadwick 1958). The latter excavation is not yet published but Hawkes has published a paper which analyses the grave alignments and interprets them in terms of sunrise bearings (1976).

The alignment of graves has been of interest to archaeologists since the middle of the nineteenth century (Rahtz 1978). In recent decades attention has been focused on the solar hypothesis which postulates that the graves were aligned such that the foot end was directed towards the sunrise on the day of burial. Thus with the seasonal movement of the sun the orientation of the graves would vary. From this variation it would be possible to determine for any individual the time of death as being one of two dates in the year. For Anglo-Saxon England, the solar model was first proposed by Calvin Wells and Charles Green for the cemetery at Caister-on-Sea, Norfolk, and for the probably monastic cemetery at Burgh Castle, Suffolk (Wells and Green 1973). Three years later Hawkes applied the model to Finglesham. While the sixth-century graves were oriented more toward SW–NE, the graves of the seventh and early eighth centuries clustered 'between the azimuths of midsummer and midwinter sunrise, and there can be very little doubt that they were dug on sunrise bearings deliberately' (Hawkes 1976, 42). In order to obtain a bearing, a watch was maintained until the sun rose. This latter idea has been rejected by Donald Bullough who presents documentary evidence that burial was on the day of death and hence that a dawn vigil could be ruled out (1983, 191).

It has been argued elsewhere that the solar model has been developed in the absence of rigorous methodological analysis and without a clear understanding of the nature of the

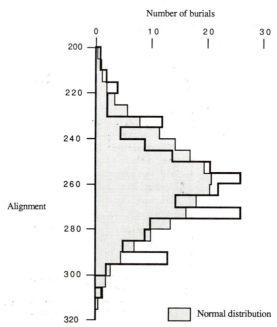

FIGURE 4 FINGLESHAM, KENT. Grave alignments compared to a normal distribution (270° indicates head to west)

underlying statistical distributions (Boddington 1987). Giles Kendall has demonstrated that the seasonal distribution of mortality suggested by the solar hypothesis is totally dissimilar to the pattern of rural mortality evidenced from later parish records (1982). In particular the archaeological distributions are peaked such that most deaths would have occurred in spring and autumn. At Finglesham four-fifths of deaths would have occurred during these seasons (169/208/81). Both Hawkes and Wells argue that such seasonal fluctuations might have occurred (Hawkes 1976, 49; Wells and Green 1973, 440). Nevertheless, such wild and regular seasonal variations do not accord with our understanding of the demography of communities of any period.

What then is the explanation for the observed distribution of burials at Finglesham and elsewhere? The solution is, regrettably, rather dull. Any attempt to align a grave on

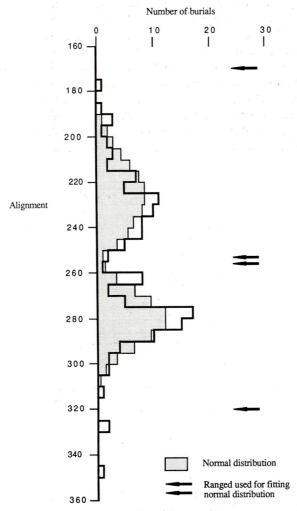

FIGURE 5   SHUDY CAMPS, CAMBRIDGESHIRE. Bimodal grave alignments compared to two normal distributions (two graves at 76° and 119° omitted)

a specific point, or in a given direction, will be subject to a limited degree of error. Small errors will occur frequently while larger errors will occur with relative infrequency. Such a distribution of errors is modelled statistically by the normal distribution (Thomas 1976). A normal distribution fits both visually and statistically to the distributions at Burgh Castle, Caister-on-Sea and Finglesham (Figure 4; see Appendix for the statistical data). To demonstrate the near universal applicability of the normal model, Figure 5 shows two normal distributions fitted to the alignment distribution at Shudy Camps. At this site two modes of orientation were used and a normal distribution can be seen to be a reasonable fit to each.

It is not intended here to suggest that alignments are of no interpretive interest to the archaeologist, simply that the solar hypothesis is untenable. Archaeologists have focused their attention on the scatter of alignments. Such scatter that there is has been over-emphasized by the 'solar arc' diagrams of alignment commonly used by archaeologists (e.g. Hawkes 1976, Figures 4–7). The more conventional histograms presented here correctly emphasize the clustered characteristic of burial orientation. When this aspect of alignment is considered it can be seen that there are interesting differences in the alignment characteristics between cemeteries. There are four primary features of alignment that are of interest to the archaeologist:

1. Alignment modes. The preferred direction of alignment. In some Anglo-Saxon cemeteries, there are two modes, one at right angles to the other (e.g. Burwell). In others the mode changes with time (e.g. Shudy Camps).
2. Random error. The 'normal' dispersion of graves (described above).
3. Chronological drift. As exampled at Finglesham.
4. Topographical drift. Parts of some cemeteries are clearly influenced by adjacent topographic features (e.g. the ramparts at Blewburton Hill, Collins and Collins 1959), or by the contours of the underlying hillside (e.g. Cannington, Rahtz 1977).

The further pursuit of this topic is beyond the scope of this paper, which must be satisfied with rejecting the solar hypothesis put forward for some Final Phase burials.

EDGE EFFECTS: SETTLEMENT, BOUNDARIES AND BURIAL

A nother peripheral characteristic of the model is the gravitation of burial grounds toward settlements. Faull saw the burial ground at Sancton as moving from the 'outer edge' of the cultivated land to the village (Faull 1976). The question of the relationship of pagan burial grounds to contemporary territorial boundaries deserves to be considered briefly here. An influential study was published by D.J. Bonney in 1966 when he demonstrated that one third of Wiltshire's known pagan burial grounds occurred on parish boundaries (20/69/29) while a further 13 per cent occurred within 150 m of such a boundary (9/69/13). Unfortunately Bonney does not publish a complete list of the cemeteries used in his analysis, so it is not possible to determine how many graves rather than cemeteries occur on boundaries.

Recently Bonney's study has been followed up in more detail, and with careful statistical reasoning, by Ann Goodier (1984). This is not the place to examine her work in detail but some points may be noted. Cemeteries are not predominately associated with boundaries (defined by her as a 200 m wide band). Indeed according to Goodier's figures, there are just 5 per cent associated with boundaries in the fifth century, rising to 25 per cent in the seventh century. Most burial sites are thus elsewhere. Goodier's statistics demonstrate that more sites (or perhaps, sightings) occur on boundaries that would be expected if there was no association between the burials and boundaries. The samples here are small and no doubt prone to sampling bias, hence we should be cautious in using them despite the statistical significance of the results. Regional differences also occur. In the south and west, and in Suffolk, 24–34 per cent of the burials are on boundaries; this diminishes to 11–17 per cent in the north, south Midlands and south-east. There is thus both chronological and regional variation. What Goodier's survey does not tell us is whether chronology or geography contributes most to the variations observed. Neither does it tell us the number of burials, rather than the number of sites. This is perhaps a crucial point. A higher proportion of the burial sites on boundaries have interments which are primary or secondary in barrows (47/135/35) compared to the proportion not on boundaries (123/619/20). As this form of cemetery (with the exception of those in Kent) tends to be smaller than average, this presumably deflates the proportion of burials (rather than sites) on boundaries still further. A rough poll of the figures suggests a mean size of nine discovered burials at barrows compared to sixteen elsewhere. Regrettably, despite Goodier's spirited attempts at quantification, we still cannot resolve whether there is a formal association of burials and boundaries. For our purpose we may simply note that a minority of Anglo-Saxon cemetery sites occur on boundaries (135/754/18).

Several authors have seen it as characteristic that pagan Anglo-Saxon burial grounds are located away from settlement. This view is epitomized by the following statement: 'Like most other late cemeteries including Polhill, Winnall II – the Christian cemetery – occupied a typically "pagan" position on high ground well away from any likely site of settlement' (Hawkes 1973, 186). Such a philosophy is also a vital part of Faull's model for Sancton (Faull 1976). A similar view was initially taken by Chris Arnold in his analysis of the cemeteries in the south of England (Arnold 1977), but he later revised this and suggested an early association of settlement and graveyards followed by a subsequent separation (Arnold and Wardle 1981).

There is now convincing evidence for the proximity of a number of settlements and pagan cemeteries. Adjacent (within 500–600 m) and contemporary settlement is known in at least thirteen sites – Alveston Manor (Warwickshire), Bidford-on-Avon (Warwickshire), Bishopstone (Sussex), Cassington I (Oxfordshire), Catholme (Staffordshire), Harrold (Bedfordshire), Heslerton (Yorkshire), Mucking (Essex), Northfleet (Essex), Spong Hill (Norfolk), Springfield Lyons (Essex), Walton (Buckinghamshire) and West Stow (Suffolk). In four other cases settlement may well be associated – Trumpet Major (Dorset), Polhill (Kent), Sewerby (Yorkshire) and Wakerley (Northhamptonshire). In two other instances isolated burials occur within settlements – at New Wintles Farm, Eynsham and at Sutton Courtenay, both in Oxfordshire. These cases demonstrate quite clearly that cemetery and settlement are not invariably, nor even normally, separated. The matter was summarized by Evison as long ago as 1970: 'Now that the number of excavated Anglo-Saxon sites is mounting it is becoming increasingly evident that the opinion that cemeteries of the period were commonly sited at a considerable distance from the houses is not tenable' (Eagles and Evison 1970, 50). It is of note that of those settlements clearly associated with settlements, only Harrold might be classified as Final Phase, though Bidford-on-Avon probably continued into the seventh century. This might be taken as support for Arnold and Wardle's model of separation of settlement and burial ground in the middle Anglo-Saxon period (1981). However, much depends on how the character of the early Anglo-Saxon landscape is viewed. Recent fieldwork and excavation has rapidly changed our view of the early Anglo-Saxon landscape. Excavations in progress at Raunds, Northamptonshire, have suggested that the earlier settlement takes on the form of loose clusters (Selkirk 1987). A similar pattern has been recovered from fieldwalking evidence from Doddington parish, about 15 km upstream of Raunds (Foard 1978). The associated pagan cemeteries have not yet been discovered at Raunds or Doddington, but a broadly similar settlement pattern exists at Brixworth, also in Northamptonshire. Here a spread of small early sites have been identified (Hall and Martin 1979) and three of the known Brixworth cemeteries lie within this cluster. Such is the poor quality of the cemetery data from Brixworth that we cannot as yet develop a coherent model for the development of its settlement and burial grounds. Nevertheless, despite the imprecise character of much of the data, it is evident that the pattern of Anglo-Saxon settlements is more complex than previously thought and that the matter of association of settlement and burial ground must be seen in the context of a landscape undergoing progressive nucleation.

THE END OF THE FINAL PHASE:
TOWARDS A NEW MODEL FOR TRANSITION

T his review of the Final Phase has not been exhaustive. Nevertheless the model has been seen to be inherently weak. While seventh-century burials are increasingly interred without grave-goods, the model does not take account of the very rich burials of that period. It also seems unlikely that the burial grounds singled out as Final Phase do in fact represent a distinct and separate phase. Rather, the cemeteries are part of the constant addition and abandonment of cemeteries as the Anglo-Saxon landscape evolved. Further, the succession of one cemetery by another nearby has only infrequently been demonstrated. The contemporary settlement has not been located, nor examined, for any of the cemetery 'pairs'. Perhaps above all, the Final Phase model is weak because it sees changes in burial practice as resulting primarily from a single factor, the conversion to christianity. More probably the changes result from an amalgam of pressures deriving from landscape, social, economic and religious change.

What sort of model should then replace the Final Phase? At this stage a new model cannot yet be fully expounded nor validated, although a few of its major components can be sketched. They indicate a necessary shift of emphasis away from the decline of grave-goods toward the location and morphology of burial grounds. Some of the components have been referred to above, others remain beyond the scope of this paper:

1. Grave-goods decline in response to a variety of factors which are economic, social and religious in character.
2. The Anglo-Saxon cemetery should be seen as a unit of landscape. Burial grounds must be expected to, and indeed do, relocate in response to the development of the landscape.
3. The timing of the change from pagan burial ground to Christian graveyard was more dependent on local factors, such as the establishment and growth of the manor or kings *tun*, than on the notional conversion of the kingdom or region to Christianity.
4. The siting of new graveyards is often closely correlated with the siting of manors, to which churches and (sometimes subsequently) churchyards were attached.
5. The adoption of Christianity leads to the convergence of the focus of worship and the place of burial. In the pagan period the temple and shrine were separate from the place of burial. In the Christian period all cemeteries appear to be associated with churches.
6. Pagan burial grounds are normally non-focal and do not cluster around rich or important graves. Burials in Christian churchyards are concentrated to the south and east of the church.
7. There is no clear evidence for pagan cemeteries being formally defined by banks, ditches or fences, although this is an essential characteristic of the Christian period.
8. The combination of church and graveyard together create a basic stability to the location of burial grounds, compared to the more transient pagan grounds.
9. Superimposed levels, or 'generations', of burial occur as a result of the confinement and longevity of the Christian cemeteries.
10. From the reintroduction of barrow burial in the seventh century onwards the emphasis is on marking the surface of the grave 'in perpetuity' rather than on display and deposition in the open grave.

APPENDIX

STATISTICAL EXAMINATION OF THE SOLAR HYPOTHESIS

The Kolmogorov-Smirnov Test (Thomas 1976) was used to examine if the distributions departed statistically from normality. Five classes were used throughout. In each case the result was not significant at the 95 per cent level.

Burgh Castle – n=112, K-S=0.102, K-S(0.05)=0.129.
Caister-on-Sea – n=96, K-S=0.035, K-S(0.05)=0.139.
Finglesham – n=208, K-S=0.056, K-S(0.05)=0.096.

Bibliography

Ager, B. 1983: "The Anglo-Saxon cemetery" in Collis, J. (Ed.) *Wigber Low, Derbyshire: a Bronze Age and Anglian Burial Site in the White Peak*, Sheffield, 101–2.

Alexander, M. 1983: Old English Literature. London.

Arnold, C.J. 1977: "Early Anglo-Saxon settlement patterns in southern England", *Journal Historical Geography* 3, 309–15.

Arnold, C.J. 1980: "Wealth and social structure: a matter of life and death", in *Anglo-Saxon Cemeteries 1979*, P. Rahtz, T. Dickinson, L. Watts (Eds.) B.A.R. 82, Oxford, 81–142.

Arnold, C.J. and Wardle, P. 1981: "Early medieval settlement patterns in England", *Medieval Archaeology* 25, 145–9.

Baldwin Brown, G. 1903: *The Arts in Early England. Volume I*, London.

Biddle, M. 1976: "The archaeology of the church: a widening horizon", in *The Archaeological Study of Churches*. Addyman, P. and Morris, R. (Eds.) Council British Archaeology Research Report 13, London, 65–71.

Bruce-Mitford, R.L.S. 1975: *The Sutton Hoo Ship Burial I*, London.

Boddington, A. 1987: "Raunds, Northamptonshire: analysis of a country churchyard". *World Archaeology* 18, 3, 411–25.

Bonney, D. 1966: "Pagan Saxon burials and boundaries in Wiltshire", *Wiltshire Archaeological Natural History Magazine* 61, 25–30.

Bullough, D. 1983: "Burial, community and belief in the early Medieval west", in *Ideal and Reality in Frankish and Anglo-Saxon Society*, Wormwald, P. (Ed), Oxford, 177–201.

Chadwick, S.E. 1958: "The Anglo-Saxon Cemetery at Finglesham, Kent: a reconsideration", *Medieval Archaeology* 2, 1–71.

Collins, A.E.P. and Collins, F.P. 1959: "Excavations on Blewburton Hill, 1953", *Berkshire Archaeological Journal* 57, 52–73.

Cook, A. 1978: "Catalogue of the Anglo-Saxon material" in "Excavations at Wakerley, Northamptonshire", Jackson, D.A. and Ambrose, T., *Britannia* 11, 228–234.

Eagles, B.N. and Evison, V.I. 1970: "Excavations at Harrold, Bedfordshire, 1951–53", *Bedfordshire Archaeological Journal*, 17–55.

Evison, V.I. 1956: "An Anglo-Saxon cemetery at Holborough, Kent", *Archaeologia Cantiana* 70, 84–141.

Evison, V.I. 1987: Dover: The Buckland Anglo-Saxon Cemetery. *Historic Buildings and Monuments Commission for England, Archaeological Report* 3, London.

Faull, M.L. 1976: "The location and relationship of the Sancton Anglo-Saxon cemeteries", *Antiquaries Journal* 56, 227–33.

Goodier, A. 1984: "The formation of boundaries in Anglo-Saxon England: A statistical study", *Medieval Archaeology* 28, 1–21.

Hall, D. and Martin P. 1979: "Brixworth, Northamptonshire – an intensive field survey". *Journal British Archaeological Association* 132, 1–6.

Hawkes, S.C. 1973: "The dating and social significance of the burials in the Polhill Cemetery" in *Excavations in West Kent 1960–70*, Philp, B. (Ed.) 186–201. Kent Archaeological Rescue Unit, Dover.

Hawkes, S.C. 1976: "Orientation at Finglesham: Sunrise dating of death and burial in an Anglo-Saxon cemetery in East Kent", *Archaeologia Cantiana* 92, 33–51.

Hawkes, S.C. 1982: "The archaeology of conversion: cemeteries", in *The Anglo-Saxons*, Campbell, J. (Ed.), Oxford, 48–9.

Hawkes, S.C. 1979: "Eastry in Anglo-Saxon Kent: Its importance, and a newly-found grave" in *Anglo-Saxon Studies in Archaeology and History I*, Hawkes, S.C., Brown, D., and Campbell, G. (Eds.) 81–114, Oxford.

Hawkes, S.C. and Wells, C. 1983: "The inhumed skeletal material from an early Anglo-Saxon cemetery in Worthy Park, Kingsworthy, Hampshire", *Paleobios* 1, 3–36.

Hodges, R. and Whitehouse, D. 1983: Mohammed, Charlemagne and the Origins of Europe, London.

Humphreys, J. et al, 1924: "An Anglo-Saxon Cemetery at Bidford-on-Avon, Warwickshire", *Archaeologia* 73, 89–116.

Humphreys, J. et al, 1925: "An Anglo-Saxon Cemetery at Bidford-on-Avon, Warwickshire: Second

Report on the Excavations", *Archaeologia 75*, 271–88.

Hyslop, M. 1963: "Two Anglo-Saxon Cemeteries at Chamberlains Barn, Leighton Buzzard, Bedfordshire", *Archaeological Journal 120*, 161–200.

Kendall, G. 1982: "A study of grave orientation in several Roman and post-Roman cemeteries from Southern Britain", *Archaeological Journal 139*, 101–23.

Leeds, E.T. 1913: *The Archaeology of the Anglo-Saxon Settlements*. Oxford.

Leeds, E.T. 1936: *Early Anglo-Saxon Art and Archaeology*. Oxford.

Lethbridge, T.C. 1926: "The Anglo-Saxon Cemetery, Burwell Cambs", *Proceedings Cambridge Antiquarian Society 27*, 72–9.

Lethbridge, T.C. 1927: "The Anglo-Saxon Cemetery, Burwell Cambs. Part II", *Proceedings Cambridge Antiquarian Society 28*, 116–25.

Lethbridge, T.C. 1929: "The Anglo-Saxon Cemetery, Burwell Cambs. Part IV", *Proceedings Cambridge Antiquarian Society 30*, 97–109.

Lethbridge, T.C. 1931: Recent Excavations in Anglo-Saxon Cemeteries in Cambridgeshire and Suffolk. *Cambridge Antiquarian Society Quarto Publications, New Series 3.*

Lethbridge, T.C. 1936: A Cemetery at Shudy Camps, Cambridgeshire. *Cambridge Antiquarian Society Quarto Publications, New Series 5.*

Meaney, A.L. and Hawkes, S.C. 1970: Two Anglo-Saxon cemeteries at Winnall, Winchester, Hampshire. *Society for Medieval Archaeology Monograph Series, 4.* London.

Morris, R. 1983: The Church in British Archaeology. *Council British Archaeology Research Report 47*, London.

Owen-Croker, G.R. 1986: Dress in Anglo-Saxon England, Manchester.

Ozanne, A. 1962–3: "The Peak Dwellers", *Medieval Archaeology*, 6–7, 15–52.

Rahtz, P.A. 1977: "Late Roman cemeteries and beyond" in Burial in the Roman World, Reece, R. (Ed.), 53–64. *Council British Archaeology Research Report 22.*

Rahtz, P.A. 1978: "Grave orientation", *Archaeological Journal, 135*, 1–14.

Selkirk, A. 1987: "Raunds", *Current Archaeology 107*, 323–39.

Shennan, S. 1988: *Quantifying Archaeology*, Edinburgh.

Shephard, J.F. 1979: Anglo-Saxon Barrows of the later 6th and 7th centuries AD. Unpublished Ph.D. Thesis, University of Cambridge.

Stebbing, W.P.D. 1929: "Jutish cemetery near Finglesham, Kent", *Archaeologia Cantiana 41*, 115–25.

Thomas, D.H. 1976: *Figuring Anthropology*, New York.

Wells, C. and Green, C. 1973: "Sunrise dating of death and burial", *Norfolk Archaeology 35*, 435–42.

Young, B. 1977: "Paganisme, christianisation et rites funeraires merovingens", *Archeologie Medievale 7*, 5–81.

CONTRIBUTORS

BARRY AGER   Department of Medieval & Later Antiquities, British Museum
CHRISTOPHER ARNOLD   University College Wales, Aberystwyth
ANDY BODDINGTON   Department of Computing Services, Open University
SONIA CHADWICK HAWKES   Institute of Archaeology, University of Oxford
JEREMY HUGGETT   North Staffordshire Polytechnic
DAVID LEIGH   The Conservation Unit, Museums and Galleries Commission
KEITH MANCHESTER   University of Bradford
MICHAEL RHODES   Museum of London
JULIAN RICHARDS   University of York
JACQUI WATSON AND GLYNIS EDWARDS   Ancient Monuments Laboratory, English Heritage
ROGER WHITE   Wroxeter Post-Excavation Project